POTUS

SPEAKS

Finding the Words That
Defined the Clinton Presidency

MICHAEL WALDMAN

SIMON & SCHUSTER

NEW YORK   LONDON   TORONTO
SYDNEY   SINGAPORE

SIMON & SCHUSTER
Rockefeller Center
1230 Avenue of the Americas
New York, NY 10020

10 9 8 7 6 5 4 3 2 1

Library of Congress Cataloging-in-Publication Data

Waldman, Michael, [date]
    POTUS speaks : finding the words that defined
    the Clinton presidency / Michael Waldman.
      p. cm.
    Includes index.
    1. Clinton, Bill, 1946–   —Oratory.   2. Clinton,
Bill, 1946–   —Language.   3. United States—
Politics and government—1993–
4. Communication in politics—United States—
History—20th century.   5. Rhetoric—Political
aspects—United States—History—20th century.
6. Political oratory—United States—History—
20th century.   7. Political corruption—United
States—History—20th century.   8. Waldman,
Michael, [date]   I. Title.
E886.2 .W35 2000
973.929'092—dc21
00-057409

ISBN 0-7432-0020-9

To Liz,
Benjamin,
Susannah,
and Joshua

CONTENTS

POTUS
SPEAKS

POTUS: Acronym for "President of the United States." Used in internal White House communications.

INTRODUCTION

IN ANXIOUS MINUTES before Bill Clinton left to deliver a speech, I stood before the ornately carved desk in the Oval Office. I was the President's chief speechwriter, and he was marking up a draft I had written for him. Glasses pushed down his nose, a black Sharpie pen swiftly scratching away, he shook his head as he encountered some high-flown rhetoric. "Words, words, words," he muttered. "Words, words, words." "That's it," whispered economic aide Gene Sperling as we walked out of the Oval Office. "No more words. Only symbols."

A presidential speech is more than rhetoric, more than a string of sound bites or applause lines. It is where policy, and politics, and presidential personality come together. The words that are chosen can define a presidency. Never was that more true than during Bill Clinton's two terms—especially because this president was so intimately involved. I was a part of that process for seven years, ultimately writing or editing nearly two thousand speeches, working with him on two inaugural addresses and four State of the Unions.

My bias should be clear from the beginning: I was proud to work for Clinton, proud of what he accomplished for the country. For all his mistakes, I think that Bill Clinton was not only a successful president, but an important one.

Clinton was the first president to come to office after the end of the Cold War. When the Berlin wall fell, our expectations of the presidency changed, too. Clinton found that out the hard way, his grand plans colliding early in his term with the reality of the public's disdain for government. Then something much more interesting happened. Not without stumbles at first, he found himself creating a new way to use his office.

Most fundamentally, he changed the way a president uses the bully pulpit to lead. Consider this fact: In a typical year, Clinton spoke in public 550 times. In a similar year, Ronald Reagan spoke 320 times; Harry Truman, 88 times. It wasn't just that Clinton liked to talk (which he most assuredly did). Rather, he was forced to find new ways to break through, to connect with the public amid the clamor of four competing twenty-four-hour cable networks, a bitterly partisan Congress, and seemingly permanent investigations. It was a new kind of presidency, less dependent on legislation, more rooted in a president's unique power to act and to speak. With his stream of speeches and announcements, he was trying, bit by bit, to restore public confidence in government, to show that it could get things done. In so doing, he framed a new approach, fiscally responsible but active. This will most likely be his lasting legacy: redefining the role of government and then successfully convincing the public to share that vision.

First, a word on speechwriting. Presidents have always had help with their speeches, from the day Alexander Hamilton wrote George Washington's Farewell Address. Lincoln's first inaugural ended with a famous passage largely written by William Seward. Franklin Roosevelt laboriously copied out by hand the typed draft of his inaugural that was prepared by Raymond Moley. For most of the country's history, presidents rarely spoke in public. But with the rise of the modern presidency, no chief executive could function without speechwriters. FDR worked closely with his. Drafting sessions would begin with cocktails, then dinner. Then, after a bout of dictation, the writers would repair to the Cabinet Room, where their all-nighter would be catered by the White House chef. (As time passed, much changed in the world, but apparently not the need for speechwriters to work all night. In his book, Lyndon Johnson's aide Richard Goodwin recalls that, faltering as he drafted the 1966 State of the Union address, he was visited by a White House physician. The doctor injected him with a red liquid, and he perked up. In the 1990s, of course, we had quadruple espressos from Starbucks.) But over the years, the writers were shunted aside, the writing divorced from policy and strategy. When Peggy Noonan wrote the brilliant speech for Ronald Reagan commemorating the fortieth anniversary of D-Day, she had never met the man.

Under Clinton, the pendulum began to swing back. He chose me to be his director of speechwriting not because of my liquid prose, but because, it was thought, I understood his policies and his mind. Speechwriters were once again privy to policymaking and political strategy. Eventually I reported directly to the chief of staff and the President, avoiding layers of editing. A team of six speechwriters reported to me. We worked on domestic issues and the international economy. Pure foreign policy speeches were handled by the National Security Council (so issues of war and peace

are largely absent from this book). We found a way to write for Clinton that he found most useful—spare, factual, shorn of fancy prose. If he were to deliver a thirty-minute speech, the draft if read aloud would last fifteen minutes. "We give him Hemingway," I would tell new speechwriters. "He'll turn it into Faulkner."

His strength was never soaring rhetoric, though when the occasion demanded, a eulogy or a ceremony or sermon, he was as eloquent as any of his predecessors. Rather, Clinton's powerful gift at communicating grew from the intensity of his connection to the audience before him—that and his love of policy and his drive to explain it, explain it, explain it. I would stand by the side of the stage and watch him, draped over the podium, searching a room as he spoke. He might dutifully read along with the prepared draft. Then, when he sensed the listeners were with him, or were resisting, he would leave the text, start dropping his consonants, and loop around and around the subject, trying to persuade the audience until he had won the point.

Another word: on scandals. I recognize that historians will assess the Lewinsky matter as part of his legacy. This book reflects my experience and those of my colleagues. Our mission was to keep doing our jobs amid withering controversy. My work and his work—even, amazingly, during the height of the impeachment trial—was focused on policy.

I'm writing this book because little of what I have read accurately captures the two terms of the Clinton presidency. The story begins in Little Rock.

ONE

HIGH HOPES

BILL CLINTON began his presidency with an enthusiastic stream of words.

On election night, November 3, 1992, the President-elect stood on a brilliantly lit stage in front of the Old State House in Little Rock, Arkansas. "My fellow Americans, on this day, with high hopes and brave hearts, in massive numbers, the American people have voted to make a new beginning," he declared. "This election is a clarion call for our country to face the challenges of the end of the Cold War and the beginning of the next century, to restore growth to our country and opportunity to our people, to empower our own people so that they can take more responsibility for their own lives, to face problems too-long ignored, from AIDS to the environment to the conversion of our economy from a defense to a domestic economic giant."

For the 40,000 people stretched out before him—for the 44.9 million who cast their ballots for him that day—this was a moment of supreme optimism and hope. For the first time in twelve years, in many ways, for the first time in three decades, those of us who had worked and voted for him would have a president in whom we believed. Our feeling of unity with America was whole and unreserved.

I stood a few yards from the side of the stage in a knot of campaign workers, standing on my toes to peer over the formidable hair of the governor's mother. "Today the steelworker and the stenographer, the teacher and the nurse had as much power in the mystery of our democracy as the president, the billionaire, and the governor. You all spoke with equal voices for change. And tomorrow we will try to give you that."

The President-elect, the Vice President–elect, and their wives waved

and pumped the hands of those in front. Gore lunged out to grab James Carville, a few rows in, with Secret Service agents holding on to his waist. The loudspeakers blared the campaign song, Fleetwood Mac's "Don't Stop Thinking About Tomorrow." To my utter amazement, that bathetic song— the same soft-rock Muzak that made me gag in the seventies—now put a lump in my throat.

More amazing was the fact that I was there at all. Four months earlier, I was a public interest lawyer in Washington, testifying and lobbying and writing books and articles. I ran Congress Watch, Ralph Nader's lobbying office. Occasionally, we blocked something bad. We never passed anything good. Four more years of George Bush was about as dispiriting a prospect as I could imagine. I wanted to wield power, to engage in the messy, compromised work of governing. I was impressed by Bill Clinton; I liked his message about modernizing the Democratic Party. Most of all, he was a Democrat who could win.

One day, shortly after the Democratic convention, the phone rang. It was George Stephanopoulos, whom I had gotten to know while I was lobbying Congress and he was an anonymous congressional staff member.

"Hi, congratulations again," I enthused. I had been helping the Clinton campaign informally by writing position papers and advising on policy. A mutual friend, historian Eric Alterman, had let George know that I wanted to join the campaign full-time. But I didn't think I would actually get the chance.

"I think it would be great if you came down to Little Rock," he said. "We have the money now and you would do great. We could really use you."

I leapt off my chair but tried to sound cool. "Wow, that's great, George. I have only one question." I felt awkward asking it. "Um, what role, what title, would I have?"

"You'll be senior. Senior," George said. "Wait, here's James."

James Carville came on the line. "Role! What role! This is the *Wah Room!*" he shouted. I had never met the man. "Pack up your toothbrush and get your ass down here!"

As I hastily prepared to leave my job, Ralph Nader called. He had been a hero of mine since grade school. Ralph was a constant goad to younger staff members whom he believed were too soft, too focused on their careers. When former assistants went into mainstream politics, he routinely turned on them. During the Carter administration, his top advisor had left to run the auto safety agency. Months into her tenure, Ralph attended one of her press conferences and demanded that she resign. I knew I might well face the same treatment. He disliked Bill Clinton, distrusted his obvious love of earthly pleasures, and had repeatedly predicted that

Clinton would never be elected. "They aren't going to trust you," Nader said. "The Cajun and the Greek. They won't trust you for a while." He paused. He wanted me to understand that my mission was to help steer the candidate in a progressive direction. "Remember. Your purpose is not only to serve but to swerve."

I met Bill Clinton a few weeks later. I was working in the War Room in Little Rock, writing policy proposals, conducting research on the Republicans, listening and watching Carville rant. In a generous effort to expose me to the candidate, Stephanopoulos dispatched me to the campaign plane to brief Clinton and Gore for a television appearance on the Phil Donahue show the next day. I knew next to nothing about the subject of the show — a government program that apparently paid American businesses to move jobs overseas. Bruce Reed, an old friend who was the deputy campaign manager and policy director, introduced me to Clinton, who had just dropped into the seat opposite me on the campaign's charter plane. "Governor, this is Michael Waldman. He is our foreign aid expert." I swallowed hard. I had, at best, a paragraph or two of things to say.

Clinton pulled out a *USA Today* crossword puzzle. Gore opened a thick, three-ring binder that his staff had prepared. I studied Clinton. His red face, graying hair, and blue eyes made him look strikingly patriotic, like an American flag. I was waiting to see if he would try to seduce me, to forge an instant connection, the Clinton technique I had read about in newspaper profiles. Instead, he frowned at his crossword puzzle and marked it up with a ballpoint pen. I didn't know whether to wait for him to look up, but eventually I began to recite facts and figures about foreign aid, and job loss in the textile industry, and what they could expect from Phil Donahue.

Gore piped in eagerly. Evidently he had studied his notebook. They began discussing "the Caribbean Basin Initiative" and "parity" and "transition assistance." Their discussion was friendly but competitive. Each seemed eager to show how well he understood policy. I sat silent, since I had little to contribute. The briefing was done. Clinton closed his eyes for the rest of the flight. When he left the plane, I pocketed the crossword puzzle. (You never know what might be valuable someday.)

The fall campaign was a sleepless blur. Carville held court from a couch at the center of an open newsroom, and he provided an electric charge that was felt throughout the old newspaper building that housed the campaign. Every attack had to be answered immediately; every fact had to be footnoted. At seven every morning, and again in the evening, dozens of campaign workers gathered for Carville's War Room meetings. (It was easier for me than for my wife, Liz, three months' pregnant with our first child, who was working as a researcher defending the governor's Arkansas record and had to haul herself out of bed each morning.) I wrote position papers

on regulatory reform and banking, went on TV to defend Clinton's record, stockpiled research on Bush, and wrote press releases every few days attacking various administration shortcomings. In truth, there was not much to show for my efforts. Clinton was relentlessly positive, rarely assailing Bush for anything other than the overall health of the economy.

On the campaign trail, Clinton was a wonder. His moist, empathetic style was becoming familiar to the country at large. More interesting was his message. For decades, the Democrats had been locked out of the White House, seen by middle-class voters as culturally out of touch, more interested in exotic issues than mainstream economic concerns. The year before, in a largely ad-libbed speech to the centrist Democratic Leadership Council, Clinton had attacked "the stale orthodoxies of left and right" and unveiled a new approach. The Democrats should offer opportunity for all Americans, he said. "But opportunity for all is not enough, for if you give opportunity without insisting on responsibility, much of the money can be wasted, and the country's strength can be sapped. So we favor responsibility from all." It's hard to remember now that for a Democrat to mention "responsibility" was innovative; some even heard it as a racist code phrase. Clinton called this social bargain a New Covenant. During the general election drive, that innovative message was lacquered over by a more orthodox populist attack on Bush's economics. But underneath, still visible, was a new synthesis.

Now Bill Clinton was the President-elect. Standing onstage, young, tall, improbably handsome, he had the makings of a transforming president, one of the greats. The ghosts of Roosevelt and Truman, of Kennedy and Johnson, all those who had used the office and relished its power, seemed present that night. The expectations were high. His exuberant words raised them. Did he realize the power of his words and how loudly they would now ring? Did he know how high the hopes were, the expectations that he excited?

As I LOOK BACK after seven years, it is clear that Bill Clinton entered the presidency with a grand and contradictory sense of the office and how he would fill it. He grew up schooled in the ideas of what has been called the heroic presidency. From the first hundred days of the New Deal to the collapse of Soviet communism, the office had been the dynamo powering the political system. We elected presidents to do big things. To conquer fascism. To win a world war. To create a strong social safety net and help usher in the civil rights revolution. And for half a century, to face down the Russians in the Cold War. Chief executives were judged by imposing accomplishments, bold strokes that almost invariably expanded the reach of the

federal government. They were to display mastery in a series of dramatic foreign crises.

Almost alone on the national stage, presidents commanded the bully pulpit. Their voices fit the media of the day: Roosevelt's tenor voice and measured cadences were perfect for radio. Kennedy's deft press conferences, vivid rhetoric, and glamour were perfect for an era when television was becoming more important, and photography was going color. Reagan's winking delivery of sound bites before beautiful backdrops fit a time when the evening news compressed political messages into small pieces. The modern presidency was televised. The very first half-hour network evening news program featured Walter Cronkite interviewing John F. Kennedy, just weeks before he went to Dallas. Congress, by contrast, spoke with a babel of voices; in fact, until recent years, congressional proceedings weren't photographed at all.

Bill Clinton was determined to fill the role of the strong modern president. His speeches were sprinkled with references to Roosevelt and Lincoln. The crowd at Madison Square Garden, at his nomination, was enthralled by the grainy film footage of a teenage Clinton shaking hands with JFK. His signature initiative, a national service program, was directly modeled on Kennedy's call for young people to serve through the Peace Corps. To interviewers, Clinton readily spoke of his affinity for young Thomas Jefferson.

But at the same time, Clinton—despite his years as a governor—had no fingertip sense of the great institutional machine that is the presidency. Few Democrats did. Over two decades, Republicans had held the White House all but four years. And in that brief interruption, Jimmy Carter had run as an anti-president—with few tangible goals other than shrinking the office and diminishing its pretensions.

Throughout this Democratic diaspora, the party had altered its view of the office. The strong presidency was created by liberals. But after Vietnam and Watergate and Iran-Contra, a generation of Democrats worried more about the dangers of an out-of-control executive than they craved the benefits of a powerful president. In the 1940s and 1950s, liberal historian Arthur M. Schlesinger Jr. wrote reverently about *The Age of Jackson* and *The Age of Roosevelt*, respectively. More recently, he had warned against *The Imperial Presidency*. Young Democratic lawyers and policymakers, excluded from the executive branch during Republican administrations, filled the growing staffs of congressional committees instead, where they found ways to trim the power of the executive. Democrats didn't defer to presidents; they investigated them. The only other source of political power for Democrats was governorships and mayorships, offices filled with men who distrusted the federal government.

When a party wins the presidency, it is a change as profound as if it had held *no* seats in Congress and now suddenly held the majority. Clinton had been thinking for years about how he would use the office. He was not ready; no Democrat was.

GEORGE STEPHANOPOULOS urged me to rush back to Little Rock three days after the election, though I had no job. Within a few days, a hiring freeze was imposed. But George was able to argue that I was already there, and secured a place for me as one of his three deputies. The transition offices occupied two floors of what passed for a skyscraper office building in Little Rock. Transitions are a tossed salad of hard, often pointless work, ennui, and hope—commingled with the terror, above all, that you might get left out. Nobody knew anything; nobody had a clear responsibility. Nobody could say for sure what his or her role would be, if any, once Clinton was sworn in. In one office, amid towering piles of paper, economic policy advisors Robert Reich and Gene Sperling began to pull together an economic plan. Two doors down, the foreign policy advisors worked, waiting for phone calls from Boris Yeltsin and trying to determine which calls were crank. A warren of offices upstairs were sometimes borrowed by Webb Hubbell, Hillary Clinton's law partner, and other ethics advisors.

Each night, transition staff members were feted by dozens of reporters at the few high-end restaurants in town: New Mexican food at the Blue Mesa in West Little Rock, steak at Doe's, ribs at a half dozen places. (Though the economy of Arkansas is heavily dependent upon poultry, it seemed nearly impossible to get a piece of chicken to eat in the state. Perhaps they know something.) The reporters had unlimited expense accounts. And they didn't even seem to care if we didn't give them any information. The journalists, especially the prominent ones, were happy to do all the talking. It was a heady and giddy time.

It was also, as it became clear soon enough, a missed opportunity. Of the wasted prospects in the Clinton presidency, the transition was not only the first, but in some ways, the worst.

There was, for starters, enormous wasted energy. The transition became the vent through which Democrats poured twelve years of frustration. Thousands of people went to work on task forces and clusters and committees. They combed through executive agencies and compiled bulky briefing books for the new cabinet. Nearly all of it was make-work. The transition's lawyers had ruled that the cabinet briefing books would become a public record, subject to the Freedom of Information Act, if they were actually brought into government by the new cabinet secretaries.

There were public miscues. The President-elect was discovering that

his words now boomed loudly, ricocheting throughout the country within minutes. Simple gimmicks that would have gotten a few hours of good press on the campaign trail were scrutinized for the character traits they revealed. One of the communications staff suggested that Clinton, jogging on the streets near the White House during a visit to Washington, stop at a McDonald's to chat with the homeless as he had done in Little Rock on his morning run. He had to endure eight years of Big Mac jokes as a result.

The biggest mistake—with consequences that would linger for months—was the failure to understand the importance of the White House staff.

Clinton spent hours each day mulling over his cabinet, not planning his White House. In part, this was because Warren Christopher, the Los Angeles attorney who was supposed to be leading the cabinet search, had been penciled in as chair of the entire transition at the last minute. Christopher seemed to have little interest in doing anything other than filling the cabinet. And when he was chosen to be secretary of state, his attention was understandably drawn elsewhere. The cabinet that resulted was one that "looked like America," as Clinton had promised: it was ethnically diverse and had more women than ever before. But it didn't think like America, or even like Clinton's new electoral coalition. It included citizens of Cambridge, Berkeley, and Madison, Wisconsin, but none from swing states Illinois, Ohio, Michigan, or Pennsylvania. And, until just days before he was sworn in, Clinton never got around to naming his White House staff.

Despite years of watching the evening news, despite H. R. Haldeman and Hamilton Jordan and Iran-Contra and John Sununu, the new president seemed not to recognize that the White House staff wields more power less accountably than nearly any cabinet secretary.

One day Harrison Wellford dropped by my office. He is a well-known Washington lawyer who had gotten his start working for Nader. He had served in the Carter White House. Now he had been given the assignment of reporting to the new administration on the possible structure of the White House staff. He showed me his report. Republicans, comfortable in the buttoned-down corporate world, generally appoint a strong chief of staff. Democrats recoil from the possibility of a powerful CEO and choose a weak chief of staff or none at all. Democratic presidents place themselves at the hub of a wheel with many spokes. Soon enough, they find that to be a recipe for chaos. Jimmy Carter started with no chief of staff. Halfway through his term he gave the title and full responsibility to Hamilton Jordan. Too late. Wellford was worried that the new White House would steer into the same swamp.

The failure to appoint a strong White House staff early meant that no-

body was focusing on how the President would seize the stage in the first days of his presidency.

Stephanopoulos was the transition's communications director. There was still early Beatlemania for George. *The New York Times* published a large photo of him, looking tousled and sexy, in front of a Patton-sized American flag. (I stood next to him. My first *New York Times* caption read: "Man at rear is not identified.") He was preternaturally savvy and idealistic. If anyone had been charged with planning the first weeks, it would have been George, but even he was not given clear responsibility.

A plan for the first weeks did circulate. It was a memo that David Gergen, who had served as Ronald Reagan's communications director, had written to the Gipper in 1980. Scrounging through the stacks of the one decent bookstore in Little Rock, we realized that the most recent Democratic book on how to use the presidency, *Presidential Power and the Modern Presidents* by Richard Neustadt, was originally published in 1960—the same book JFK had relied upon when he was preparing to take office. It warned that presidential transitions were the most perilous time, and that few administrations knew what they were doing when they took power. Ha! At least we won't make that mistake, we thought.

As Christmas approached, the pace quickened. Every few days, Clinton would announce a new batch of cabinet nominees. And they would be subject to a grilling from the press.

"Senator Bentsen, you have been accused of being in the pocket of lobbyists and moneyed special interests. You had to cancel your 'breakfast club' when you would meet with lobbyists because of appearances. Doesn't this send the wrong signal?" I finished my question, playing a reporter, with perhaps just a little too much body English. We were in the den of the Governor's Mansion. Lloyd Bentsen had just committed to leaving the United States Senate to be nominated as secretary of the treasury. In a few minutes, his appointment would be announced to the press. The regal Texan was submitting himself to mock interrogation by the communications staff of the transition (it would have taken three of us to exceed his age). He bristled and glared. "I strongly support campaign finance reform. I have supported it throughout my career. And no one can question the way in which I have conducted myself in office." I knew how Dan Quayle must have felt when he faced Bentsen in the vice presidential debate. Clinton watched, amused. "None of the real questions are as tough as these guys," he observed.

Most of the domestic cabinet nominees were to be announced on December 11. We gathered in the mansion's living room to prepare them. Stephanopoulos, communications aide Ricki Seidman, press secretary Dee Dee Myers, and Gene Sperling faced them on a couch. Bob Boorstin, one of the other deputies, and I sat on chairs. Nearly all of us were in our

early thirties. Warren Christopher sat bolt upright, neatly pressed and silent, in the corner. Mack McLarty, a polite Arkansas businessman and old friend of Clinton's, was there. (We weren't sure why; the next day he would be named chief of staff.) Hillary wandered in and out, and finally sat by the door.

The last to be mock-grilled was Carol Browner. She was thirty-six years old. I knew her from her days as a congressional staff member and environmental activist in Washington, before she returned to Florida to become that state's environmental commissioner. Now she was being nominated to head the Environmental Protection Agency, with a budget of $5.9 billion. We pushed her with tough questions. "You used to work for Citizen Action, a left-wing environmental group. Aren't you too extreme?" "What about the Florida Everglades?" Browner earnestly rebutted each charge. We were done.

Hillary looked up. "You didn't ask her the most obvious question."

"What's that?" we asked.

"Aren't you too *young* to be in the cabinet?" She looked at us. "But *they* wouldn't ask that." She smiled. (I think.)

STEPHANOPOULOS HAD ASSEMBLED for Clinton a thick three-ring notebook of memos and essays from supporters and friends with advice for the new president's inaugural address. Among others, the great living Democratic speechwriters were contacted—Ted Sorensen, Dick Goodwin, Arthur Schlesinger Jr. For Clinton, it was a way of tweaking his current staff: get me some *real* speechwriters. They were also a good source of lines and ideas. (The line in Al Gore's 1992 convention speech used to great repetitive effect—"It is time for them to go!"—was plucked by Bruce Reed from a memo by Goodwin, who had written some of Lyndon Johnson's and Robert Kennedy's greatest speeches.) For Clinton, I suspected, it was also the baby boomer's thrill at being able to summon up all his political heroes, akin to asking the Stones to play at a pool party.

I was assigned to write a memo about political reform. I wrote a broader treatise, suggesting that the inaugural focus on the need to renew our democracy. "Winston Churchill once was asked what he thought of a pudding. 'It lacks theme,' he replied. An inaugural address, to succeed, cannot 'lack theme.' " The memo continued, "In crafting an inaugural address, the major question to be asked is: what is the condition of the country, what is the situation, that is to be confronted by the address? (The great inaugural addresses deal concretely with national moods or crises, tying them into more timeless themes.) In other words, what is the pivot? And in what direction does the new President want to push?

"I would suggest that the need to rebuild the economy, while obviously the main reason Gov. Clinton was elected, is subsumed within an even greater imperative: *Citizens are deeply cynical about government and politics, and thus distrust governmental solutions to problems. But they want to believe in the political system, and in the idea of the United States as a functional and thriving democracy.*" I urged that Clinton make the renewal of our democracy his central theme.

I finished it past the deadline and faxed it to the Governor's Mansion in Little Rock. I wasn't being devious or bureaucratically deft—just disorganized. In any case, Nancy Hernreich, the governor's executive assistant, slipped it into the front of the briefing book.

A few days after New Year's, I was back in Little Rock. Stephanopoulos' assistant called me up to his office, one flight above mine. There was barely room for him, his desk, and me. He looked up with studied cool. It was the political equivalent of Ed McMahon arriving at your door with an oversized check.

"Governor Clinton wants you to work on the inaugural address."

TWO

FORCING THE SPRING: INAUGURATION DAY 1993

ON A CHILLY SUNDAY in early January 1993, Bill Clinton was at the dining room table in the Governor's Mansion in Little Rock. George Stephanopoulos, speechwriter David Kusnet, and I sat with him. It was our first session to discuss his inaugural address, the speech that would be his first words in power, to be delivered for the ages. Clinton leaned across the table.

"Ask not what your country can do for you," he intoned. "You have nothing to fear but fear itself. If you can't stand the heat get out of the kitchen. Live free or die. And in conclusion: read my lips!" Clinton pinkened with laughter. He was reciting a speech made by Eddie Murphy in the movie *The Distinguished Gentleman*, which had arrived in Little Rock cinemas the week before. Murphy plays a con artist who talks his way into Congress. His victory speech is a hilarious collection of political clichés.

We laughed along with Clinton—partly in memory of the movie, partly at the insider tingle of hearing the President-elect deliver the same lines. And in my case, at least, partly in secret exultation: the new president, I thought, understood the film's subversive message—the pressing need for change, the urgent need to break Washington's racket.

Few things equal the dizzying thrill of working on a new president's inaugural address. Power and energy seem to flow to the new leader, cascading from unseen and untapped sources, pooling in this one person who will briefly embody the nation's hopes. The document will set the tone for a new administration, chart the course for the politics of an era, and, possibly, change the way a country sees itself. This meeting was my first wet bath in Clinton's charm and intellectual energy. His words flew quickly and his

southern accent thickened. At the same time he seemed disorganized, even then exhausted by the task he had set out for himself.

Clinton had not taken a vacation after the election—he had no country home to retreat to, and chose not to head to the Caribbean. The only real time he took off was around New Year's, when he and his family went to Hilton Head for the annual Renaissance Weekend retreat. This was an invitation-only gathering of media and government strivers. There were encounter sessions and workshops, all very earnest. The papers were full of photos of Clinton playing touch football on the beach.

Now he was back, his synapses firing, his head filled with ideas from the dozens of people he had seen and spoken to. We sat around his formal dining room table, softly lit by a chandelier. As I was to learn over the next seven years, drafting a major speech with Clinton is not a solitary exercise—for the speechwriter or for the President. He did not want a polished and perfect draft. Our job was to capture his thoughts, feed him ideas, try to wrestle it into some sense of structure and organization. We sat with a tape recorder, and pen and paper. He, in turn, decided how to act by reacting—to our drafts, to the urgings of others. He often found his organizing principles by dissecting contrary advice.

Clinton had decided to focus the speech, he said, above all, on the theme of "a re-creation—a renewal." He had outlined the themes, and tested out much of the language, in a speech he had given just before midnight on New Year's Eve. He had spoken on a panel with elderly Supreme Court Justice Harry Blackmun. The topic was "changing of the guard." He wanted to give an address with a heavy focus on generational change.

"We have changed the guard," he now repeated. "And now, each in our own way, we must answer the call. It's a timeless mission. We have to march to the music of time, but ours is a timeless mission."

Clinton had campaigned as a candidate who understood the middle class, and who opposed austerity economics. His theme in the primaries was rejection of the idea that the middle class was pampered and needed to sacrifice for the sake of its soul. Now he was shifting course, contemplating an economic plan that emphasized deficit reduction. "We have to do two things at once," he said. "We have to do something the American people have never had to do: deal with an enormous amount of debt and increase our investment. Nobody's ever had to do this."

Stephanopoulos pointed out that twelve years before, in his first inaugural, Ronald Reagan had announced that government is not the solution, government is the problem. "We have to say what the government's about," Clinton responded. He rarely said no to a direct suggestion. But he didn't jump at the idea of a rebuttal of Reagan. This speech would not offer a reconsideration of the role of government. That could come later.

Clinton observed that we needed to address political reform. The Eddie Murphy movie was a parable about Washington and its corruption. It was a parody of the disdain for politics, the anti-incumbent anger that had been lit by the savings and loan scandal, the congressional pay raise, and the stubborn stall in wages and family incomes. We commented on how striking it was that this sentiment was now so widespread that it was fodder for Hollywood. "You know, the character of the committee chairman is based on a real person," I tendered. Dick Dodge, gruff and cynical chair of the dominant Power and Industry Committee, was plainly based on John Dingell, longtime chair of the Energy and Commerce Committee. By 1992 that committee had jurisdiction over some 35 percent of the legislation that went before Congress. "Really? Was the character based on him?" Clinton asked. He looked at Stephanopoulos, who had been the top aide on the House floor for the Democratic leader.

Clinton remembered one Arkansas congressman. "He used to bring these lobbyists down for retreats," he smiled. "I didn't think that was very good." His tone was partly of disapproval, but with more than a twinge of amusement. Clinton's love for the human comedy of politics undercut any puritanical drive to reform it. But at this moment, the cheers of the campaign trail still fresh, he recognized that some fundamental anger at politics was abroad—and he wanted to address it.

AN INAUGURAL ADDRESS is one of the only times that a president knows for sure that his words will be remembered in history. The Government Printing Office publishes a book of every president's inaugural remarks. The speeches have ranged from eloquent to awful. The shortest was Lincoln's breathtaking second inaugural, in which he said the Civil War was God's punishment for the sin of slavery and called for reconciliation. The longest was so protracted that President William Henry Harrison caught a cold and died of pneumonia a month later. Most inaugural addresses aren't very good.

Kennedy's was the only inaugural in the twentieth century to achieve bracing eloquence without a crisis. And it is the one everybody knows. As we worked, mock inaugurals were arriving by fax and Federal Express at the transition offices because applicants for speechwriter jobs had been asked to produce a draft speech. Many included "ask not what your country can do for you" paragraphs. It reminded me of the scene in Mel Brooks' *The Producers*, where one bad actor after another auditions to play Hitler in "Springtime for Hitler." I wrote out a set of rules and taped it on the wall behind my computer. NO QUOTING DEAD PRESIDENTS. NO REVERSIBLE RAINCOAT SENTENCES. (The phrase, coined by hu-

morist Calvin Trillin, denoted Sorensen's neatly balanced and inverted sentences.) We kept being pulled back to Kennedy's speech. Clearly, it was the pattern imprinted on Clinton's mind.

David Kusnet had written a skeleton first draft. He was the campaign speechwriter who had stayed in Little Rock and sent out drafts to the traveling party. He was famous in political circles as a character in an anecdote about Michael Dukakis: the Massachusetts governor had ordered Kusnet not to use "country club Republicans" as a pejorative since lots of nice people go to country clubs. Kusnet had written a book, *Speaking American*, teaching liberals how to talk to ordinary people instead of just to themselves. The book is full of growled anecdotes from life as a union organizer, disdain for woolly-headed and academic liberalism. I expected to meet a longshoreman. Kusnet was shy and gentle, with studious glasses.

Kusnet's draft was polished and moving, but it did not yet have a sharp focus. It began with a tribute to George Bush and the generation now departing power. It dwelt at length on the history of the nation. And it refashioned a line that Clinton had used frequently on the campaign trail. "Every problem in America has been solved somewhere," Clinton would say, speaking like an inventive governor whose mission is to find successful pilot programs and employ their lessons. Kusnet had molded this practical thought into a sweeping, Kennedyesque sentence that was obviously intended to be the "line" from the inaugural. "There is nothing wrong with America that cannot be cured by what is right with America."

Clinton asked for another try, along with a series of one-liners, bits of rhetoric, and a conceptual outline. He asked for it to be eight to ten minutes long. Over the next few days Kusnet and I wrote another draft. It began with an image that had been passed on to Clinton by Stephanopoulos. Father Timothy Healy, the Jesuit priest who had headed Georgetown University and for whom George had briefly worked at the New York Public Library, was at work on a memo and draft speech for Clinton when he died. "We hold this ceremony in the depth of winter," Healy's notes read, "but in another sense, by the words we say and the faces we show to the world we are indeed forcing the spring. This occasion is indeed May–winter, spring, 'Pentecostal fire in the dark time of year.' " "Forcing the spring." It sounded nice. But what did it mean? Apparently, forcing a bulb means to cause a plant to bloom ahead of its natural schedule. It was, in some ways, a worrying metaphor.

Clinton liked the new draft, but one thing wasn't right, he said at our next meeting. We had not hit political reform hard enough. I had written, "Together, we can take back our government from the special interests. Together, we can make sure that the power of money will never shout down the voice of the people."

Clinton bit his pen. "No, this isn't enough. This is what I want to say." He dictated rapid fire, with surprising vehemence.

"This capital, like every capital since the dawn of civilization, has been a place of intrigue and calculation. Powerful and wealthy people come here and maneuver with an obsessive concern about who is in and who is out, who is up and who is down, often forgetting about the people whose toil and sweat sent them here.

"In the past year, I met Americans by the tens of thousands who deserve better. And I know that in this city there are hardworking people who want to renew our public life. So let us resolve to reform our politics, so that the power of organized money no longer can shout down the public interest. Let us put aside the petty politics of personal advantage, to hear the pain and see the promise of America, and to give this capital back to the people to whom it belongs."

WITH THE SPEECH UNFINISHED five days before the inaugural, the Clintons were leaving Little Rock to begin the long processional into Washington. Their entourage would go with them.

Kusnet and I stood in front of our offices in the emptying transition building. Our luggage had been sent ahead. Laptops were at the ready. I carried William Safire's book of great speeches, a Bible, and a frayed collection of presidential inaugurals. The wipable board from the campaign headquarters four blocks away still read, in magenta Magic Marker, "Themes: Change Versus More of the Same. The Economy, Stupid. Don't Forget Health Care." It had already entered political lore, it was already part of the legend of James Carville. Shouldn't it go in the Smithsonian? Our assistant gently wrapped it up and loaded it for the trip. It would be put on display at an inaugural eve party. It was never seen again.

The first leg of the trip was to take us from Arkansas to Virginia. An emotional crowd of the Clintons' old friends saw them off at Little Rock Municipal Airport. Their daughter, Chelsea, brought high school classmates along. It was the last flight on a charter plane, with the press and staff and President-elect all in the same cabin.

The flight was quiet, just the whine of engines. Each of us nursed our reverie. For me, it was a romantic fantasy: a reformer, a rebel, having left Washington for the hinterlands, returning with the conquering general to clean out the infidels.

The journey was an exercise in carefully choreographed spontaneity, designed to recapture the campaign's populist energy. Buses. Casual clothes. Young people. Small towns. The speechwriters were assigned to one of the buses.

We stopped at Monticello, where Clinton talked about Jefferson, the young man as national leader, the president who believed in permanent revolution. In Washington, he was scheduled to visit John F. Kennedy's gravesite, and would speak at an event honoring Martin Luther King Jr.

We fell silent as our bus drove over Memorial Bridge and pulled up in the traffic circle behind the Lincoln Memorial, four days before the inaugural ceremony, where an open-air pre-inaugural concert was being held. Military jets streaked overhead. I found my wife and we embraced. Hundreds of thousands of revelers watched a performance staged on the steps of the memorial. The highlight was a handful of the world's greatest saxophonists, lined up in tribute to Clinton, bleating "Heartbreak Hotel."

BUT THE SPEECH WASN'T DONE. More to the point, it was growing. With each draft, Clinton was crossing out other people's writing, composing in between the lines in his tight left-leaning scrawl and assigning us to draft new sections that were nearly doubling it in length. As the streets filled with the party faithful, Kusnet and I went to an office at George Washington University, and worked all night on separate computers to recast and condense the latest draft. At dawn, we walked to Blair House, the President-elect's quarters across Pennsylvania Avenue from the White House.

The official guesthouse for the United States government was a scene of elated and feverish activity. From the street, its façade is modest. It looks like a townhouse. In fact, the front door opens up to a series of interconnected mansions nearly a block long, with the floors mismatched from one building to the next.

The halls were crowded with luggage and boxes. A monogrammed golf bag, with Clinton's name on it, leaned against a wall. We worked in a sitting room that had been converted into a staff office. Large gilt-framed portraits peered down on us. At one end of a table, an old Little Rock friend sat, counting out tickets and assigning seats for the inaugural platform. (At one in the morning, as I worked through the second night on the speech, I asked her for a ticket. She snorted.) At the other end of the table, Nancy Hernreich worked with Clinton's new secretary, Betty Currie. They would soon be sharing the space outside the Oval Office. Betty was one of us; an experienced political operative who had worked in the War Room for Carville and then as Warren Christopher's secretary.

I began to learn that for Clinton, a major speech doesn't merely involve the ideas of his friends. The friends show up. Throughout his career, he cultivated friendships. He had his fundraising friends, his policy friends, his golf and card friends. He had a circle of literary friends, too. They were part of any speechwriting ritual. Whenever Clinton faced a

nerve-fraying public performance, his college roommate Tommy Caplan materialized.

Caplan was an historical novelist living in Baltimore. And when he sensed Clinton needed a steadying hand, Caplan would move in, literally. His droll enthusiasms and slightly off-the-point comments kept Clinton loose. But his political judgment was sound; he had hung around the Kennedy White House as a high school student. Tommy had a graceful pen, usually focusing on the peroration, the part of a speech when the policy is done and the poetry can take over. He sat down and began thinking out loud to Kusnet and me about ways to lift the language. Clinton had written, "Our Founders saw themselves in the light of posterity. We can do no less." "How about this?" Caplan asked in his singsong voice. "Anyone who has ever watched a child's eyes wander into sleep knows what posterity is." When Clinton saw the draft, he added, "Posterity is the world to come—the world for whom we hold our ideals, from whom we have borrowed our planet, and to whom we bear sacred responsibility."

Shortly after, another old Clinton friend arrived. Taylor Branch had won the Pulitzer Prize for the first volume of his biography of Martin Luther King Jr. Clinton knew him from the McGovern campaign in 1972, where they had the improbable assignment of managing the peace candidate's campaign in hawkish Texas. Branch had not heard from Clinton consistently over the years. But as this biggest speech of his life approached, Clinton had reached out to the most prominent writer he knew well. Branch began tweaking lines.

Clinton went out into the cold to speak at a Martin Luther King Day observance at Howard University. The holiday was a fortunate accident of timing. Branch had brought a quote from a speech King had delivered in Harlem upon returning from Oslo, where he received the Nobel Prize in 1964. "For the last ten days," King had said, "I have been on a literal mountaintop, having transfiguring experiences. We've had the privilege of meeting and talking with Kings and Queens, meeting and talking with Prime Ministers of nations. . . . I wish I could stay on this mountaintop. I wish I could stay here tonight, but the valley calls me." Clinton told the hushed crowd that "God did not drop me from a mountaintop. I was born in the valley"—applause washed over him. "Let us begin, with energy and hope, with faith and discipline, and let us not quit until our day is done. The Scripture says, 'Let us not grow weary in doing good, for in due season we shall reap if we do not lose heart.' Martin Luther King Jr. never lost heart. Let us spend ourselves in the valley in the quest for which he gave his all." Clinton came back fired with the music, the prayers, and the affirmation of the black audience. His extemporaneous riff would now become the peroration for the inaugural.

INAUGURAL EVE. Upstairs, in his dressing room, the President-elect sat down with a copy of the speech. He was already changed into his tuxedo for the televised inaugural gala. Hillary was getting ready in the next room, visible through an open door. He wanted to strengthen the statement on the budget deficit. After weeks during which his economic advisors had urged him to make deficit reduction the priority of his economic plan, Clinton was beginning to realize he needed to shift his emphasis. But he didn't like it. "You know, I hired people like Leon Panetta for their technical expertise on the budget," he told a few of us, putting aural quote marks around the word "technical." "But these people have no idea how the middle class has suffered." Clinton was acutely aware of issues of class and economic power. He saw himself as the mediator between the voters and the elites.

That night, the Clintons attended the inaugural gala at a suburban sports arena. We waited for them to return. Clinton was planning to rehearse in a downstairs library off the entrance foyer of Blair House. Every once in a while, one of the military personnel who would be operating the teleprompter would stick his head in the door. Are we really planning to do this? Yes, they were assured, we're going to rehearse. Finally the President-elect returned. Early in the morning, Clinton took his place behind a mock podium in the dark-paneled room. Gore sat there, posture perfect, his head dropping and jerking awake.

Clinton decided to begin, not with a long list of acknowledgments, but as Thomas Jefferson had, with a republican "Fellow Citizens." He changed words: "commerce and communications are global, investment is mobile, technology is—not 'transportable,' how about, 'technology is almost magical.'" He rewrote the passage on deficit reduction. We must choose "sacrifice not for its own sake but for our own sake."

He cut out words, lines, and whole paragraphs, slicing out a page of challenges that embodied his "new covenant" of opportunity and responsibility. "We will offer every worker a lifetime of learning," he cut, removing a paragraph that continued,

> but you must build your skills and prepare yourself for the new world marketplace. We will offer industry incentives to succeed—but you must respond by investing in America. We will provide a higher education for every student who wants it—but you must meet a higher standard of service in return. We will make health care affordable—but you must do more to care for yourselves. If we succeed, we will have shaped a new ethic of citizen responsibility.

The result was a speech that was lean and high-minded, a brisk over-
ture. It struck an invigorating note of sacrifice. Like Kennedy's, it referred
to generational change. But it missed an opportunity to redefine how a progressive might describe the role of government. It didn't challenge the listener as vigorously as many of his campaign speeches had done. It cited
Roosevelt's call for "bold persistent experimentation," but not his admonition, in a different speech, that "new conditions impose new requirements
upon government."

ON THE DAY ITSELF, the quibbles faded. As the President-elect called on the
President at the White House, Kusnet and I left Blair House and blinked in
the sunlight. We each had a copy of the inaugural address on a floppy disk.
An advance man pointed us to a police car, which drove up a deserted
Pennsylvania Avenue toward the Capitol, siren wailing. We handed the
disks to a military officer in a tiny, windowless wooden compartment alongside the inaugural platform, and left to find our seats. I turned to look at the
Mall. Hundreds of thousands of people filled the space, first in neat rows,
then in a multicolor profusion of parkas and ski hats, stretching all the way
down toward the Washington Monument, filling the side streets and perch-
ing on the edge of fountains.

Eight times in the speech's fourteen minutes, Clinton spoke about
change and renewal. William Safire would point out that the sense of re-
birth of a nation subtly echoed Lincoln at Gettysburg. His delivery was
brisk and strong.

Perhaps the most surprising moment came when Clinton read the
paragraph on political reform with some force—his personal pledge to
cleanse democracy's temple of the money-changers. "Let us give this government back to the people to whom it belongs."

He waited for applause. The officials and dignitaries on the platform
clapped politely, and he began to read the next paragraph. But as his words
echoed off the monuments a mile away, a wave of loud applause answered
back. It began at the far end of the crowd, by the Washington Monument,
and grew in strength as it approached the dignitaries on the inaugural platform, washing over the stand after a few seconds.

Sitting on a folding chair in front of the Capitol, hearing the new president reading words I knew so well, was nerve-fraying and exhilarating. The
sweep of the Capitol, the height of the stage, the pomp and solemnity—
hearing the phrases we had nursed for days—all was unforgettable. I wasn't
teary or overcome with joy. Mostly, I was tired.

Later that day, I fought through the crowds on the Mall, through Chi-

natown, and through the gates of the White House complex for the first time. A guard checked my ID, my driver's license, waited for a computer database (known as the WAVES system) to confirm that I was not a terrorist, looked up, and smiled. "Go on in."

A half dozen young staff members prowled the empty echoing halls of the Old Executive Office Building, where I (and most presidential aides) would work. The departing Bush assistants had left signs of their departure, the campfire still warm. I noticed a few strange artifacts. Next to cavernous offices, each with a single clean desk in the middle, were narrow offices that appeared to be for their secretaries. These were stocked with typewriters and quaint little plastic bottles: Wite-Out. Gentlemen, apparently, don't type. It looked like the Man in the Gray Flannel Suit had just decamped on the 5:40 back to Greenwich, circa 1958. *Wow*, I thought. *At least I know how we won.*

I approached the West Wing, across the parking lot that was grandly known as West Executive Avenue. Already, only a few hours into the new term, the walls of the West Wing lobby were lined with large color photographs of Clinton and Gore. The furniture was heavy and formal, the ceilings low, the hallways narrow, like an old New England bed-and-breakfast. You twist and turn and there you are: the Oval Office.

A uniformed agent stood guard. Could I go in? Sure. The room was empty, but the feeling of seeing that office for the first time has stayed with me. It is the brightest room I have ever seen: glorious windows, carefully recessed lights (designed for television cameras). It's impossible to escape the feeling that you have been there many times, and you have—in your fantasy life, reading novels, reading history, watching television. You could navigate the furniture with your eyes closed. At that moment, in that bright room, anything seemed possible.

THREE

CLINTONOMICS

RENEWING THE ECONOMY was Clinton's central promise as a candidate, and it would be his most visible achievement as president. To implement his plan he had to defeat the Republicans, who bitterly resisted his deficit reduction package (including a tax increase). And he had to overcome the Democrats, who resisted his free trade measures beginning with the trade pact with Mexico.

It's hard to remember now, after such a long stretch of prosperity, what it felt like in January 1993. Growth over the previous three years had been the slowest since before World War II. Manufacturing workers who once had counted on a lifetime of employment were being discarded by businesses in a massive cost-cutting wave. And it seemed that the government was powerless to do anything about it. A best-selling book of the previous year was entitled *America: What Went Wrong?*

When Clinton had met with his economic team for the first time in early January, they presented him with new and alarming estimates of the growing budget deficit. Twelve years into Reaganomics, the annual budget deficit was $290 billion, and by the end of a five-year budget cycle, it would be $346 billion. This was much worse than the Bush administration had admitted during the previous year's campaign. As a candidate, Clinton had argued above all for investment as the answer to the country's long-term economic woes. Keynesian theory, and liberal politics, suggested a surge of spending. His economic plan, unveiled in *Putting People First*, had called for $200 billion in new investments—in education, training, technology, and other programs—to help people survive economic change.

But those plans came directly into conflict with an approach urged by

his chief economic advisors. In addition to Lloyd Bentsen as treasury secretary, Clinton had chosen Robert Rubin, the co-chair of the Wall Street investment house Goldman Sachs, to be director of a new White House National Economic Council. Rubin and Bentsen made a novel argument. Something fundamental had changed, they said. The markets—the bond markets, the stock market—were now controlled by the collective opinion of financial analysts. If they were impressed by an economic plan, one that emphasized deficit cuts, the result would be a reduction of interest rates, and that far more than an investment scheme would improve the economy. Clinton was grumpy about their argument. But in one of the most important decisions of his presidency, he sided with them. It was a bank shot of historic proportions.

CLINTON WAS TO PREVIEW his economic proposals in a brief Oval Office address to the nation on February 15, and then to unveil them in an address to a joint session of Congress two days later. The success of these speeches was vital to the strategy. They would signal to the market that the President was willing to seek sacrifice. They would have to persuade the public to accept an unorthodox mix, one that was not expected of a Democrat.

There was a problem, however. For a month, the President held a floating seminar on economic policy in the Roosevelt Room, personally reviewing every line of the budget—something no other president had attempted to do. But as the elements of the economic plan shifted, no one told the speechwriters. A constantly expanding group of aides was drafting a February speech based on the economic assumptions and policy prescriptions of the previous June. And no one in the White House had composed anything as complex as a message to Congress.

When Clinton summoned speechwriters and communications aides to the Oval Office to discuss the congressional address, his instructions were ambitious, wide-ranging, and indiscriminate. "What do I—the voter, Congress—get out of this?" he asked. Notes from that meeting list a dizzying string of answers: child-support collection, community development banks, urban enterprise zones, reinventing government, national service, lobby registration and campaign finance reform, welfare reform, immunization of children, rebuilding the infrastructure, job training and conversion from military production into peacetime enterprise, increased cutting-edge research and development, full funding for Head Start preschool and the Women, Infants, and Children nutrition program, one million summer jobs, more police on the street, and so on. The speech had to explain "to ordinary Americans why the deficit matters," Clinton said. "We need a label, a slogan that ties this all together," Clinton said repeatedly.

I was not a speechwriter—I was working on the policy side—but I was asked to join Kusnet and begin drafting the speech to the Congress. Deputy Communications Director David Dreyer and Paul Begala, the campaign consultant, would start writing the Oval Office address. They were alumni of House majority leader Dick Gephardt's Capitol Hill office. Kusnet and I had come out of liberal social movements. No one charged with writing either speech was from the party's centrist New Democrat wing, and none of us were regularly in the Roosevelt Room, so our efforts were largely guesswork. Was the budget to be sold as investment or deficit reduction? How strongly should the arguments about fairness be made? Were we still putting people first?

The Oval Office address, as it turned out, was sharply partisan and accusatory. It called any opponents of the plan "the defenders of decline." It argued that the rich needed to pay their fair share (i.e., more); it put forward the populist arguments that had been so effective on the campaign trail. Coming from the President, in the Oval Office, it was jarring. The President had not yet mastered the ability to hover above the entire political landscape. There was the snap of a backlash. Chief of Staff Mack McLarty worried to me that a large number of businesspeople and lawmakers thought the speech had proposed class war. At one level it was a success: the broad public liked the idea of the rich paying more, and liked the cuts the speech discussed in government and the White House staff. In the Washington echo chamber, it was seen as a failure.

The unanticipated letdown raised the stakes for the address to Congress. But there was no direct and linear conversation instructing us to change direction—or, indeed, what direction we should take.

The day before the address, Gene Sperling was allowed out of the Roosevelt Room to tell the speechwriters what was in the budget. He had been the campaign's economic policy director. After months of constant work, he was feverish and bleary with a bad flu. In an all-night writing session in David Dreyer's corner office in the Old Executive Office Building, Sperling was propped up in an easy chair, covered with blankets and coats. Every so often, when we writers needed an explanation of a policy, or confirmation of a fact or figure, we would call out the question to him. Sperling would remain immobile. But after a few seconds, his eyes closed, he would give the answer we needed. Then he would relapse.

When the sun rose, the speech was adequate, but still pitched to an investment-oriented economic plan, not a deficit reduction strategy. It stressed the need for spending to restart the stalled economy—the so-called stimulus bill that would be introduced before the overall budget. Then it emphasized the need for long-term investments. Then, finally, the need to reduce the deficit. It seemed to present a conventionally liberal plan far

more enthusiastic about expanding government than trimming its excesses. Bruce Reed and Jeremy Rosner, a former Democratic Leadership Council aide who now wrote speeches for the National Security Council, drafted a new more centrist opening section. The President sent word that he wanted their beginning used. Rather than resolve the tensions between New and Old Democrats, Clinton papered them over by including dissonant notes from both songbooks.

Despite Clinton's importunings, we hadn't come up with a catchy slogan or label. Begala suggested something as simple as "New Direction." In the end, the speech proclaimed, "America needs a New Direction, and I intend to lead us there." It was even capitalized in the text. But nobody seemed to notice very much. The New Direction would join the New Covenant on Clinton's slogan compost pile.

ON WEDNESDAY MORNING, February 17, the day of the speech, Hillary Clinton erupted. She thought that the draft was a mess, that the competing and sometimes inconsistent elements of policy jangled discordantly. She sat at the head of the conference table in the Roosevelt Room of the West Wing, in front of the flags of the military services. She read each paragraph aloud, soliciting comments and dictating changes. The President was in his private dining room, trying to sell the plan to the three network anchors, and then in his office, working down a list of telephone calls to congressional leaders and opinionmakers. Entire sections were being lopped off. Reed was summoned to provide a New Democrat perspective. At Hillary's request, Bob Rubin provided a paragraph on the benefits of deficit reduction. The noon deadline for sending the speech to the printer came and went. (It would be the first time in twenty years, the *New York Times* noted with disapproval, that such a speech had not been distributed in advance on Capitol Hill.)

The President burst in through a side door. He was smiling and energized, seeming not the least concerned that a dozen of his advisors were rewriting the speech, even as the House chamber was being readied for his arrival.

"I just talked to Ross Perot," he said enthusiastically. "Here's what he said. 'I don't care what you say but you've got to talk about campaign finance reform.' That's all he wanted to talk about." He looked around the table, finally focusing on me. "We've really got to do campaign reform. We've really gotta work with him." Clinton often conveyed messages to one person by directing them at another. In this case, he was telling McLarty to get cracking, and he did it by addressing me in front of his chief of staff.

We moved to the family theater, a movie theater in the East Wing of

the White House that was equipped with a teleprompter for rehearsals. Now Clinton began aggressively editing and rewriting, writing in the margins of his reading copy. Begala and Dreyer tried to keep up with the changes. One key element was still missing: the President had asked for a list of specific cuts in government programs, but one after another, he rejected including them. He had been willing to make the cuts in the budget, but he was reluctant to brag about them, to use them to show his toughness in opposing entrenched interests. Cutting rural electrification seemed like an easy one; after all, this was 1993, and there were precious few acres of the country that lacked electricity. Clinton erupted, apparently for the second or third time. "It's easy for you to say," he groused. The urban, East Coast aides in a Democratic White House can feel tough and proud of themselves for cutting rural electrification. But he knew these people.

I left for the Capitol as the last changes were being typed. Sperling and I were wedged into a side aisle among a throng in the well of the House of Representatives.

The annual ceremony of democracy is never as exhilarating as when a new president unveils his freshman program. On television, the House chamber looks stately and spacious, laid out in neat rows like a formal garden. But from ground level, filled to capacity, it is small and clubby. The Supreme Court sits in the front row in black robes, with the cabinet across from them, minus one member chosen to stay behind in case a terrorist blows up the Capitol. Dozens of ambassadors, hundreds of congressional staff members, photographers, and high school pages fill the aisles. The Democrats were spread across most of the room, some of them having arrived hours early so that they could be photographed shaking the President's hand as he walked in. They were beaming at the thought that one of their own would deliver the speech instead of a dreaded Republican.

At the center of it, raised above the crowd like a preacher, stands the President. That was where Roosevelt had announced war. Where Truman was handed a note announcing a settlement just as he was proposing to draft striking railway workers. Where Kennedy called the nation to put a man on the moon. Where Reagan—just weeks after being shot—gallantly returned. This was a rostrum used to stately, mannered symphonies. It was about to hear a jazz performance by a skilled soloist working off a pedestrian score.

The text Clinton had before him was disorganized. It identified four priorities and two great goals; it was supposed to be just about the economy but it addressed nearly every other topic as well. There was a real risk that the speech would cloud the impact of the plan he was proposing. Clinton sensed that. As he moved through the speech, seeing lawmakers stir and respond to points and fall silent for others, he began to feed off their response.

He began to riff—to ad-lib, to revise entire paragraphs. His voice rose and fell, his tempo quickened and slowed.

When he got to the health care section, he stopped. "But all of our efforts to strengthen the economy will fail—let me say this again, I feel so strongly about this—all of our efforts to strengthen the economy will fail unless we also take this year, not next year, not five years from now but this year, bold steps to reform our health care system." The audience was transfixed.

On the House floor, standing on tiptoes, Sperling and I were scanning our single-spaced copies of the speech. "He's ad-libbing! He's ad-libbing the State of the Union!" we shouted, and gave each other a high five. We were proud of Clinton, of his ability to rise to the occasion, to surmount an inadequate draft. Our jostling brought stares from those around us. Just who were these obnoxious people?

The politicians in the audience knew how remarkable this was. They had been accustomed to Reagan's stagy mannerisms and Bush's drone. This—well, this was *interesting*. The Republicans laughed when Clinton cited the "independent figures" of the Congressional Budget Office. He turned to them. It was like an actor breaking through the fourth wall, suddenly addressing the audience directly. "Well, you can laugh, my fellow Republicans," he joked. "But I'll point out that the Congressional Budget Office was normally more conservative on what was going to happen and closer to right than previous presidents." When he called on Congress to pass campaign finance and lobbying reform, lawmakers of both parties applauded—and then laughed. Clinton caught them. "Believe me, they were *cheering* that last section at home," he lectured, waving his finger.

"We must scale the walls of the people's skepticism, not with our words but with our deeds. After so many years of gridlock and indecision, after so many hopeful beginnings and so few promising results, the American people are going to be harsh in their judgments of all of us if we fail to seize this moment," he concluded. The sight of the new president, playing off the reaction of the crowd as if it were a local church congregation rather than a joint session of Congress, sent a real jolt—a surge of possibility and urgency. It seemed as if the country might finally be ready to break the habit of political gridlock.

In one way, the signature moment of the evening had come before Clinton entered the chamber. Lawmakers gazed up and saw Federal Reserve chairman Alan Greenspan seated next to Hillary in the First Lady's Gallery. It has been widely reported that the economic plan was drafted with an eye toward the likely reaction of the Fed chair. If the elected officials agreed to make deficit reduction the centerpiece of the economic plan, the Fed would lower interest rates. It was a savvy move to put the con-

servative Republican Fed chair next to Hillary. The tentative alliance it signaled would prove durable.

IT WAS HARD FOR THE PRESIDENT to admit it; harder still for his communications advisors, nearly all of whom were more liberal than he was: the economic plan had become principally a deficit reduction package. The
White House was almost apologetic.

The administration was confronting a dilemma that had bedeviled
presidents and prime ministers before Clinton: a possible revolt of the financial markets. The British Labour Party in the 1970s, Jimmy Carter and
the Democrats in 1979, the French Socialists in 1982, all had seen their
economic program wrecked by capital flight and gyrating interest rates.
The growth of highly dynamic global capital markets made the threat even
greater. Clinton was choosing to make peace with the markets. He would
be the first center-left head of government in years to serve without a crisis
of confidence in the financial markets. And the success of the program
turned it from a tactical bargain to a new tenet. In the era of global markets,
fiscal responsibility—which led to lower interest rates—was a more potent
stimulus than the traditional tools of tax cuts or spending.

For all its reliance on the market, Clinton's economic program was
seen as a pivot in economic policy. *Time* magazine dramatized it by putting
on its cover a photograph of Ronald Reagan—upside down. Within its arcane provisions, there were subtle but notable shifts in the role of government. Most important, it significantly expanded the Earned Income Tax
Credit, tax relief given to 15 million working poor families, which over the
course of the decade would prove to be the country's most effective anti-
poverty program. This quiet initiative was a major step toward fulfilling
Clinton's campaign pledge to "make work pay." At the same time, by hik-
ing income taxes on the highest earners, it rendered the code more
progressive. The budget launched a new urban policy by authorizing
"empowerment zones" that would combine tax cuts and economic development spending to revitalize inner cities. It focused new funds on the
poor, with an expansion of food stamps and Head Start and child immunization, and set the stage for more spending on education.

The struggle to pass the plan would consume months. The White
House had hoped to follow the model of Ronald Reagan's first budget—a
big announcement, a tidal wave of popular support, a reluctant Congress
bowing to public pressure. It would be an epic crusade for the new president. But the old methods no longer worked. First, the economic stimulus
bill was defeated on the floor of the Senate by a Republican filibuster—a
hammer blow to the new administration's momentum. Then the overall

budget passed only after gruesome public negotiations with Clinton's jealous rivals within the Democratic Party, among them Senator Bob Kerrey. The impression hardened that Clinton was less a commander in chief than the putative leader of feuding factions on Capitol Hill.

Republican lawmakers unanimously opposed the budget. Robert Dole, the Senate minority leader, said, "The American people know this plan doesn't tackle the deficit head-on." House minority whip Newt Gingrich predicted, "This will lead to a recession next year." John Kasich, the ranking Republican on the House Budget Committee, announced, "This plan will not work. If it was to work, I'd have to become a Democrat." It passed, in the end, by only one vote in each chamber. The night the Senate approved the measure, with Vice President Gore breaking a tie, Clinton spoke in the Rose Garden. "What we heard tonight at the other end of Pennsylvania Avenue was the sound of gridlock breaking," he said.

That was wishful thinking.

FOUR

CAMPAIGN FINANCE REFORM

At Clinton's first press conference at the Old State House in Little Rock after the 1992 election, a reporter had asked a sharp and pertinent question. How would the new president avoid Jimmy Carter's mistake of clogging the Congress with too many pieces of legislation too quickly? Clinton had answered confidently: "One of the things that I think is important that we do is to set priorities and to proceed with discipline. I think that there are some clear priorities that we have to pursue." He listed them. A plan for economic growth and deficit reduction. A plan to deal with health care. And third, "we have to have a plan for political reform, something I campaigned on and I believe in." (National service was fourth.)

Slap! Bob Boorstin, my office-mate, pounded my back in quiet congratulations. A half dozen reporters looked over to the side of the stage where we were crouching. A friend in the press corps caught my eye and winked. I was elated. After years in which I fought for reform against the incumbents of Congress, we finally had a president who would get it done. It didn't matter that he rarely brought up the subject unless asked. In fact, that was better; you needed a Lyndon Johnson, a real politician, to squeeze through the laws, to work the system and stroke the egos and make the compromises.

By 1992, the campaign finance system was a growing and widely recognized national scandal. The capital was now immobilized, with *Fortune* magazine estimating that over 80,000 people were involved in lobbying in Washington. Candidates and parties, in turn, were becoming consumed with a fundraising arms race. Officials were spending huge amounts of their time fundraising instead of doing their work. Most House incumbents

outspent their challengers 3 or 4 to 1. Because of the cost of campaigns, a growing number of senators were millionaires who could, as the professionals said, "self-finance." And presidential candidates, who had pledged to limit their spending in exchange for public funding from the taxpayers, had begun to raise so-called soft money—virtually unlimited contributions directly from corporations, labor unions and wealthy individuals. In 1992, it seemed like a scandal rotting away at democracy. (Now, alas, it seems like the innocent good old days.)

It was my personal crusade. I had written dozens of op-ed articles, co-authored a book, worked late nights for reform for a decade. Less than a year before the election, I stood with picketers outside a Republican fundraiser at the Washington, D.C., convention center, chanting, "Hey hey, ho ho, soft money's got to go!" I bellowed through a megaphone at the donors, in evening dress, who were lining up to go inside. "May I have your attention, please. This is the G Street entrance. If you have purchased an ambassadorship, please use the G Street entrance. If you have purchased tax loopholes and regulatory relief, please use the Eleventh Street entrance. This entrance is for ambassadorships only."

Before the presidential election, the Democratic Congress had passed a strong bill to curb the role of campaign spending. It would have provided public financing to congressional candidates who agreed to limit their spending. It would also have banned the soft money used by parties. The Democrats had many reasons for their courage. Most important among them was their certainty that President George Bush would veto the legislation. Support for reform, at least verbal support, was the norm for Democratic presidential candidates. The citizen group Common Cause had gotten each of the Democratic hopefuls to sign a pledge supporting the legislation. Clinton was the last one to sign.

When Ross Perot ran for president, one of his principal selling points was that he could pay for his own campaign, and thus would not have to raise funds from special interests the way the other two candidates did. In *Putting People First*, Clinton devoted a chapter to reforming politics. Especially when Perot, who had dropped out of the race, reentered, Clinton would discuss it. "I'm the only guy running who's ever done anything to restrain the influence of lobbyists and the only guy running for president who's never been part of the Washington establishment," he said on the stump in Seattle.

Perot's strong results—coming, as they did, after he showed himself to be flakier than a fresh croissant—made an impression. On election night, Clinton addressed the need for reform directly. "I heard tonight Mr. Perot's remarks and his offer to work with us. I say to you of all the things that he said, I think perhaps the most important that we understand here in the

heartland of Arkansas is the need to reform the political system, to reduce the influence of special interests and give more influence back to the kind of people that are in this crowd tonight by the tens of thousands—and I will work with him to do that."

As the first press conference broke up a few days later, and Clinton greeted me by name—the first time! from memory!—I was short of breath. When I returned to my office, phone messages from reform advocates and reporters had already begun to pile up. Speed was of the essence. Perhaps a deal could be cut with Congress soon, as the press was speculating, even before the inauguration.

WARREN CHRISTOPHER, the transition chairman, had a small but tidy office on the top floor. The senior staff met every morning in a narrow conference room a few feet away. We were leaving the meeting a few days after Clinton's press conference when I walked past a nervous, owlish man who was waiting to see Christopher. It was Howard Paster, the newly named legislative director for the President-elect. We were introduced.

When he heard my name, his fidgeting became even more pronounced. He leaned in to me and said, almost in a whisper, that he needed to talk to me—immediately—in private. We went back into Christopher's conference room and closed the door.

Clinton had reached into the heart of Washington in hiring Paster, who had begun as a lobbyist for the United Auto Workers and become a lobbyist for corporate interests.

"I need to talk to you about campaign finance reform," Paster said. "What I want to know is, are we going to work *with* Congress? Are we going to work *with* Congress?" He waited for my answer.

"Sure," I answered. "With Congress. We'll work with Congress." *What does he think? They make the laws, last I heard.* He visibly relaxed. I had passed the test, whatever it was. Or I had given in. Or something.

Paster leaned in close again. "You know, when the President interviewed me, he told me he had one question: did I believe in campaign finance reform?" I was expected to look impressed, so I did. That was it. We parted.

ON FEBRUARY 3, 1993, the new president met with the Democratic leaders in a formal session to discuss campaign reform. It was a high-water mark for the issue, though nobody knew it at the time. Arrayed around the table in the Cabinet Room were Speaker of the House Tom Foley, majority leader Dick Gephardt, Senate majority leader George Mitchell—who would all

be key to passage of the economic plan. These were the barons on whom the sovereign depended.

One key ally was missing. Mike Synar was a young congressman from Oklahoma who had played Ross Perot in the mock debates a few months before. He was the most prominent and ardent campaign finance reform advocate among the Democrats. But he was smart-alecky and controversial. When the list of attendees arrived from Capitol Hill and his name was not on it, we called Foley's office and were told, no, Synar most definitely could not come.

Synar called me, furious. "Listen to me, sonny boy, the White House can't mess with me like that," he shouted. We didn't know what we were getting into, he said. Foley and the rest of the Democrats didn't want reform. We would be sucked into their game of delay. We would regret it. I couldn't tell Synar that Foley had kept him out; it would look as if the White House was double-crossing the leadership. I stammered something noncommittal and hung up.

With Synar absent, the blood sugar in the room was dropping very low. A few minutes before the lawmakers arrived, a handful of us had met with Clinton in the Oval Office. The question being pressed upon us by members of Congress—and echoing in the press—was not whether there would be public financing, or what limits would be imposed on spending. It was far simpler. When would the legislation take effect? Lawmakers wanted to be sure that, whatever dreamy scheme was enacted, it would not affect their next race. (Saint Augustine put it succinctly: "Lord, give me chastity. But not just now.")

"Well, it's OK with me to have the effective date after the election. That seems right," the President said offhandedly. That would smooth the passage.

Clinton opened the meeting in a soft, distant voice. He knew from being on the campaign trail that the public wanted reform. This was something that could be accomplished to show that we had heard the message of the voters. He wanted to work with Congress to get it done. This would be their accomplishment. Gore reminded the Democratic leaders how the crowd had responded to political reform on inaugural day.

Foley answered in a slightly indignant, almost patronizing tone. He wanted to make it clear he was for reform. But nobody should be under any impression that passing it would be easy. And we would need the votes and goodwill of rank-and-file members of Congress to pass the tax increase, budget cuts, and health reform the President wanted so badly. The most important thing was that Clinton should not demand that Congress act within a deadline. A deadline would be counterproductive. The Congress had to do this itself.

Senate leader George Mitchell observed dryly that the Senate would be happy with a deadline. Senator David Boren of Oklahoma urged Clinton to challenge Congress. Clinton slumped in his seat and listened passively, occasionally taking notes. There was no table thumping, no LBJ-like harangue about the need for action. The meeting ended with a pledge to negotiate a proposal that the White House and Democrats in both chambers could introduce.

I was dispatched to Capitol Hill for two months of "consultations" with members of Congress. I met with dozens of Democrats in their offices. One after another, they lacerated the bill, explaining how it would cause them to lose their next election and what they would do instead—a cacophony of inconsistent proposals. As the weeks went on, the sense of urgency dissipated.

In the meantime, we accidentally spent the money that was to pay for public financing of elections. Clinton was uncomfortable with public financing. Campaigning, he had proposed that broadcasters be required to provide free television time to candidates—in part as an alternative to public funding, to avoid the political problem of taxpayer funds going to politicians. It was partly a regional response. In keeping with their anti-government animus generally, southerners were especially nervous about public funding. One day in the Oval Office, Bruce Lindsey, the White House personnel director who was Clinton's former law partner, was standing over the President's shoulder as we discussed the plan. "Public financing?" Lindsey said, and made a face much like the "yecch" face designed to scare children from drinking floor polish.

For years, corporations had been able to deduct the cost of lobbying Washington, just as they would any other business expense. Private citizens, by contrast, could not. On the campaign trail, Clinton had proposed closing the "lobbyists' loophole" by ending the tax deductibility of lobbying expenses. This would provide just enough revenue to pay for public funding of campaigns. It was politically deft: taxing the lobbyists to pay for reform.

Shortly before Clinton was to address Congress on the economy, I was walking past the Roosevelt Room when the door opened and Gene Sperling looked out, arms bulging as usual with folders and paper. "Great news," he said. "We included the lobbyists' provision in the budget. It's in." Gene was proud to have shepherded yet another campaign promise a few inches closer to enactment. I groaned. "That's not good. If it's in this budget, they'll want to use it for deficit reduction. We'll never get it back." He looked stricken. But apparently it was too late: the money was now accounted for in the budget. We decided, in effect, to put an asterisk next to the proposal in the budget, saying that the lobbyists' deduction could be used to pay for campaign reform if it ever passed.

As the negotiations dragged on, the pressure mounted from all directions. The Democratic National Committee worried about the wording of soft money restrictions. Every possible change in soft money language was leaked, presumably by proponents of reform. Negotiators for Congress pushed back in the other direction. I was urging a proposal to give candidates access to free postage. "That would help challengers," I argued. A Democratic aide who was negotiating for the Congress glared. "You don't get it. We're not in the business of helping challengers."

On March 15, we met with the President to go over negotiation positions for our talks with the Hill. When Clinton walked into the Roosevelt Room, he discovered that twenty people had come to the meeting, many of whom had invited themselves. Clinton looked weary of the subject. "I talk to these members. They don't understand. They think that they win or lose elections on their money. But that will be happening less and less. They need this." We went over a list of options. Each time, Clinton chose the most stringent reform. Then, as the session dragged on, his eyes closed. I heard later that he was furious that the meeting was as large and unproductive as it was. It had been a fake occasion and we had forced him to sit through it.

While members of the administration were exhausted and fretful, our attention wandering elsewhere, members of Congress grew increasingly apprehensive. What if this actually passed?

MARCH. A RESTAURANT JUST OFF K STREET. A blustery, wet day. A top Democratic Party operative, who had helped guide fundraising when commerce secretary Ron Brown was the party chair, wanted to have lunch. We met, each of us with an aide, at a noisy restaurant. He had a simple, earnest question. Did the Democratic National Committee need to stop raising soft money? If we were for reform, wouldn't we need to do that to avoid charges of hypocrisy? Clinton was due to start fundraising soon. Was that a good idea?

I pondered for a minute. Campaign reform would surely pass by the end of the year. In the meantime, the party had to keep raising funds. No, I told him, the key was to pass the legislation. They should keep going.

He was an idealist, and was perhaps a bit disappointed in my answer, but mostly relieved. I was giving advice I would have denounced a year before. When I got to the coat rack after lunch, I pulled on my coat and headed back to the office. In the cab, I realized that someone had mistakenly taken my coat—a ratty, fraying blue number that dated from my Nader days. I had walked out instead with an expensive, sleek blue cashmere coat. A lobbyist's coat. Nobody claimed it, and I kept it.

The Capitol. Dick Gephardt, the majority leader of the U.S. House, smiled as he quieted the crowd. We were in a room on the floor below the House chamber. Three of us from the White House—Mack McLarty, Steve Ricchetti, and I—sat at a card table in the front of the room. Before us were two dozen House Democrats. More of them crowded into the room as the session wore on.

Gephardt introduced us. "We are happy to be joined here by some representatives of the White House. They wanted to make it clear that it is a high priority for the President. I thought it was important that they hear from you, directly, what some of your concerns are on campaign finance reform."

John Lewis, the civil rights hero from Georgia who had been beaten on Edmund Pettus Bridge in Selma, Alabama, stood up. "I would not have been elected if it were not for the support of PACs. Very few African-American members of Congress would be," he declared. He said that PACs were an issue of "civil rights," and he could not tolerate any legislation that cut down on the ability of labor union PACs to help members from poor districts.

John Dingell of Michigan, the chairman of the House Energy and Commerce Committee, was scowling at me. Nader and he had been at war for decades over auto safety. Public financing would just help their opponents, he said. "Why are we putting up with all this *Nader* shit?" Vic Fazio, the California congressman who was chair of the Democratic Congressional Campaign Committee, was sitting next to me. He patted my arm. "I think you should take that personally," he smiled.

One after another, members of our own caucus expressed their anger about the proposed reforms. On most issues, lawmakers defer to the expertise of others. On campaign finance reform, they saw themselves as having earned a Ph.D. the hard way. They regarded any change in the rules with the same fears as senior citizens worrying about a trim in Social Security. Will we have to eat cat food?

When it was over, Gephardt smiled broadly, though his eyes were blank. "I think this has been a very productive chance for our friends from the White House to hear some of your concerns." He turned to us. "As you can see, there are strong feelings and a number of contentious issues that need to be resolved." In part, he was signaling to us, *We're in this together. But see what I have to put up with? Don't push me too hard.* In part, he was signaling, *Did you enjoy that? Wait 'til you try to actually pass this.* Mack McLarty was looking noticeably pale. "Well, Mike, I would say there were some strong feelings in that room," he observed as we rode in a White House car back to the West Wing. I responded with some heat. "The bill won't affect the Congressional Black Caucus' receipts from PACs. They

think it will, but it won't. The numbers don't add up." Mack's enthusiasm for reform, never torrid, was cooling rapidly.

The Old Executive Office Building. We were sitting in front of the marble fireplace in one of the offices of the counsel to the President. Perhaps surprisingly, this was one of the few times that corporate lobbyists, so bounteous a source of campaign cash, have weighed in. It's not the tobacco industry or the waste haulers. It's the broadcasters—lobbyists for one of the television networks. Our reform plan was expected to include measures to trim the rates charged by broadcasters to candidates. It was a form of subsidized time. "When free time has been offered to candidates, they haven't used it," one executive insisted. He slapped his knees. "You don't really want to do this, right?" We all know what this is really all about, he implied—getting credit for reform without really passing it. The TV network he was lobbying for had excoriated Clinton regularly for failing to tame the Washington system.

The White House kept announcing, and then postponing, the day the plan would be proposed. For weeks, negotiations stalled over the size of a maximum contribution from a certain type of PAC. Senators John Kerry, Bill Bradley, and Joe Biden met with Clinton to press him to support more dramatic reform, full public financing. Clinton didn't commit. (Kerry and Biden did all the talking. Bradley was virtually silent, sullenly eyeing Clinton.) Texas governor Ann Richards, calling on behalf of EMILY's List, a political action committee that collects funds for women candidates, lobbied against a limit on the bundling of campaign checks.

Finally, the bill was ready. It was the White House's turn to balk. At the behest of the Democratic National Committee, we tried to weaken, ever so slightly, the proposed limits on soft money. David Boren, who was closest to Common Cause—and who was busy working to block an energy tax increase that was key to the economic plan—planted himself in Mack McLarty's office and declared he would walk away from the bill if we weakened the soft money provision. There was no reason to move forward with a plan that Common Cause and other reformers would blast. We in the White House all agreed with that. The provision stayed as it was.

After all the delay, negotiations, and compromises, it was a proud day when Clinton, Foley, Gephardt, and Mitchell stood on the South Lawn to announce a strong campaign finance reform bill. It would limit spending and replace much of private campaign contributions with public funding. It would end soft money—ban it outright. It would curb PACs.

That evening, I sat on the edge of a receptionist's desk in the press office, with a remote control in my hand. I flicked from channel to channel to watch the coverage. ABC News had no story. I turned to NBC. Nothing. I turned to CBS. The only story was by Eric Engberg, focusing on the loop-

holes in the proposal. A CBS correspondent later apologized; a straight story explaining the reform had been taped, but was cut from the broadcast for length.

The Senate debated the legislation first, in June. Bob Dole and the Republicans filibustered it, forcing proponents to round up sixty votes to close off debate. The bill was weakened. A handful of recalcitrant Democrats led by Senator Carl Levin of Michigan insisted on stripping the public funding out of the bill. But after weeks of hard pressing by Senator George Mitchell, the Senate passed the measure.

The House would prove harder. Many House Democrats believed that they held their seats only by their fingernails—due to favorably drawn congressional districts and the ability of incumbents to outspend their challengers. The Democratic House's most skilled electoral strategist told me point-blank, "If we pass reform, we will lose the House."

The fact that we had carelessly mislaid the source for public funding made matters worse. Dan Rostenkowski, the chairman of the House Ways and Means Committee, was trying to craft a difficult tax bill as part of the President's budget package. He was happy to end the tax deduction for lobbying. But he had no intention of using the money for anything other than deficit reduction—and the chance to sabotage campaign reform was an added plus. The President was given the assignment of asking Rostenkowski to relent. I stopped by Howard Paster's office every few hours, waiting to find out if the call had been made. Finally, Paster came up from the Oval Office and confirmed that Clinton had spoken to the Chicago bull. "What did Rostenkowski say?" He said no, Paster said sorrowfully, with only a hint of merriment showing.

In the end, the House passed its own version of reform in November 1993. The House leadership and the White House pressured a reluctant rank and file to go along. The next step was for the Senate and House to negotiate a compromise. Usually, a conference committee would negotiate the details, but the lawmakers and reform advocates agreed that the details should be worked out in a pre-conference. The legislation had taken far too long, and the President had refrained from using his public voice to press Congress. But it seemed, for now, at least, that reform would happen.

As I wrote in a memo to Clinton, "we seem to be on the verge of compromise."

That optimism turned out to be a tad premature.

FIVE

NAFTA,
'CAUSE WE HAFTA

ON SEPTEMBER 13, 1993, I stood in bright sunlight with three thousand others on the South Lawn of the White House. On a low stage, in a simple ceremony, the leaders of Israel and the Palestine Liberation Organization were signing the Oslo Accords. Presidents George Bush, Jimmy Carter, and Gerald Ford sat beaming in the front row.

"I can't believe this. I can't believe the two of them are standing there together," whispered my assistant, whose family had strong ties to Israel.

"Rabin and Arafat. It's pretty incredible."

"No! Rabin and Peres. They *hate* each other." I started to say something, but she poked me hard and pointed. I turned back to the stage to witness the tableau: Yitzhak Rabin and Yassir Arafat reluctantly shaking hands, gently cajoled by Clinton, arms wide and practically embracing them. We cheered as if years of fear and violence could be washed away with applause.

Even so, my mind was elsewhere. The next morning, the President would be launching a fight for the North American Free Trade Agreement. And to my great chagrin, I was writing the speech.

Negotiating NAFTA had been a central achievement of George Bush's presidency. By linking the United States with the markets of Mexico and Canada, it would create the world's largest free trade zone, 367 million consumers with no tariffs.

But NAFTA exposed a deep schism within the Democratic Party. Clinton believed in free trade; he thought that economic change was a powerful and largely positive force, and couldn't be resisted in any case. As governor of Arkansas he was used to trying to lure businesses to locate in his

state, or to keep them there. But most Democrats, including labor unions and environmentalists, were opposed to the trade pact. Because no other border in the world spliced such extremes of wealth and poverty, they argued, integrating our economy with that of Mexico would drive down wages and undercut environmental standards. During the campaign, Clinton had temporized and tried to put off a decision on whether to back the pact. Finally, in October 1992, just before the election, he had announced he would support the agreement, but would insist on new "side agreements" to lift labor and environmental standards. "If it is done right," he said then, "it will create jobs in the United States and in Mexico."

By the summer of 1993, the agreement appeared to be dead. The Democratic whip in the House, David Bonior of Michigan, announced that he had 218 votes opposed to NAFTA—enough to sink the agreement. Within the White House, competing factions jockeyed. Supporters of health care worried that the President should not risk party unity over George Bush's agreement. James Carville proposed a trade: if business wanted NAFTA so badly, it should support health care.

Finally, in August, after the economic plan passed narrowly, the President decided to press for enactment of the agreement. (One reason he was not caught in the trap of wavering and trimming was that the trade pact would be brought up under "fast track" procedures—a single vote, up or down, with no amendments.) To win, Clinton would need to rely principally on Republican votes, and the GOP had made clear it would produce 118 votes only if 100 Democrats voted for NAFTA. Newt Gingrich, the minority whip, pronounced the President's efforts "pathetic."

NAFTA's backers in Congress were insistent that the President had to mount a full-fledged campaign. Not really to persuade the public: that goal was seen as nice, but unattainable. Rather, the drive would show the Republicans that Clinton was willing to bleed a bit, to spend more of his political capital, already depleted by the budget struggle.

Instead of assigning the responsibility to an existing White House office, Clinton and McLarty decided to create a freestanding operation that would be removed from the indecision and infighting that plagued the rest of the White House staff. In part, this was meant as yet another sign of commitment. Carville had a war room; health care had a war room; NAFTA should have a war room. I was assigned to be the communications director there. That was the problem.

I had been a public and somewhat prominent opponent of NAFTA. As I pointed out in an anguished memo to my superiors, the consumer group I worked for had helped to lead the effort, in 1991, to deny President George Bush the fast track authority to negotiate the agreement. Nader and

I had written an article for *The New Republic* attacking Bush's "Mexican Mistake." I had even had the idea to send jars of water to every office on Capitol Hill, each affixed with a label that said "WARNING. DDT. This could be on your food if NAFTA passes." We had lost the vote when the House majority leader, Richard Gephardt, decided to support Bush. As I warned, "I wasn't exactly Ross Perot on the issue, but I was out there."

The summons to work for NAFTA was a primal loyalty test. Clinton had made his decision; he had a right to expect his staff to implement it as best it could. And I had known he was for NAFTA when I voted for him. On the other hand, couldn't they have gotten someone else? I agonized, called several friends inside and outside the government. Finally, I decided that my choice was to work on NAFTA or leave.

Still, I waited for a summons telling me I didn't have to do it. What I got instead was a phone call from Mickey Kantor, now the U.S. trade representative, and his chief of staff, Tom Nides. "So, congratulations. I'm really glad you're going to be doing this," Mickey drawled into their speakerphone. I wriggled. "Uh, look, I don't really know if I am doing this. I'm resisting it. You see, I was strongly against NAFTA." Nides cackled. He had been a senior staff member for the House Democrats. "Who wasn't!? You're stuck!" Kantor said soothingly that he was glad that someone with my reservations was involved. I agreed to write a speech.

The NAFTA "czar" brought in to head the war room was Bill Daley, a quick-witted and polished lawyer. He was the son of the legendary Chicago mayor, and was regarded as the brains behind the political career of his brother Richard, now the mayor there. Daley had been scheduled to be transportation secretary. Denver mayor Federico Pena was named instead.

Daley was not overawed by the White House. His first day on the job, I was told, a young staff member was showing him around. As they walked past the press briefing room, the aide announced, "That's the pressroom. It used to be the pool." Daley smiled. "I know. I used to swim there." Daley was installed in a small, bare office in the Old Executive Office Building. Sitting on his desk, he spun out the arguments that he thought should animate the speech I was to write. We should avoid the trap of charging that treaty opponents are protectionist. "This has to be argued as a choice between hope and fear. The old ways simply don't work. That includes the old ways of trade with Mexico. The *maquiladora* [the unsafe factories that already operated near the border]—that's the old way, too." He was aware that NAFTA was splitting the Democratic Party and urged that the speech openly acknowledge that fact. "That's no surprise. That's always what happens when you have great change."

. I WROTE A SPEECH that made the strongest case I could conjure. The draft raced through the arguments, with temporary numbers—many of them guessed at—to be adjusted later. It said, for example, that NAFTA would create one million jobs in the first five years. In later drafts, I revised it, plugging in accurate facts. I brought it over to Sylvia Mathews, an earnest former Rhodes scholar who had been Gene Sperling's deputy during the campaign. She was now Rubin's assistant, and he had conveyed to her his own sense of nervous precision. She checked every fact. The correct number of jobs to be created, for example, was 200,000 in two years.

At the time Yassir Arafat and Yitzhak Rabin were shaking hands on the South Lawn, the speech was in good shape. I prepared to print it out. Then the computer, a relic (it was at least three years old!), crashed. I struggled to recover the file. The hours dragged by. Then David Gergen's assistant stopped by. That couldn't be good news. Gergen, who had served in several Republican administrations, had joined the White House staff as counselor to the President several months before. With his arrival, Stephanopoulos was pushed out as communications director and given a new job and an office next to the President. Now I—and others on the communications payroll—reported, somewhat circuitously, to Ronald Reagan's communications director. Gergen was friendly and usually helpful, but he had played this game many times before. He was not shy about swooping in and making his voice heard at the last minute. His assistant said that David wanted me to know that he was going to write up a version of the remarks in talking point form as well, in case the President preferred to speak off the cuff. At last I reopened the file, printed it out, and walked across West Executive Avenue to Gergen's office.

Gergen's door was closed. He was typing. I implored his assistant to let me know what was going on. The door swung open and Gergen ambled out with the talking points. I looked over his secretary's shoulder as she formatted and printed them out. They were talking points, in the sense that the beginning of each paragraph had an asterisk. Otherwise, it was a full speech, entirely new, with a very different approach. Gergen's speech was lofty, less intent on rebutting economic anxiety and more on expressing the need for America to retain world leadership.

I was demoralized and frustrated—certain, in the Washington parlance, that I was being "bigfooted." "Look, what you've done is perfectly fine," I said. "Why don't you just give him yours?" No, Gergen said amiably, he thought the President should have the choice. I handed his assistant my disk and the single-spaced copy, and went home.

The next morning, the President was due to look at the speech for a few minutes before delivering it in the East Room on the first floor of the residence. In the grand foyer of the White House, Secret Service agents

stood sentry at regular intervals. Andrew Friendly, the President's personal assistant, barred the door to the Red Room. "He's in there with the other presidents. You can't go in." He opened it a crack: the room was full of presidents, all right. "I need to be there when he looks at the speech," I insisted, but my heart wasn't in it. I made my way into the East Room.

Apparently, Gergen had shown Clinton both drafts: the talking points and a single-spaced draft copy of the speech. Clinton had scanned both and said emphatically, "Why, what's wrong with the speech? I like the speech." Clinton would read the speech text from separately printed "speech cards," like index cards, with large type text printed on them. Friendly put the cards in a gray folder with a presidential seal, and jogged down the hall. He put them in the lectern.

The East Room was hot and jammed. Academics can debate whether there is an Establishment or whether it exerts any power—or whether it has been supplanted by newer and younger Establishments—but that morning, there was an Establishment, enough to fulfill the fantasies of any Trotskyite. David Rockefeller and James Baker and Carla Hills and a dozen ambassadors. Business executives, much of the cabinet, governors, members of Congress. This room wanted Clinton to show his stuff, would be watching every nuance to see if he *meant* it. It was jammed as tight as a mosh pit at Bohemian Grove. I stood near the wall.

The military aide announced the President's arrival. He walked onto the stage accompanied by Bush, Carter, Ford, and Vice President Gore. Each of them seemed more impressive standing with the other. In this century only four presidents have been beaten for reelection, and three of them were standing here, but they looked formidable nonetheless. Disneyland's Hall of the Presidents Endorses NAFTA. Gore introduced Clinton, who basked in the applause, seeming to stand straighter than usual. He began by thanking his predecessors.

"These men, differing in party and outlook, join with us today because we all recognize the important stakes for our nation in this issue." I was elated. These were my words, and he was reading them.

"Yesterday we saw the sight of an old world dying, a new one being born in hope and a spirit of peace. Peoples who were for decades caught in the cycle of war and frustration chose hope over fear and took a great risk to make the future better." These were my words too. But there was something odd. They hadn't been in the final draft. They were in the *first* draft.

As Clinton spoke, chopping the podium for emphasis, an iron ball grew heavier and heavier in my stomach. He was, somehow, reading cards drawn from the wrong draft of the speech. The one with the made-up numbers. "I believe that NAFTA will create a million jobs in its first five years alone," he announced, to thunderous applause. Someone had

printed out the wrong file onto speech cards. Because I had stalked home, I hadn't been there to correct them. I came as close to fainting as I ever hope to.

I steadied myself and searched frantically for Gergen. There he was, a head taller than everyone around him, about fifty people away from me. I swam through the crowd, trying to look calm. I found my way to his elbow. "David," I whispered, trying not to move my lips. "He's . . . reading . . . the . . . wrong . . . speech! The . . . numbers . . . are . . . wrong!" Gergen glanced at me quickly, and then looked back at Clinton. He thought about it for a few seconds. Then he just shrugged. "Don't worry about it." Perhaps he was just trying to calm a jittery young colleague. But even in those first few seconds, I realized that Gergen knew something I didn't. The press would give the President's numbers a great deal of deference. There was time to fix any mistakes.

I wriggled my way to the back of the room, wincing when Clinton turned his card and found a notation telling him that the following paragraph was taken from a recent speech by Robert Reich, and that in the next draft we would rewrite it. His eyes bulged briefly as he realized something was amiss. He began to ad-lib—seamless paragraphs, new arguments, flowing effortlessly. Some of these, I recognized too: in the instant that he had scanned the speech draft in the Red Room, he had absorbed large chunks of the arguments.

"Ours is now an era in which commerce is global and in which money, management, technology are highly mobile. For the last twenty years, in all the wealthy countries of the world, because of changes in the global environment, because of the growth of technology, because of increasing competition, the middle class that was created and enlarged by the wise policies of expanding trade at the end of World War II has been under severe stress. Most Americans are working harder for less. They are vulnerable to the fear tactics and the averseness to change that is behind much of the opposition to NAFTA.

"But I want to say to my fellow Americans, when you live in a time of change the only way to recover your security and to broaden your horizons is to adapt to the change, to embrace it, to move forward. Nothing we do, nothing we do in this great capital can change the fact that factories or information can flash across the world, that people can move money around in the blink of an eye. . . . In a fundamental sense, this debate about NAFTA is a debate about whether we will embrace these changes and create the jobs of tomorrow, or try to resist these changes, hoping we can preserve the economic structures of yesterday. I tell you, my fellow Americans, that if we learned anything from the collapse of the Berlin wall and the fall of the governments in Eastern Europe, even a totally controlled society

cannot resist the winds of change that economics and technology and information have imposed on this world of ours. That is not an option. Our only realistic option is to embrace these changes and create the jobs of tomorrow."

Bush followed Clinton to the podium. They had debated less than a year before. "Now I understand why he's inside looking out and I'm outside looking in," Bush said.

A reception was held in the State Dining Room. Little pastries were laid out on a broad table. Tuxedoed waiters circulated. I felt like a spy in a room full of NAFTA supporters. A leading corporate lobbyist approached me. "We're very uneasy about you," she said. "Good. Tell my superiors," I responded heatedly. I hadn't asked for the assignment. "We'll be paying attention," she added.

In the next few hours, we waited tensely to see our mistakes become public. A harrowing mental movie kept replaying: those early rockets that got a few feet off the launchpad before the engines shut down, with the parachute popping out. Sandy Berger, the deputy national security advisor, sent a dry but unmistakably angry memo to the President noting the factual errors. Later in the day, Dee Dee Myers, the White House press secretary, casually announced that the million jobs figure was wrong, "due to a staff error." Some of the facts were corrected; others were interred. A few now had to be defended, and we struggled to find arguments to prove they were right. Remarkably, the opponents of the agreement never caught up to our mistakes.

The President asked McLarty what happened; the chief of staff asked John Podesta, the staff secretary; Podesta asked us. I conferred with Gergen's staff and wrote an explanation. I believe it was never sent in. The President's attention had shifted to other things. And the next week, a much larger, more disastrous speech snafu made headlines. On September 22, when Clinton went before the Congress and the nation to present his health care plan, the teleprompter showed the wrong speech—the speech from the previous February. For ten minutes, he spoke from memory while aides frantically tried to find out what went wrong. The press was filled with admiring commentary. The next day, Ted Koppel gushed at the President's performance skills. I breathed a sigh of relief. Someone else messed up, worse, and more publicly, than I had. I was off the hook.

THE SUCCESS OF THE SPEECH also meant that I was *on* the hook—I was now assigned to the NAFTA war room, running the communications effort. Staff members from different offices in the White House, from the Treasury and Commerce Departments, and from the trade negotiating office

were assigned to work together in a warren of borrowed offices in the Old
Executive Office Building. Some were ardently pro free trade; others were
disgruntled Democrats. At our first meeting I greeted Susan Brophy, who
would be the top lobbyist for the agreement. We reminisced about the first
time we had met: she was a congressional aide, and we were both working
against NAFTA. Our slogan was "NAFTA, 'cause we hafta."

On the day after the East Room event, only sixty-five Democratic
House members had supported the trade pact. At our first meeting, Daley
was emphatic. "The East Room event stopped the bleeding. Now we have
to hold people off from making a decision. The later they decide, the more
likely it is they will decide with us." Lawmakers needed cover, public arguments that they could use to explain their vote, and a sense that the White
House was kicking up some dust trying to win. First, we would seek to neu-
tralize the argument that NAFTA would cost jobs, some 5.9 million of
them, according to Ross Perot. Then, we would focus on the broader benefits of exports and trade. Finally, in the last week, push a warning of the foreign policy consequences of a defeat.

For two months, the White House staged a massive public campaign
for the agreement, scheduling eighteen presidential events, releasing studies, ghostwriting op-eds. We staged another White House ceremony with
former secretaries of the treasury and state, including Henry Kissinger
(Clinton joked that the agreement had been endorsed as well by Otto von
Bismarck), another with governors. Because the regular Democratic congressional whip operation was working against the pact, we built a jerry-
rigged system in which cabinet secretaries were assigned to keep in touch
with lawmakers. Dozens of congressmen who professed to be undecided
pestered the White House with elaborate and increasingly expensive demands. The White House had not seen such transactional gusto in years.

One morning, Brophy took her seat and related a call she had received
from a reporter the day before. Had the White House promised a congressman a project in exchange for his vote? She denied it to the reporter —
flatly, and, as it turned out, accurately. The lawmaker had sought nothing,
and had pledged his support on the merits. A few minutes later the phone
rang again. It was the congressman. "Did you get a call from the press?"
"Yes, don't worry, I denied it." "What the hell are you trying to do to me?"
he sputtered. "My constituents will think I'm a sucker."

Not every event was worth the effort. We launched the "exports" phase
of the argument in a tent on the South Lawn of the White House with a
"Products Day," hosting dozens of firms that made products for export to
Mexico. We even found an actual union local that supported the agreement. The event didn't exactly convey the message intended. There
weren't rows of gritty turbines or lawn mowers. There were boxes of cereal,

however, and chocolate mousse pie from Sara Lee. The only gripping image, which attracted photographers, was of a large White House constructed entirely of Legos. The President and his entourage stopped to admire it. He turned to labor secretary Reich, who stands less than five feet tall. "Secretary Reich could almost live in there," he joked. Reich actually laughed. Within an hour, reporters deluged the press office at the Department of Labor, demanding confirmation of the rumor that Reich would be leaving his job and moving to the White House.

On November 4, the President traveled to Lexington, Kentucky, to speak to the employees of Lexmark International, a manufacturer of laser printers. This was supposed to be a visit to the lions' den; we hoped he would be challenged by angry and anxious workers. The factory was a long, flat building in the middle of a county full of horse farms. As the presidential party entered—the press, who had flown in a few hours earlier on a chartered plane, were already in place—we saw with satisfaction that the factory looked like a factory, high ceilinged, drafty, with gunmetal gray machinery everywhere. But some of the workers were wearing *ties*. Despite the best efforts of our advance people, we could not conjure up a workforce that looked like Charlie Chaplin's *Modern Times* any more. Clinton was passionate. "That one fellow talks about the giant sucking sound," he said, paraphrasing Perot's charge that jobs would slosh down the drain to Mexico. "Let me tell you something, folks. I know a little about this. I was a governor of a state that lost plants to Mexico. . . . The short of it is that everything bad that everybody tells you about with this agreement can go right on happening if we don't adopt it. If we do adopt it, it will get better." The questions from the workers—instead of being confrontational as we had hoped—were polite and often supportive of NAFTA.

Daley and I were standing alongside the photographers' platform, chatting with reporters. Jim Miklaszewski of NBC told Daley, "We hear a rumor that the Vice President is going to debate Ross Perot on *Larry King*." Daley scowled. "No. No way. Why would he do that? It would just elevate Perot. That hasn't even been discussed. No." At that precise moment, Clinton and his entourage walked by. Miklaszewski swiveled and called out, "Mr. President, is the Vice President going to debate Ross Perot on *Larry King*?" Clinton smiled and kept walking. "The Vice President has challenged him to a debate on *Larry King Live*; let's see if he accepts!" The reporters rushed to phone the news. Daley shook his head and said ruefully, "The czar is always the last to know."

GORE DEBATED PEROT on November 9 and triumphed. The vote approached. Democratic lawmakers were still holding back—still caught, in

primal, almost physical agony, between their labor supporters and their president. Many unions threatened to run primary candidates against Democrats who supported NAFTA. Clinton had spoken to the AFL-CIO in October. He was supposed to argue to them for the agreement, and he did. But he softened his appeal—even going so far as to avoid saying the word "NAFTA" for fear it would elicit boos.

Now the Democratic members of Congress were begging for help from the White House. Clinton would have a chance to address the issue on *Meet the Press*, which was interviewing him for its anniversary edition. The day before the broadcast, we met with the President in the White House. He had just played golf with three Democratic lawmakers. He ambled in, still in golf togs, singing, "NAFTA, 'cause we hafta." Before the meeting began, he announced, "Who can I download their stuff to?" I quickly jotted down the requests and concerns of the lawmakers. Maybe I should push back at labor, Clinton mused. That's what the Democratic congressmen really needed. The staff argued against attacking labor. We still needed them on health care. Clinton agreed.

The next morning, in the first question, Tim Russert, the show's host, asked Clinton about Ross Perot. Instead, Clinton heatedly attacked labor unions. His voice low with anger, he said that unions had threatened to withhold campaign contributions from Democrats who backed the agreement, calling it "real roughshod, muscle-bound tactics." We were shocked. How had that come out? David Gergen rushed off to read the AP wires, already humming with stories about a Democratic president's surprising assault on his most powerful constituency. During a commercial break, he brought Clinton a wire story. When the program resumed, the President tried to smooth it over. "Did you see what Gergen just did?" Clinton asked Russert. "He brought in this thing saying that the headline is now that Clinton accused labor of roughshod tactics. I mean, those guys are my friends. I just don't agree with them on NAFTA. We're all going to work together."

In the last few days, dozens of lawmakers announced their support for NAFTA, just as Daley had predicted. After the debate between Gore and Perot, support for the agreement jumped in public opinion polls to 57 percent. It was clear that standing for principle, against the wishes of his own party, was paying off politically for Clinton. I urged that he deliver an Oval Office address the night before to call on Congress to act. "This can lift us above the 'let's make a deal' dynamics that we are seeing in the press," I noted. In his office next to Clinton's, George Stephanopoulos shook his head, looking downcast. It would be seen as rubbing it in, he said, as saying, "We won this victory over the Democrats."

In the end, as Clinton and Gore stood in the library on the second floor of the residence and watched the vote tally on C-SPAN, it wasn't all

that close. NAFTA passed the House by 234–200. Only 102 Democrats voted for it.

RALPH NADER was roaring in frustration. Because he had helped Jerry Brown in the primaries in 1992, he was regarded as an opponent from the first days of the administration. I had kept in close touch with his aides but had not spoken to him in months. To my surprise, he never called to lobby, to urge one course of action or another. When I saw him at a political fundraiser that spring, he greeted me gruffly and asked why I hadn't invited him to lunch at the White House mess. I chuckled nervously.

My work on behalf of NAFTA sent Nader over the edge. When I was given the assignment, he wrote a syndicated column saying I had "crossed the Rubicon without [my] conscience." One of Nader's aides, whom I had hired out of law school, told the *Wall Street Journal* that I was a "Benedict Arnold." The morning after the vote, my phone lines were lit up. One after another caller was screaming, demanding a list of all the bribes paid to congressmen to win their votes. Apparently, Nader was appearing on a series of right-wing call-in shows, giving callers the desk phone numbers for me and for Daley's deputy Rahm Emanuel. At my instruction, my assistant gave out Nader's phone number to callers who were yelling at us. Briefly, we tied up their phone lines too.

It hurt a bit to have my former mentor attack me in that way, but I wasn't surprised. I had decided to work for Clinton and the President had decided to push NAFTA. I owed him my best efforts. The trade agreement, too, had changed, and now contained protections, however weak, for labor and the environment. But there was something more. Perhaps it was simply a matter of psychological self-protection, but I had come to believe that NAFTA was right—or at least, not nearly as wrong as its critics said. I didn't think that the best course for the United States was to pull back from open markets. There had to be a way to protect consumers and workers, and control the behavior of corporations, that did not repudiate the benefits that came from free trade. I suspect that my evolution mirrored that of many other Democrats. As I watched Clinton persuade them, I found myself becoming persuaded, too.

IN THE WAKE of the NAFTA victory, Clinton's popularity began to rise. For the first time as president, he was seen to have shown a strength born of a willingness to stand up to friends as well as opponents. It was a first true test of the rhetorical power of his presidency—the first time he had turned public opinion and won a victory by using the full strength of his office.

It was significant in another respect. With NAFTA, the distinctive elements of Clinton's economic agenda had now dropped into place. By the end of 1993, the budget was headed toward dramatic deficit reduction. While it shrank the size of government, it increased spending in so-called human capital. By 1999, as the budget was balanced, federal spending on education and training would nearly double. And—with increasing self-confidence—free trade was being presented as a third essential plank in the platform.

One month after the passage of NAFTA, the United States and 116 other nations agreed to a worldwide trade agreement in Geneva known as the Uruguay Round of the General Agreement on Tariffs and Trade. This was the completion of trade talks that had stretched over a decade. It lowered tariffs worldwide on hundreds of products. In total, it amounted to the most significant single tariff reduction in history. It also created a new international organization, the World Trade Organization, out of an earlier and weaker trade group. The WTO would prove to be controversial, its procedures shrouded in secrecy. But it was the first new international organization to be founded after the end of the Cold War.

And what about NAFTA itself? Was it a success? Seven years later, it is clear that neither the sweeping optimistic predictions nor the dire warnings were borne out. NAFTA created some jobs—but not the 200,000 that we expected, let alone the one million we initially announced. One of the arguments made for NAFTA was that the United States was already running a trade surplus with Mexico, selling more products than we were importing from them. In 1995, the Mexican peso collapsed in value, and it was clear that the trade surplus had been the product of an inflated currency. The surplus became a trade deficit. Yet at the same time, NAFTA did not destroy the American working class. During the economic boom of the 1990s, trade grew by one third, and ended up accounting for one fifth of the overall expansion. In the end, the fight was probably more significant for its symbolism than its substance. As the world's economy was becoming increasingly integrated—a trend that would accelerate dramatically throughout the decade—the struggle over what was to become known as globalization would recur, over and over, in new forms. This was the first real political contest over the terms of global trade, over how to advance cherished goals in a potentially untamable marketplace.

And with NAFTA, whatever turns out to have happened, I can say with confidence: I was right.

THE FIRST YEAR of the new president's term was ending with his public image finally coming into focus. He had fought hard, taking on the Repub-

licans and his own party, to put in place a new economic approach. With the NAFTA win, he seemed at last to have learned the lesson that a president succeeds when he avoids being ensnared in the gears of the legislative process. Now, looking forward to 1994, we had a chance to press through the fundamental reforms that had been promised: health care, welfare, campaign finance.

SIX

COLLAPSE

In 1994, THE EXPANSIVE PROMISE of the presidency was supposed to be redeemed. Working closely with its allies in Congress, the White House would produce acres of progress, passing reforms, writing bold new laws. The reality: 1994 was the year it all fell apart—the year that Clinton's vision of his presidency collided with the resistance of Washington to change, and the plain fact of the public's contempt for government.

For starters, the administration almost immediately was sideswiped by scandal. A visitor to the West Wing in the first weeks of 1994 would have seen huddled and anxious clumps of aides. Allegations that years before the Clintons had been involved with a shady savings and loan operator— which had emerged briefly during the 1992 campaign—had resurfaced, and the White House had released incomplete information, whetting appetites. The administration was disorganized. No single person or office had responsibility for calmly answering questions. There was a feeling of plummeting, and not knowing when your feet would touch bottom, if ever.

In those first unnerving days, individuals were pulled almost at random into "damage control." These meetings generally ended as sessions in which worried staff tried to keep track of newspaper accounts. I even served my time for a few weeks on Whitewater damage control. (I have the lawyers' fees to prove it, after I subsequently turned over to the White House counsel some subpoenaed documents I found during an office move.) The press, the Republicans, followed soon by many Democrats, demanded the appointment of a special prosecutor. Stephanopoulos among others had argued that the issue was not whether a special prosecutor would be named—that was a foregone conclusion—but how much politi-

cal capital would be spent trying to fight it, political capital that should be husbanded for health reform and other priorities. Bernard Nussbaum, the White House counsel, argued strenuously that special prosecutors are not predictable, prone to tangents and crusades. In a phone call from Air Force One on the tarmac in Moscow, Clinton gave the OK to ask Attorney General Janet Reno to name a special prosecutor. I stood along the wall of the White House pressroom, along with other aides, as Stephanopoulos announced the President's request. This time, when the *New York Times* ran my photo without an identifying caption, I was relieved.

The next day, as I was dashing down the stairwell in the West Wing, Nussbaum was coming up. We nearly collided. "Well, at least that's done with," I said, referring to the appointment of a prosecutor. He looked at me urgently. "Look, someone is going to write a book about all this—probably you. It should be you! You're gonna write a book! And I hope you write that this was one of the most selfless acts you have ever seen. Because in order to save their health care plan, the Clintons have just sacrificed an enormous amount. Money. Peace of mind. Their friends. This was a very selfless act."

Shortly after, Attorney General Reno appointed Robert Fiske, a Republican former U.S. attorney, to serve as special prosecutor. The President replaced Nussbaum with Lloyd Cutler, well known to Washington's legal and journalistic communities. Responsibility for dealing with the scandal, and its offshoots, was centralized in the Counsel's Office. The rest of the White House staff tried to go back to business. But in reality, an endless cycle of investigations had begun that would beset the White House through nearly two entire terms. And time and momentum had been lost.

With the budget passed, with NAFTA won, with Whitewater, as we hoped, "out of the way," the administration could now focus with intensity on passing health care, welfare reform, a crime bill, and campaign finance reform.

Health care was all-important—and all-consuming. Some 37 million Americans lacked health insurance; millions more had inadequate coverage. Loss of a job often meant loss of insurance. In proposing national health insurance, Clinton was seeking to patch the major remaining hole in the social safety net, indeed to finish the work of the New Deal. The President raised the bar as high as he could in the State of the Union address as he pulled out a pen and declared, "If you send me legislation that does not guarantee every American private health insurance that can never be taken away, you will force me to take this pen, veto the legislation, and we'll come right back here and start all over again." It was a breathtaking gamble, if not entirely a conscious one. Presidents are unique in that they write the exam on which they are then graded. This one defined his own success or failure as whether he would win a program no president had achieved.

As the administration concentrated on health care, other priorities slipped. Campaign finance reform, for one. Clinton no longer talked much about it. The speechwriters rarely included it in the list of administration priorities. The White House scheduled no speeches, radio addresses, or "message events" on the subject.

Differing versions of campaign reform had passed each house of Congress by November 1993, but as the winter became spring and spring summer, the House and Senate never appointed negotiators to iron out the final legislation. Instead, Democratic aides met privately to try to craft a plan that would then be presented to the conference committee. Gephardt's staff director worked with the Ways and Means Committee, while we consulted with the Treasury Department, to try to find a way to pay for public financing. That effort took months.

Ultimately, the negotiations bogged down over an issue of almost entirely symbolic importance: the size of the maximum contribution that a political action committee could give to a lawmaker. Senators backed a proposal, first made by Clinton on the campaign trail, to reduce the size of an individual PAC gift. The House, in turn, limited the total volume a candidate could receive from PACs. In fact, the distinction was largely irrelevant: few candidates received the maximum from any individual PAC. But the editorial boards, prodded by reform advocates, insisted that a lower PAC contribution was essential to any plan's "credibility."

For months, neither the Senate nor the House gave any indication of moving off their obstinate negotiating positions. I bombarded McLarty and others with a series of increasingly frantic memos. In June, I sent a missive to the presidential party in Europe, where Clinton was commemorating the fiftieth anniversary of the Normandy invasion, headlined "POLITICAL REFORM D-DAY." It implored McLarty to have Clinton call a meeting of the Democratic leaders to hammer out a deal. It never happened.

The next issue to singe the Democrats was crime. Here, the damage was doubly unnecessary: Congress *did* pass anti-crime legislation. But the tortuous effort laid bare the divisions between the urban and rural wings of the Democratic Party.

Crime was more than an inflammatory political symbol. Especially in the wake of the spread of drug gangs, crime had become increasingly violent and random. Part of Clinton's New Democrat appeal was rooted in the sense that he shared the public's revulsion against lawlessness, and that he supported the death penalty. But beyond this, Clinton embraced the experimental community policing approach being tried in Houston and other cities that took officers out from behind station house desks and put them on the streets, once again walking a beat. In *Putting People First*, Clinton had proposed to deploy 100,000 additional community police, a

proposal that was tough, stressed prevention, and rested on the latest academic thinking.

The first legislative foray on crime was a success. In late 1993, Congress passed the Brady bill, requiring a waiting period and background check for the purchase of a handgun. It was the first significant legislative defeat for the National Rifle Association, which intimidated lawmakers with its electoral marksmanship.* The fight had stoked a fierce anger on the part of politically active gun supporters. Now the proposed crime bill would ban certain kinds of assault weapons. At the same time, the provisions in the legislation that made it easier to use the death penalty were provoking a very different kind of rebellion. The Congressional Black Caucus was demanding a provision that would let defendants argue that the death penalty was being used disproportionately against African-Americans. When that provision was omitted from the bill, ten members of the caucus vowed to oppose it.

The showdown came on the "rule" governing debate in the House of Representatives. For a governing party to lose on a rule on a major piece of legislation is almost unheard of. It signals a loss of operating control. Staff members gathered in communications aide Rahm Emanuel's small West Wing office, which looked out over the driveway, to watch the vote on TV. Rahm, who had raised campaign money for dozens of House members, predicted we would lose. I stood in front of the window to block the view of the office in case news cameras were trained on us. They would have seen a picture of dejection, as the rule went down to defeat. An hour later, like family members converging on a wake, two dozen staff members had gathered in the communications director's office. The President came in to rally the troops, to remind us how important it was, to agree to travel to Minnesota the next day to stump on the issue. We cheered. He seemed energized. Clinton's bursts of activity sometimes seemed to come after defeat.

The congressional leadership told Clinton that they could easily pass the bill if he dropped the assault weapons ban. He refused. It took a month of frenetic effort, but the crime bill finally passed, with the weapons ban included. In dozens of congressional districts, the NRA was further inflamed. More time was lost.

Meanwhile, the Whitewater-torture of scandal and allegation continued. A host of aides were called before a grand jury probing contacts between the White House and the Treasury Department. More headlines were made when it was reported that Hillary Clinton had made $100,000 on the commodities market. The Senate Banking Committee held weeks

---

* In the first five years it was in effect, the Brady law would result in 500,000 felons, fugitives, and stalkers being turned away when they tried to purchase a handgun.

of hearings on Whitewater. Then, just as the hearings drew to a close, a panel of federal judges removed Robert Fiske and installed as independent counsel Kenneth Starr, a far more partisan figure who had been mulling a U.S. Senate run as a Republican in Virginia. The investigation would start all over again.

That spring, the President realized that everything was on the line. He replaced Mack McLarty, his first chief of staff, with Leon Panetta, the former House Budget Committee chairman who was heading the Office of Management and Budget. At last a politically savvy, strong chief of staff would be empowered to guide strategy. But that wasn't enough.

Month by month, as 1994 limped along, one after another of the Democratic Party's sweeping reform proposals expired.

The first to go was welfare reform. Clinton's promise to "end welfare as we know it" had been key to his argument that he was a different kind of Democrat. Aid to Families With Dependent Children (AFDC) had been created during the Great Depression as a small widow's pension, but then had dramatically expanded in the 1960s. It was now widely agreed that the welfare system was failing: while many received welfare as a stopgap between jobs, about half the recipients were on it for years, sometimes for generations. The Democratic Leadership Council urged Clinton to move on welfare reform early, to show a willingness to tackle Democratic shibboleths. Bruce Reed led an effort to devise a welfare reform plan that had some semblance of Democratic Party support. In June, the administration finally unveiled its proposal. It would cut off welfare after two years for most recipients and require them to work. It also included over $9 billion of spending on job training, child care, and other steps to help people enter the world of work. In the end, there simply was no time.

By the summer, health care reform had barely a pulse. We tried to recapture the populist imagery and energy of the election campaign; a nationwide bus cavalcade converged on the White House. But the health insurance industry mounted a $15 million advertising campaign to defeat reform, and to the public, their attacks rang true. Any universal health insurance system was bound to mean greater regulation and deeper government involvement in the industry. Americans simply didn't believe government could handle it. The Republicans decided that no reform was better than a compromise that would give the Democrats a victory. In any case, the Democrats, with responsibility for the proposal divided among feuding congressional committees, never agreed on a single plan. On September 26, Senator Mitchell pulled the plug. There was no vote on health care in either chamber of Congress.

Campaign finance reform was the last of the administration's proposals to expire. For nearly a year, Congress took no public action. Then, in

late September, a week before the end of the congressional session, the Senate and House Democratic leaders finally settled on a compromise bill, agreeing to split the difference on political action committees (along lines that both had rejected for months). By then, it was too late. Now the Republicans, their corporate money-flow mortally threatened by reform, mounted a fierce filibuster, which required a supermajority of sixty votes to overcome—a response made even more difficult by the fact that it was so late in the session. Republicans blocked both chambers from formally appointing negotiators to finalize the deal.

As the final vote approached, a handful of Democrats and some moderate Republicans were still undecided. I wrote memos asking that Clinton call the wavering lawmakers. The night before the vote, Clinton drove to Senator Edward Kennedy's house in Virginia for a fundraiser. Kennedy was facing unexpectedly tough competition from a wealthy businessman. I rushed to the chief of staff's office to find Harold Ickes, who would be accompanying Clinton to Kennedy's house. Ickes had already gone. In frustration, I stood at his phone, calling the White House operator and placing pages reminding everyone I could think of to have Clinton make the calls.

I will not forget the scene the next day in the lobby off the Senate floor, an ornate marble chamber. A uniformed guard had a tiny television set. On its fuzzy screen, with a wavy picture, I watched campaign reform die a few feet away on the Senate floor. Nearly every Republican voted to block debate, even those who supported reform. The chance to deny the Democrats credit for reform was simply too sweet to give up. The chance had slipped through our fingers. It was an opportunity that came rarely, and would not come again soon.

I returned to the White House, deeply dejected. As I was walking up the steps, Pat Griffin, a genial former Hill aide who had replaced Howard Paster, was coming down the steps. He offered what he thought would be cheering words. "The President never got the word that he was supposed to make calls. He was mad. He said, 'Why didn't you tell me? Why didn't you give me something to do? This is something that I *care* about.' "

A MONTH LATER, on election night, we watched the results in the communications director's windowless office in the basement of the West Wing. The young staff, Clinton's thirtysomethings, sat jammed on couches and in corners. I sat on the floor as the balloon-like face of Newt Gingrich, the Speaker in waiting, filled the TV screens.

The Republicans won control of the House of Representatives for the first time in forty years, and control of the Senate for the first time in a decade. Speaker of the House Tom Foley was defeated for reelection by a

novice candidate who boosted term limits. Senator Harris Wofford, whose election in 1991 had launched the health care issue, was rejected. Prominent Democratic governors including Mario Cuomo of New York and Ann Richards of Texas lost. The governors of nine of the ten biggest states were now Republicans.

The Democrats went down for many reasons. In large measure, the relatively small voting public was reacting to specific, difficult issues that Clinton had taken on. In the middle South and much of the Northwest, the gun lobby exacted its revenge. First-term lawmakers and those from states such as Washington with term limits movements lost because Congress refused to change its own behavior by passing political reform. Many others were hurt by their vote for a tax increase at a time when the positive impact of deficit reduction was not yet being felt. And all Democratic candidates were devastated by the health care proposal—by the sweep of the plan, by the unreconstructed liberalism of its construction and salesmanship, and, of course, by its ignominious end.

But it was more than a repudiation of specific votes.

That night, it was clear that a host of assumptions—about liberalism, the Democratic Party, and the presidency—had been rejected by the voters. Clinton had run as a different kind of Democrat, and he often governed that way, but he had staked everything on a health care plan that was seen as a return to liberal fundamentalism. He had tried to work the machine of the presidency, tried to summon the public to pressure the system, but the public wasn't interested in big gestures and large ambitions. It simply did not trust government. What it had seen of Washington during the first two years of the Clinton presidency did little to encourage such trust. The health care industry easily played on that skepticism. For decades, confidence that Washington could meet its large goals had been eroding. With the end of the Cold War, what was left of it had silently collapsed. By the end of 1994, confidence in government had fallen in the Gallup poll to 15 percent, its lowest level in history. That trust would have to be rebuilt, slowly and consciously, before the public was ready to embrace a progressive agenda again.

It was also clear that Clinton had tethered his fortune to the Congress. When he spoke, too often it was as a legislative leader, worrying about subcommittee votes and the details of bills. He would need to learn how to speak as president—both as head of state, for the whole nation, and as the sole chief of the executive branch.

In the coming months, as his shock subsided, Clinton understood the rebuff as a fundamental breakpoint in the public's relationship with government. Shortly after the election, at a Camp David session with some professors, he told them that he had underestimated the public's distrust of

government. "We'd better start having some small successes"—and soon—he said. In the Cabinet Room a few months later, the President talked about term limits, which he had opposed during the campaign. Bruce Reed and I urged that he at least consider a plan to allow states to set term limits rather than risk a move toward a constitutional amendment. Clinton accepted that approach and explained why it was better. It has been an anomaly in our country's history, he said, that the public wanted a strong, semi-permanent governing class—a desire bred by the history of the Depression, world war, and Cold War. Now it had rejected that view. But someday, he said, it might change its mind. "We don't want to create an obstacle if they do again." He saw the 1994 results as a profound rebuke—not just to him but to the approach to the presidency that he (and other Democrats) had taken. It was the beginning of a process that would lead him to reconstruct his presidency bit by bit.

As THE YEAR TURNED, the conversation in the White House mess was even more hushed than usual. A group of us mid-level aides were seated at a round staff table near the door, for which reservations were not required. Crisply dressed servers, drawn from the navy's mess staffs, quietly delivered food and removed china with the presidential seal on it.

I was halfway through lunch when I looked around the room and my eyes fell on a corner table. "Look at that!" I blurted out.

Ira Magaziner was having lunch with a guest. Imperious, intellectually arrogant, he had crafted the health care plan. A few months ago he was at the center of a whirlwind of activity. Now he was in limbo, with few responsibilities, his phones silent.

At the next table, with his back to Magaziner, was an elderly gentleman, with his hair slicked straight back, his clothes baggy but impeccable. Robert McNamara. Kennedy's and Johnson's defense secretary. The architect of the Vietnam War.

And as we watched, Magaziner and McNamara turned and greeted one another and began a genial, earnest conversation.

Our entire table watched transfixed. "OK," someone finally said. "Captions."

"You destroyed a Democratic presidency? Hey, that's amazing! I destroyed a Democratic presidency too!" I offered. Someone else suggested, "Have you read The Best and the Brightest?" Laughter mounted—though we tried hard to stifle it. Finally, Cliff Sloan, an associate presidential counsel, brought the discussion to an end. In the voice of a Jeopardy announcer, he said, "And the topic is—flow charts."

SEVEN

THE COMEBACK
BEGINS

A FEW HOURS before the President was to deliver the 1995 State of the Union, two groups of speechwriters huddled over two keyboards in the White House family theater, shortening it. Advisors sat in expectation. Military teleprompter operators stood. Only the President was missing. He was still upstairs, writing the speech with Hillary, we were told. Pages that he had written out were arriving as the hour approached. He did not come down to rehearse.

Al Gore had been summoned to the family theater to work with Clinton on the speech. Now he stood in the aisle, his eyes cold and his jaw muscles clenched, as he surveyed the scene. His fury—at Clinton, at the disorganization, at the spot the administration was now in—was obvious. Watching him from a nearby seat, I imagined his thoughts. *When I am president, this will not occur.* After moments of silence, he turned and left.

For those who had worked with the President, the preparation of this speech had been painful. A draft would be delivered to Clinton, who would respond by rejecting it and sending back a wholly different draft. Rather than coming together, the number of drafts continued to grow, each prepared on a parallel track. One night in the Roosevelt Room, before sending the speechwriter back over to the residence to meet with Clinton, Leon Panetta said plaintively, "Tell him we like our speech better."

By the time Clinton arrived at the Capitol podium, the speech was slightly over an hour long. By the time he finished delivering it, it was an hour and twenty minutes. He returned to the themes he had articulated so forcefully in the early days of his primary campaign—before the effort to open the military to gays, the tax hike, and health care erased his distinctive

political brand. It was the first time in two and a half years that a wide audience heard Clinton describe his policies as a "New Covenant"—a renewed bargain between the citizens and the government, opportunity and responsibility. It seemed that Clinton had hit rock bottom. The promise of his presidency seemed ashes. In fact, his comeback had begun, though that wouldn't be clear for some time. It would be more than a personal return to power. Throughout 1995, in fits and starts, and amid fierce feuding among his advisors, Clinton began to build a new kind of presidency. It was a presidency that depended far more than ever before on the bully pulpit, on his speeches and statements, and on actions he could take on his own. It would spell out a new role for government.

The Republican ascendancy on Capitol Hill was a tremendous event. The nation saw a congressional political party that was self-confident, seemingly with an agenda and mandate to govern that had previously been the province of presidents. On the day he was sworn in as Speaker, Newt Gingrich spoke to the House, quoting Franklin Roosevelt's 1933 inaugural address and setting out an agenda for the first hundred days of the term. The Republicans sought a radical reduction in the role of government. They pressed for a balanced budget constitutional amendment, tried to eliminate four cabinet departments, and sought to scrap the Public Broadcasting System and the national service program. A regulatory reform bill would have hamstrung environmental and safety regulations. Legal reform would have required a consumer who filed suit against a corporation to pay part of the corporation's legal fees if the lawsuit was unsuccessful, overturning two centuries of American law. Capping it all was a series of spending cuts and tax cuts.

In the spring of 1995, the right had a churning intensity. Conservative talk radio hosts now reached millions of listeners, mostly angry working-class men. The National Rifle Association sent out a fundraising letter referring to federal law enforcement agents as "jackbooted thugs." It was an ugly season. To top it off, Gingrich had made clear that the Congress would relentlessly investigate the administration—probing Whitewater one more time and using myriad committees to cross-examine other areas of the administration's conduct.

For the first months of 1995, Clinton appeared to feel trapped: still bound by alliances and commitments with the institutional Democratic Party; torn between his desire to lash out at the Congress, his natural instinct for conciliation, and his dismay at his opponents' occupying the political high ground. It wasn't much fun for those who worked for him, either. The communications department where I had spent the first two years was broken up. I moved into the Domestic Policy Council. The liberals on the staff—George Stephanopoulos and Deputy Chief of Staff

Harold Ickes—had lost Clinton's ear. Centrists such as chief speechwriter Don Baer and Bruce Reed often seemed to feel snubbed by their colleagues.

Clinton was restless and probing, looking for allies on his own staff. I was helping conduct a review of regulatory policy for the Vice President. Along with Elaine Kamarck, the political scientist who headed Gore's reinventing government effort, I had met with the President to go over a speech that would announce reforms in government services. "Yes, yes, this is what I want. I want you to show how I support cutting regulation. Only when you have made that case can you then successfully make the argument against the Republican approach." Later, he paged me to press his message. I practically drove off the road when I saw the page: OPERATOR 1: PRESUS HOLDING. "This is what we should be doing. This is exactly the kind of thing we need," he said.

One day, I was pacing around Bruce Reed's office, fuming about the inactivity and lack of direction in the White House. Reed and I had adjoining offices at the far corner of the Old Executive Office Building—as far removed from the center of the action as it was possible to be without crossing Connecticut Avenue. Reed's massive desk held four neatly stacked, foot-high piles of paper. He looked impish. "Something strange is going on. Things are going to change. I can't tell you what's going on, but things are going to change."

The end of the first hundred days of Gingrich's set of campaign commitments, the Contract With America, was approaching. Clinton was going to break his silence with a major speech before the American Society of Newspaper Editors. This would be an efficiency drill for the entire White House staff. The President would speak. The press office and communications staff would amplify his message with fact sheets, while other administration officials would reprise the President's approach in their own speeches. All this would be coordinated with Democratic members of Congress, who would talk in Congress and to their constituents. I was drafted to help produce the fact sheets that would be distributed to party supporters.

The President had agreed to focus on education, a subject dear to his heart. The talk would be forward-looking, almost ignoring the overheated activities of the Republican Congress, turning instead to an issue on which the Democrats were trusted.

The day of the speech, my college roommates were visiting. I proudly took them to lunch in the White House mess and led them around the West Wing. Clinton was delivering his remarks at that moment in Dallas. We looked into the chief of staff's outer office. The television was on CNN, and Clinton was discussing the Contract With America. "In the first one

hundred days, the mission of the House Republicans was to suggest ways in which we should change our government and our society. In the second one hundred days and beyond, our mission together must be to decide which of these House proposals should be adopted, which should be modified, and which should be stopped." He continued:

> You know, our country has often moved forward spurred on by purists, reformists, populist agendas which articulated grievances and proposed radical departures. But if you think about our most successful periods of reform, these initiatives have been shaped by presidents who incorporated what was good, smoothed out what was rough, and discarded what would hurt. That was the role of Theodore Roosevelt and Woodrow Wilson in the aftermath of the Populist era. That was the role of Franklin Roosevelt in the aftermath of the La Follette Progressive movement. And that is my job in the next one hundred days and for all the days I serve as president.

"That's odd," I told my roommates. "I don't remember that being in the speech."

We gazed into the Vice President's outer office. Staff members were staring at the screen, some with their mouths open. "We stand at a cross roads. In one direction lies confrontation and gridlock; in the other lies achievement and progress. I was not elected president to pile up a stack of vetoes." Clinton began scrolling, item by item, through the Contract With America, saying which measures he would sign, which he would block, and which he would accept with specific changes.

George Stephanopoulos strolled by. We had both attended Columbia University, and he knew one of my roommates. He nodded toward the TV. "What's going on? How's the speech?"

"I don't think it's an education speech. He's about halfway through the Contract With America, saying what he'll sign and what he'll veto. Right now he's up to tort reform." Stephanopoulos looked as if someone had told him his office was on fire. He bolted down the hall.

My friends looked at me for an explanation. "Um, it's not always like this. Something strange is going on."

It certainly was. Clinton was giving an entirely different speech from the one expected by most of his senior staff and the congressional Democrats. What had happened?

Later, Don Baer explained. Baer had joined the staff as director of speechwriting in 1994 in one of several efforts to improve the communications operation. He was a lawyer and a well-regarded journalist. As an editor

for *U.S. News & World Report,* he had written a profile of Clinton, and was taken with the Arkansas governor. They were both southern progressives who felt out of step with the mainstream of the Democratic Party.

Baer and a fellow speechwriter had written a draft on education. They had finished it in the early-morning hours of the day before the speech, had circulated it to the rest of the White House, and sent it in to Clinton. At that same moment, in a meeting in his residence, Clinton had decided not to focus on education after all.

A few hours later, at 6:45 in the morning, Baer received a call at home from Harold Ickes. "Come straight to my office," Ickes said. Baer was instructed to go to political consultant Bob Squier's firm in a townhouse on Capitol Hill. Upon arriving, Baer sat alone in a room until an unfamiliar man entered, carrying a detailed outline of a new and very different speech. It was Dick Morris, and together, along with Bill Curry, an associate of Morris', they wrote a new speech.

At the time, Morris, a Republican political consultant and pollster, was a little-known figure in the White House. But before that, he had been Clinton's chief political advisor during his rise in Arkansas. Baer now understood that Morris was the hidden influence on Clinton he had detected in recent months. It turned out that Clinton had not been with Hillary alone in the days before the 1995 State of the Union. Morris, too, had been there. When Baer or another staff member arrived, the advisor would make himself scarce. Only Panetta had an early inkling of what was going on. Morris accidentally faxed a memo on the State of the Union to the chief of staff's office. His aides told me later that Panetta had thrown a fax machine.

The speech drafted by Morris and Baer was far better than the one on education endorsed by the White House staff. With it, Clinton began to reestablish himself as a force in Washington. Over the next four months, Clinton ascended the pulpit with an effectiveness unprecedented in his presidency. He still faced enormous obstacles in his effort to be heard. On April 18, he held a prime-time press conference in the East Room. Only one television network covered it live. When he was asked about the lack of coverage, he declared, "The Constitution gives me relevance. The power of our ideas gives me relevance."

Just how relevant would be tested within hours.

Shortly after nine the next morning, a terrorist bomb destroyed the Murrah Federal Building in Oklahoma City, killing 168 people, 19 of them children, in the deadliest terrorist act on U.S. soil. It was the kind of galvanizing, traumatizing event that can put a president at the center of things.

Panetta, military aides, and Justice Department officials met continuously in the Situation Room in the West Wing basement. The Sit Room is

the closest thing most White House staff ever see to the "war room." In
those tense close quarters, Clinton was deciding how to react and what to
say. Shortly before he was due to speak to the nation, someone remembered to call speechwriting.

Baer and Jonathan Prince, the youngest and fastest speechwriter, had
already dashed off a statement. It offered condolences and vowed to capture those responsible, branding the bombing the work of "cowards." Clinton added that the bombing was the work of "evil cowards." Those words
made banner headlines in at least one newspaper.

Early suspicions had fallen on international terrorists. But within a
few hours of the bombing, police arrested Timothy McVeigh, a right-wing
anti-government extremist. Two days later, he was charged with the crime.
Clinton seized this moment. Four days after the catastrophe, he joined a
prayer service at the Oklahoma state fairgrounds. "You have lost too much,
but you have not lost everything," he told the mourners. "And you certainly
have not lost America, for we will stand with you for as many tomorrows as
it takes."

Since Pericles spoke in ancient Athens, eulogies have followed a classic form. Honor the dead. State why it is appropriate that we do so. Take
from their deaths a lesson as to how we should live our lives. Clinton had
delivered many such speeches during twelve years as chief executive of a
small state. His touch was sure. Novice orators go overboard. Clinton knew
that. "Our words seem small beside the loss you have endured," he said.

"To all my fellow Americans beyond this hall, I say one thing we owe
those who have sacrificed is the duty to purge ourselves of the dark forces
which gave rise to this evil. They are forces that threaten our common
peace, our freedom, our way of life.

"Let us teach our children that the God of comfort is also the God of
righteousness. Those who trouble their own house will inherit the wind.
Justice will prevail.

"Let us let our own children know that we will stand against the forces
of fear. When there is talk of hatred, let us stand up and talk against it.
When there is talk of violence, let us stand up and talk against it. In the face
of death, let us honor life. As Saint Paul admonished us, let us not be overcome by evil, but overcome evil with good."

It was the nation's first exposure to Clinton as mourner in chief, a role
at which Ronald Reagan had excelled. In fact, it was the first time Clinton
had been a reassuring figure rather than an unsettling one. For many people, during those days, for the very first time, he truly became a president.

He also saw the political opening the bombing had created, for while
Timothy McVeigh was planning an anti-government explosion in the
heartland, the Republicans in Congress were proclaiming an anti-

government "Republican Revolution" in Washington. The President scrapped a planned commencement address topic at Michigan State University. The speech he delivered just a few hundred miles from the wooded retreats where racist militias practiced their gunplay carefully drew a line against anti-government militancy—and in so doing, seemed implicitly to marginalize the Republican Revolutionaries. "There is nothing patriotic about hating your country," he told the graduates, "or pretending that you can love your country but despise your government." Historian Carol Gelderman noted that despite criticism of the President for politicizing the tragedy, he dominated the nation's response to it. "Once again he had fulfilled one of the major duties of a president, which is to speak out in public about a clear danger to the nation's peace and to take steps to meet the danger."

Clinton continued to reassert his presidency, delivering major speeches on values, on the budget, on affirmative action. Each of them was the cause of a tug-of-war between White House factions.

It has been widely recounted that that spring Morris was urging Clinton to "triangulate"—to position himself between and above the liberal Democrats and the conservative Republicans in Congress. I think the key to understanding Morris—his hold on the President and his success at helping Clinton reassert himself—is that he was not bound to what passed for reality in Washington. Clinton would want to support a balanced budget. His political staff would remind him of the web of commitments and alliances that made it impossible for him to do so—his previous statements, his previous budgets, the depth of the cuts required, the sentiments of congressional Democrats and the party's interest groups. For Panetta and Stephanopoulos, sensitive politicians, it might be possible to thread a path to a balanced budget, but to do so required exquisite political footwork. Morris would simply look at his polls, tap a question on his handheld computer, and announce, "The President should come out for a balanced budget."

THE CHIEF OF STAFF TO THE PRESIDENT occupies a large corner office in the West Wing, down the hall from the Oval Office and next to the Vice President's office. Unlike most rooms in the White House, this office is large and airy, with high ceilings, a garden patio, a fireplace, and bookshelves. The walls were filled with photos of Panetta as a young Nixon official who was sacked for enforcing the civil rights laws. (It is not clear whether Panetta was fired or quit. Once I asked one of Panetta's aides about it. "Depends on what day you ask him," he explained.) Mack McLarty had built a small phone booth into the wall so that calls could be taken in con-

fidence while a larger meeting continued. Panetta's office was often filled; his role was close to that of prime minister, with a long rolling meeting and decisions made at a level below the President. He was plainly mortified about what he saw as a lack of proper decision making that accompanied Morris' brainstorms.

One day in April, I was summoned to sit at Panetta's conference table. With a look that was equal parts indignation and amusement, he gave me an assignment. "Mike, the President wants to ban foreign lobbying. Foreign lobbying. Can we do that?" This would be announced in a speech in the spring, maybe in the commencement address Clinton would be delivering at Dartmouth on June 11.

I thought quickly. "Well, I think there are constitutional issues. Lobbying is protected by the First Amendment—the right to petition your government. So there may be constitutional ways to do it, though it wouldn't be easy. The bigger issue is, is this a good idea? I think this is a cheap hit. It would take our attention away from the real reforms—lobby registration and campaign finance reform. We're not exactly doing a lot on those. The administration is full of former foreign lobbyists. We'll look silly." I pointed out that the biggest problem relating to foreign lobbyists had been solved. Upon taking office, Clinton had barred his trade representatives from switching sides and lobbying for foreign firms and governments after leaving government, as the trade representatives for Reagan and Bush had done.

Leon looked relieved. He had probably worried that I would hear the idea and start singing the "Marseillaise." "Look, I agree with you. But the President thinks this is a good idea. So we have to look at it." That day, and in a series of meetings afterwards, I was instructed to look into the policy ramifications, the legal implications. I quietly slipped to Panetta and Ickes a list of former registered lobbyists for foreign governments and companies who now worked for the administration.

I thought the idea had been quietly rebuffed until I got a phone call, my first, from Morris. His metallic voice sounded as if it was generated by a computer. "Mike, I'm Dick Morris. The President has asked me to work with him. I am told that you are the person who knows everything about political reform. We want to ban foreign lobbying. I would like you to get it done." I explained why it wasn't a good idea, told him the work I had been doing on it. I quickly let Panetta know that our stake had apparently missed the heart of this proposal.

The Dartmouth commencement address was now formally scheduled to be a speech on political reform. It would be Clinton's first full-length talk on the issue since May 1993. Delivered in New Hampshire, the first primary state, it would have an unusually large impact. It would give Clinton a chance to open a new front against the Republican Congress.

They seemed less eager to reform themselves than the Democrats had been, and had invited corporate lobbyists to do much of the work of writing their environmental program. The speech would include new proposals on lobbying and campaign reform. As for a ban on foreign lobbying, the idea had seemed successfully smothered.

A few days later the phone rang again. Morris introduced himself again. "We need to get moving on this. The President is becoming very impatient. I would like you to send out a memorandum to the rest of the White House staff instructing them to move on this." He began to dictate. "To: Members of the White House staff. From: Leon Panetta." He dictated a full memo and told me to send it out to the staff, without showing it to Panetta. "Dick, I don't think I can send out a memo under Leon's name without his seeing it." I explained that I was for reform and against foreign lobbying, but this was a bad idea.

Harold Ickes, who regularly dismissed utopian political reform measures with a jovial epithet, instructed me to canvass the agencies of government. He knew that the proposal would provoke a paper storm. The State and Commerce Departments sent long memos on the benefit to the United States of hearing from foreign governments. The Justice Department argued against its constitutionality. When we met in Panetta's office, I thought some of the agency officials would get the vapors, they were so upset. Leon took the memos to Clinton. It seemed once again that the idea was dead.

Meanwhile, I poured myself into writing the commencement address. It would be the speech I had always dreamed of my president giving. It avoided stunts such as pretending to ban foreign lobbying. Instead, for the first time, it would give Clinton a chance to lay out a clear theory of meaningful reform.

In the Oval Office, a few days before the speech was due to be delivered, the President seemed unhappy. A few months before, Senator Robert Dole had proposed that a bipartisan commission be established to draft campaign finance reform legislation. The commission would be modeled on the Base Realignment and Closing Commission, a panel which had chosen which military bases were to be closed, providing a list to be sent on by the President and voted up or down by Congress with no changes. "What's wrong with that? That seems like a good idea," Clinton said. I had canvassed the campaign finance reform groups and Hill allies, and I explained that this would be seen to be taking the Congress off the hook, delaying reform until a distant date. Clinton marked up the speech, and said he liked it. But there was something hesitant in his manner. "I'm not sure he wants to do this," Don Baer remarked to me.

Matters were complicated by the fact that Newt Gingrich was due to

be in New Hampshire at the same time as Clinton. The Speaker invited the President to join him at a town meeting. Clinton quickly agreed.

The speech was to be delivered on Sunday. Late Saturday morning, Don Baer and I sat outside the Oval Office. When Clinton opened the door, I leapt to my feet, pen ready, with the latest draft of the speech fit for editing. The President spoke to us just inside the doorway of his office, his face inscrutable. "You know, I don't think I want to do this topic. It just doesn't feel right. I would rather speak about education." He looked at Baer. "Do you think you could do that?" He quickly escorted us out.

I don't know who was more stunned. I had just seen the work of several months cast aside. Baer had just been given the assignment of writing a commencement address from scratch in a few hours. At least I got to go home.

I was at home the next day, when a deputy White House press secretary called from New Hampshire. "Turn on CNN." Clinton had given an address on education at Dartmouth, then headed to the town meeting. There, a retired steelworker who was dying of cancer asked the Speaker and the President to agree to a bipartisan commission to draft campaign finance reform legislation. He even asked that it be modeled after the base closing commission. Gingrich and Clinton looked surprised, and they quickly agreed. In an image replayed several times that afternoon, they stuck out their hands and shook on it.

We quickly assembled a team of Justice Department lawyers and legislative experts from the White House to draft a bill that would create a political reform panel. Within days, the proposal was scrubbed clean and ready to send to Gingrich. We drafted a letter from Clinton. Pat Griffin, the legislative director, called the Speaker's office. And all hell broke loose.

Gingrich was livid that we were sending him a proposal, Griffin explained. "He met with his guys. His guys said this is bullshit. They don't want to do it."

"What do you mean they don't want to do it? He shook hands. In public. On TV."

"I'm just telling you. They won't do it."

In public, Gingrich's press secretary attacked the President for politicizing the proposal. In private, the plan was all but dead.

We made one more run at reviving it. Someone suggested that we name our two members to any panel that might be appointed. The logical choice was Mike Synar, the congressman who had been excluded by the House Democrats from our meeting two years before. Synar had lost his seat in Congress over his support for gun control. He was now starting a bipartisan organization seeking to mobilize public opinion for campaign reform. When I briefed Clinton, he was signing letters at his desk, but looked

up sharply when he heard Synar's name. "That's a great idea. I'd love to do that. But I just got a call today. He has cancer." Synar died within months.

Leon Panetta suggested John Gardner, the founder of Common Cause, a liberal Republican who had been Lyndon Johnson's secretary of health, education and welfare. We added Doris Kearns Goodwin, the historian whose history of the Roosevelts during World War II was a bestseller the previous year. The two agreed to come to Washington, where they met with Clinton and held a joint press conference to urge Gingrich to act. Gingrich would not meet with them.

That Clinton-Gingrich handshake was a double irony. It followed a pattern—Clinton giving the right response on reform just hours after shrugging off the chance to speak on it. It was also genuine: Clinton ardently supported the political reform commission. In the instant when the insincerity of the political system's commitment to reform was memorialized in a photo, Clinton had meant it.

One day that summer, Baer and I were waiting for a meeting with the President to begin. Baer pointed his head into the Cabinet Room and closed the door. "There is a chance I'm going to be named communications director," he whispered. "If that were to happen, I think you would be the right choice to be director of speechwriting." I would not get the formal title for another six months, but during that time I filled much of the role—working on the key speeches on the budget showdown with the Republican Congress.

THE BUDGET DEBATE OF 1995 was one of those rare moments when fundamental principles are at stake, or at least, are at the center of the public discourse. The Republican Party was explicit about wanting to pull back on the social welfare programs that had been on the books for years. On one day in October, Senator Dole bragged that he had voted against the creation of Medicare, and Speaker Gingrich told another audience that his goal was to make changes in the program so it would "wither on the vine." The conservative movement had gathered force thirty years before, when millions of southern Democrats, resisting civil rights, began voting Republican, first for president and then for Congress. The steam of that movement had propelled the anti-tax revolt of Proposition 13 in California in 1978, then Ronald Reagan's election, and now the Contract With America.

Clinton and the Democrats were in a politically difficult spot: in 1993, they had raised taxes and cut spending to "reduce the deficit" by more than half, as it turned out. But they were still opposed to "balancing the budget," fearing that it would require excessively deep cuts. Yet to the public, "balancing the budget" was as much a statement of values as of economics. It re-

flected a desire for the government to get its act together, in commonsense terms, in a way that the anodyne "deficit reduction" did not. In June, Clinton had announced that he, too, was for a balanced budget. The dramatic declaration, made in an Oval Office address, provoked sharp public rebuke from the Democrats in Congress (which may have been part of the point).

Now that Clinton had come out for "balancing the budget," he felt on secure ground to engage in the debate on what kind of balanced budget. He began to stress that he was for "a balanced budget that honors our values." But having donned the robe of fiscal responsibility, it was important not to seem to support spending indiscriminately. The congressional Democrats believed that Medicare, above all, was the vulnerable point in the Republican plan. Stephanopoulos, backed by Panetta, urged a constant focus on defending the popular program. Medicaid was also affected by the GOP budget: it would be eliminated as a federal guarantee altogether and converted into a block grant of funds for states. Politically, Medicaid was seen as principally helping poor people, though in fact it also paid for nursing home care for all families. Education was Clinton's most cherished priority, and the Republicans wanted to eliminate the Department of Education and proposed slashing student aid. Gore insisted that the environment be added to the list of priorities. Soon Clinton and all the members of the administration began pounding on the same theme: "a balanced budget that honors our values—by protecting Medicare, Medicaid, education, and the environment." MMEE.

In the spring of 1995, Dick Morris had been right to argue that the President should bluntly declare support for a balanced budget. Now he was anxiously urging a deal with Congress. In the fall of 1995, Stephanopoulos was right to resist—and to insist that Medicare could win the next election for the Democrats.

Throughout the fall, the confrontation with the Republicans on the shape of the government gathered momentum. The Republican majority had decided to try, in enacting its first budget, to dramatically reshape the government. The shape of the budget was fixed early on: a balanced budget, with a $245 billion tax cut (principally benefiting upper income taxpayers) and a simultaneous $270 billion cut in Medicare. The Republicans assumed that Clinton would flinch and give in to their demands. So early on, they announced a strategy of threatening to shut down the federal government—refusing to provide the funds to keep it operating—as a means to force him to sign their plan. At the same time, they were planning to allow the U.S. government to approach default on its outstanding debts by refusing to raise the debt limit, also as a means to force the administration to capitulate.

On November 13, 1995, Clinton vetoed the debt limit bill sent to him

by the Congress, which would have conditioned the raising of the debt limit that allows the government to keep borrowing in the marketplace on acceptance of their budget terms. At midnight, the government was due to shut down.

Clinton was scheduled to speak to the annual meeting of the Democratic Leadership Council, the organization that he had headed but which just a year before had been witheringly critical of him. He worked hard on the speech. Our draft had included a line from the poem "The Second Coming," by William Butler Yeats, about how this would be a test of whether the center can hold. A few minutes before leaving, Clinton called for a copy of the poem and read it to a rapt audience: "The best lack all conviction, while the worst are full of passionate intensity."

The key to Clinton's strategy was never to allow the Republicans to be "for" a balanced budget and himself to be "against" it. We realized that the press would be more likely to reprint the most confrontational sentences, and that even a balanced, nuanced speech could be reported as if it was a partisan rant. So the speech was careful to stress Clinton's support for a balanced budget, even within a sentence.

"I support a balanced budget, but I oppose the Republican budget plan," he said to applause. "I believe we have a duty to care for our parents so that they can live their lives in dignity. That duty includes securing Medicare, slowing the rate of growth of inflation, protecting our senior citizens and giving them every opportunity to maximize the options that are out there. But the Republican budget rests on massive cuts—three times bigger than any previous ones in our history—designed apparently to let the system wither away."

He concluded with an unaccustomed Churchillian flourish, surprising the audience—possibly surprising himself. "As long as they insist on plunging ahead with a budget that violates our values in a process that is characterized more by pressure than constitutional practice, I will fight it. I am fighting it today. I will fight it tomorrow." He talked through their applause. "I will fight it next week and next month. I will fight it until we get a budget that is fair to all Americans."

That night, the operations of the federal government partially shut down. Most federal employees were furloughed; federal offices were closed. The Statue of Liberty, the national parks, the passport office, all were shown in the newspapers, closed. The White House was emptied of all except "essential" staff. (In our little world, only Baer and I worked. The rest of the communications staff stayed home.)

In a crisis atmosphere, negotiations continued—and each day, Clinton spoke to the country. His words were a mix of reassurance, defiance, and carefully crafted declarations.

The first day, in the briefing room: "On behalf of the American people, I said no."

The next day, in a television interview: I will hold firm, "even if it's 90 days, 120 days, or 180 days."

The next day, in the Oval Office: "If I were to sign their seven-year plan, in effect, I would be approving these cuts. I won't do that because I believe it would be bad for America."

Before each statement, advisors gathered in the Oval Office or in the President's private dining room to pore over the text and debate the nuances. Gore would demand a firm stand; Panetta, bloodied by his days negotiating with the Republicans, worried about the damage being done by the shutdown. One Saturday morning, Baer, Sperling, and I leaned over a computer, writing a battle-ready radio address to replace a conciliatory one written the night before. Stephanopoulos was nervously shuttling between the strategy session in Panetta's office one flight above and our drafting session in the basement. The radio address would be broadcast live to the country in minutes. "Last night I went the extra mile to bring Republicans and Democrats together," the President began. "But this morning it looks like this chance to reopen the government may be slipping away." We stood quietly in the back of the room, our pagers turned off so they would not beep during the broadcast, watching him deliver it.

Finally, after a six-day shutdown, a temporary compromise was achieved, when the Republicans and Democrats agreed to balance the budget in seven years, but pledged to do so in a way that preserved our priorities—Medicare, Medicaid, education, and the environment. But the Republicans would not simply declare victory and withdraw, a course once urged during the Vietnam War. In early December, they passed their budget to send to the President—giving him an opportunity to dramatically veto their measure.

At a planning session in the Old Executive Office Building, I proposed that we employ some obvious political symbolism: Since we were insisting this was a fight about Medicare, the President should veto the bill with the same pen used by Lyndon Johnson to sign Medicare into law. The pen was sent by overnight mail from the LBJ Presidential Library in Austin. We met with Clinton in his dining room, down the private corridor from the Oval Office. He was busy crossing out lines and rewriting when the provenance of the pen was explained to him—and as it sunk in that the pen was thirty years old, he looked at me. "Was this your idea?"

"Yes, sir."

"Pretty good," he smiled. "Let's hope it works." He practiced a few strokes, dipping into the inkwell.

Clinton went into the Oval Office. Surrounded by families who

would be affected by the cuts in Medicaid and education, bathed in television light, he looked every inch the president. Just as the Oklahoma City bombing had brought him into focus for the first time as a truly national leader, now the contest with the Republicans showed him standing firm for political principle.

"Throughout our history, American presidents have used the power of the veto to protect our values as a country. In that spirit today, I am acting to protect the values that bind us together in our national community," he declared sternly. He pulled out the fountain pen and began to sign his name. Nothing happened. He bore down harder. Finally, he looked up, calling out in an LBJ voice, "Can you bring me some ink, boys?" The staff secretary dashed from the back of the room, jumping over television cables and narrowly avoiding lamps. They fiddled with the inkwell, and finally the pen worked.

That night, the television news showed Clinton struggling with the pen. "It ran out of ink today and had to be refilled in mid-ceremony. But the President had no shortage of reasons why he said he had to do this," Brit Hume reported on ABC. "As it turns out, we wouldn't have gotten on the news if the pen had worked," Stephanopoulos reassured me.

The stalemate continued. Clinton's resurgence was visible. But—as the Republicans voted to shut the government down a second time—it was still unclear whom the public would blame.

EIGHT

STATE OF THE UNION

IN THE EARLIEST DAYS OF 1996, Washington was snowed in, the government was shut down, and it still seemed likely that it would be Bill
Clinton's last year in office. I delighted in pointing out at staff meetings that
the last Democratic president who left office without being either dead, defeated, or politically demolished was James K Polk in 1848.

Capitol Hill was testy, even gloomy. The Democrats still distrusted
Clinton and ached from their loss of power, the Republicans were angry
with their leaders over the botched shutdown. The polls had shifted dramatically, with the President having recovered much lost ground; but it was
far from certain who was winning the battle of public perception.

The mood in the country was little better. The economy had been
growing, rising by 3.5 percent in 1994 and 2.1 percent in 1995. But in the
public mind, times were still hard—and the fear facing working people was
the prospect of a sudden downward plunge in status and income. A front-
page story in *USA Today* in January was headlined "70% Say Economy Is
Fair to Poor." One third said that the economy was getting worse. And three
quarters of the electorate was dissatisfied with the way things were going in
the country. On the newsstand a *U.S. News & World Report* cover asked: "Is
the American Worker Getting the Shaft?"

Three weeks into the New Year, Clinton was scheduled to deliver
the State of the Union address. It would have to frame the tumultuous
year that had just ended and declare who had "won" the battle of the
budget. Because Bob Dole had chosen to deliver the Republican response that would follow immediately, it would launch the election
campaign.

And this would be my first big speech as director of speechwriting. In the first years of the administration, the writing of the State of the Union was a chaotic process that mirrored the President's uncertainty about direction. This year, Clinton—working through Dick Morris—tapped a network of junior aides, scattered throughout the White House, to craft the policy agenda for his reelection campaign.

SOME OF AMERICA'S FOUNDERS had an inkling that the State of the Union would veer close to royal pageantry. The Constitution requires the president to "from time to time give to the Congress information of the state of the Union" and make legislative recommendations. George Washington and John Adams went before Congress to present their reports. But Thomas Jefferson thought it was presumptuous, even kingly, for a president to go before Congress and tell it what to do. He sent his State of the Union in writing, and that is what presidents did for another century. Woodrow Wilson, who sought to create a strong, personal twentieth-century presidency, broke precedent by motoring to Capitol Hill to deliver a speech in person in 1913.

With a few exceptions, these annual speeches have been dull, dutiful recitations of legislative agendas. Only FDR's 1941 "Four Freedoms" speech, in which he laid out the war aims of the United States, was particularly memorable. Then Ronald Reagan realized that the State of the Union was a perfectly designed platform for his skills—well lit, hundreds of applauding extras, a chance to provoke his opponents into looking churlish. He used the addresses to cast a mood—patriotic, defiant, optimistic—and to highlight heroes who embodied his individualistic ethos. His addresses were rarely used to advance new policies.

Watching the speech is one of the few remaining civic rituals in America; voting, newspaper readership, and party affiliation are down, but tens of millions of people still watch the speech. It is the only time each year when a president can be assured that his words will directly reach the public without first being sliced, sautéed, or roasted by the press.

For this reason, policymakers wage fierce competition to have their proposals included in an address. The difference between a program being "a" priority and "the" priority can mean billions of dollars. The role of the speechwriter is to help the president sift through the dozens of competing visions for the speech. You need to deflect gently the proposals of agency heads who plead for their pet projects, knowing that a presidential reference can imply billions of dollars when the budget is written. And you need to boil down gallons of advice into a few tablespoons of intense sauce.

WHEN I TOLD PEOPLE that I was working on the State of the Union, they didn't ask about tone or policies. They said what my mother said when I telephoned her, "That's wonderful. Make it short." More than a few of them remembered Clinton's disastrous 1988 speech nominating Michael Dukakis for the presidency. The nominator had been supposed to speak for fifteen minutes and droned on for a half hour. Television cameras focused on the red light and delegates making the "cut" sign across their throats. The 1995 State of the Union wasn't remembered much more fondly. It was the longest State of the Union ever delivered—one hour and twenty minutes, much of it extemporaneous.

The first White House staff meeting on the 1996 State of the Union was held in late 1995 in the Ward Room of the White House mess—a small, dark-paneled dining room decorated with etchings of soldiers. Twenty people crammed into the room, and it seemed as if the only topic anyone wanted to discuss was the length.

Press secretary Mike McCurry, averse to meetings, pushed his way into the crowded room. He was emphatic. The 1995 State of the Union had been a failure, he said. It was way too long, too rambling, and had too many policies. Dick Morris, who was making a rare appearance before a large group of staff, reddened. "The State of the Union moved the President a permanent seven points," he said curtly. Elites hadn't liked it, but the public did. In fact, the ratings for the speech had gone up as it went along.

McCurry didn't buy it. He knew that the speech was seen by journalists as a caricature of everything that was wrong with Clinton. He had an alternative proposal. "I think the speech should be a tone poem." It should express broad themes, eloquently, without a lot of proposals. A separate message, proposing policies, could be sent to the Congress in writing.

I winced. *Tone poem*, I thought. *That's code for "get someone who can write poetry to write it."*

The matter was settled by consulting the entrails of public opinion. Mark Penn, a pollster from New York who was now working for the President, told me that he and Morris had polled the question: How long should the State of the Union be? Twenty minutes? An hour? Forty minutes? Should it present broad themes or detailed policies? The people had spoken: forty minutes was OK, lots of policies, no tone poem. I was relieved. Citing polls, however absurd, could be an efficient way to bring an aimless meeting to an end. But I was also amazed at the process. I could imagine a typical family, cleaning up after dinner, trying to watch television, annoyed when the phone rang and a stranger began asking questions: how long should the State of the Union address be?

As I DROVE NORTH late one night on I–95 with my family toward New York for the holidays, I fretted on a cellphone with Penn. "Look, don't worry," he said. "You know how this is going to go. We have to see what happens with the government shutdown. We're not going to know until two weeks before the speech. So just relax. Get some sleep and we'll deal with it then."

When we returned to Washington, with the government still closed, we had to begin assembling a speech. With three weeks to go, our efforts would be compressed. And there were questions to answer. What should its tone be? What should its focus be? What policies should it advance?

Clinton was voracious for ideas, advice, even scoldings. Much of it was contradictory, and nearly all of it was lofted at a level of generality that rendered it useless. Part of my role was to organize the "process." Before Christmas, we had sent Clinton a book of memos from two dozen writers and academics—from Arthur Schlesinger Jr. to Garrison Keillor. Cabinet secretaries were encouraged to send in memos, too. Robert Rubin warned against adopting a demagogic anti-business tone. Donna Shalala asked for more funding.

Don Baer and I met with the cabinet secretaries in the Roosevelt Room. It was a bit of a ritual: The secretaries knew that such a meeting was unlikely to have a major impact on the final speech. But it was a part of any State of the Union process, and it couldn't hurt. Alice Rivlin, the Office of Management and Budget director, was tart. "In the past, we have made a mistake. There have been too many ideas, not well developed. We should choose a few of these things and do them well." Bob Reich agreed. "Let's help him [the President] make decisions about the focus. We should ask, 'what's the headline that we want, what's the headline going to be?' " Mickey Kantor, the trade representative, warned, "Don't get into a debate over whether we are for or against government. We should not do the 'role of government' as a theme. We're not the party of government; we're the party of the future." We nodded and took notes.

The President also heard from the congressional Democrats. The message was loud and sharp. The vast majority urged the President to focus on economic anxiety. They believed that the 1994 election losses could be traced to discontent among working people. Stanley Greenberg, who had been elbowed aside as the President's pollster, argued that the loss in 1994 was due almost entirely to the defection of "downscale" Democrats—poor and working-class families who had cast their votes in hope for Clinton in 1992, but who felt betrayed by NAFTA and deficit reduction and the failure of health reform. Many in the administration allied themselves with this view. America's middle class, Robert Reich argued, had become an "anxious class" — "millions of Americans who no longer can count on having their jobs next year, or next month, and whose wages have stagnated or

lost ground to inflation." The President approvingly circulated Reich's remarks to his staff.

To add to the din, the President had asked that a "thinkers' dinner" be convened at the White House. On January 7, the day after the second government shutdown had officially ended, the government was shut down again, this time by the weather. Washington's sense of itself as a sleepy southern city was mocked by a deep blizzard (Washington has not moved on the map in two hundred years, but everyone is still surprised every time it snows). The streets were deserted.

Wearing suits and sweaters and L. L. Bean snowshoes, we shook off our coats and gathered in the Red Room. Musicians in military dress quietly played chamber music. The room was full of boldfaced names from the *New York Review of Books*. Henry Louis Gates, the voluble head of the African-American studies department at Harvard. Ben Barber, whose book on globalization had caught the President's fancy two years before. This year's hottest catch was Robert Putnam, whose article "Bowling Alone" chronicled the decline in communal activities (like bowling leagues) and civic activity, and had been cited in numerous op-eds and editorials. Moving among the intellectuals was Bill Galston, a sociologist who had served on the White House staff.

Everyone was quietly giddy; those invited were genial to one another, but one sensed that inside, they were rehearsing what they would say to Clinton. The President and First Lady glided in. We were ushered across the grand foyer, through the state dining room, and into the family dining room. A long table was covered with flowers, silver, and crystal. Engraved name cards and a menu were at each china plate. The President and Vice President sat across from each other. Staff and officials were arrayed around the ends of the table.

When the conversation began, mini-sermons shot sparks off in a dozen directions. But for all the disparate talk a commonality could be discerned. There was very little said about government and what it could do. Civil society was badly frayed, the academics argued. The web of associations—churches, schools, unions, neighborhoods—that had undergirded life for middle-class people was under assault. The President took notes and nodded. Occasionally, he would interject political strategy and note the harsh public mood in response to the academics' airy talk of community. Plainly, he was continuing to probe, to see how far he could push progressive ideas on the country. He appeared to love a setting like this—high-minded, crosscurrents of thought and talk. He absorbed it all somehow. A word, an idea, a phrase jangled around in his head. It was fascinating. But it was a bit depressing, too. And it wasn't clear that it would be very helpful.

Henry Cisneros, the secretary of housing and urban development, sat

at one end of the table. After the dessert plates were cleared away, as the academics dispersed (pocketing their name cards as souvenirs), he pulled Baer and me aside. He believed that the only way to cut through the gloom—the only way for Clinton to reshuffle the deck—would be to surprise everyone with a confident, optimistic, even ebullient speech. Cisneros had sent Clinton a note and wanted to show it to us. He had attached a page from Thomas Flexner's biography of George Washington. "As he approached his 7th State of the Union," Cisneros wrote, "President Washington was under severe criticism. His opponents were ready to attack him for what they expected would be a bitter, divisive speech. Instead he completely disarmed them by delivering an optimistic vision of America's many blessings and its future. This might be a wonderful moment for exactly that kind of 'jujitsu.' " Flexner wrote that his opponents "were so devoted to controversy that their first reaction was that Washington had raised the white flag of surrender. . . . But it quickly became clear that Washington had made a master stroke. . . . The pendulum, which had swung so far against Washington, was swinging back."

Mark Penn had come to the same conclusion. His polls showed a surprising result: Contrary to the sense of pessimism that seemed to pervade the country, people were strikingly optimistic about their own economic futures. When asked about the country, however, they were negative—reflecting back to their leaders and the media the sense of gloom they were constantly being told they felt. Penn believed that the President had to break the cycle of pessimism that was causing people to doubt the success of his policies.

I, too, turned to history. On a cold Saturday afternoon during the government shutdown, I opened a notebook my staff had compiled: SELECTED STATE OF THE UNION ADDRESSES 1936–1988. It included addresses delivered by presidents who were running for re-election.

Jimmy Carter, in 1980: "This last few months [sic] has not been an easy time for any of us." Ouch. Malaise. Carter lost.

George Bush began by apologizing for not being Barbara Bush. Then he actually made a joke about having been sick on the prime minister of Japan. (Note to self: no barf jokes.) Then he went on to express optimism about the future—but first, he apologized for not seeming to care about the end of the Cold War or the economy. "Even as president, with the most fascinating possible vantage point, there were times when I was so busy helping to manage progress and helping to lead change that I didn't always show the joy that was in my heart." Message: I am queasy. Bush lost.

I turned to Ronald Reagan's 1984 speech. For him, 1983 had been a hard year. A terrorist bombing had killed 241 U.S. Marines in Beirut. The

deficit was worsening. While the economy had begun to recover, that fact had not really sunk in. But confidence surged from the page. The opening paragraph had a jaunty momentum. "Mr. Speaker, Mr. President, distinguished members of the Congress, honored guests, and fellow citizens: Once again, in keeping with time-honored tradition, I have come to report to you on the state of the union, and I'm pleased to report that America is much improved, and there is good reason to believe that improvement will continue through the days to come." We're used to thinking of Reagan as presiding over an exuberant boom—and that's true. But in January 1984, people didn't yet believe the boom was real. After this speech, they did. Reagan won forty-nine states later that year. As he said, "America is back, standing tall."

Even Richard Nixon, in 1972, was happy and optimistic, bragging about ending the turmoil of the 1960s. If Nixon could do it, anyone could.

The lesson was surprisingly clear-cut: when it comes to the State of the Union in an election year, the optimistic presidents win. Presidents are held accountable for the country's overall direction. And when a president accentuates the negative, the public assumes things are worse than they really are. Clinton's natural optimism, far from a liability, was politically the right thing as well.

DURING THE FIRST WEEK in January, we gathered in Don Baer's office. The West Wing is far smaller than it seems in movies or on television. The tone is hushed, not so much because of the weight of history as because talking loud means being heard in other offices down the hall. Baer had moved into an ample but windowless office in the basement of the West Wing, across the hall from the White House mess. The walls were bare, save for his children's drawings.

The people gathered in the room might be the generators of ideas and energy in the White House, but they did not generally hold the top jobs. Bruce Reed was suffering through his third year as deputy to the domestic policy advisor. Rahm Emanuel was nominally a communications aide but with Reed actually ran the administration's policy on a number of social issues, especially crime. Gene Sperling was the deputy to Laura Tyson; he had run the campaign's economic policy. For months, these staffers had been preparing policy ideas, gathering them up from the bureaucracy and from informal networks. We had quietly been passing the ideas on to Morris, sometimes without our supervisors knowing about it. We were all in our mid-thirties; we had all been in Little Rock or on the campaign trail; every one of us had been straining at the bit. This speech would be our chance — our White House coming of age.

Penn put a transparent cell on the overhead projector. He had divided the electorate into universes. "Clinton base voters" were Democrats who would vote for Clinton without much prodding. They couldn't be ignored, but the election would be won elsewhere. "Swing One" voters were independents who leaned toward Clinton but who distrusted the Democratic Party's approach to values. They were married people with children. They were to become known as soccer moms. "Swing Two" voters were angry, mostly men. They were more interested in punishing crime than anything else. ("Rahm's people," we called them. We joked that they were happier punishing crime than preventing it.) Seen this way, the election seemed suddenly winnable. For voters overall, the top issue was the need for "strict laws to keep insurance companies from denying coverage/allowing people to keep coverage with a job change." That was the Kennedy-Kassebaum bill, a measure that was designed to revive the issue of health care, albeit incrementally.

Swing Ones, the soccer moms, stressed crime prevention. They were for measures that would reach young people and teach them values — such as the V-chip that allows parents to block their children from watching violent television programs. For Swing Twos, the most popular proposal was extending federal sentencing standards so that inmates would serve 85 percent of their sentence.

In short, the biggest worry on the part of a growing number of Americans was not economic. It was a sense that their values were under threat — not by the forces of "secular humanism," as the religious right would have it, but by an increasingly coarse and commercialized culture. If we could answer this concern, then we could win the suburban vote that had been long denied to the Democrats.

A few days later, we gathered in Baer's office again. This time, we chewed over "thematic paragraphs." These would be brief and condensed statements of possible organizing principles — a few sentences that would set the tone for the speech.

Everyone had been encouraged to suggest chunks of useful rhetoric. Penn would test them to see if the tuning fork vibrated. One rhetorical device, suggested by Baer: "Our challenge at the dawn of a new century is to help our children know again that they can have dreams, that work pays, and that we are one nation." Another option: "America must return to its core values. We have to recognize that family is the cornerstone of our nation, and we must reorient all of our tax and welfare policies to promote families." Another on the millennium: "The most important job of our next president is this: to see into the next century, to be able to lead our country into the new millennium. This new era will be a time of peace, of spiritual awakening, a golden age . . ."

Bruce Reed was quietly mortified. This exercise seemed so empty and contentless. Bill Clinton had been unique among Democratic presidential candidates in demanding responsibility, not just offering more programs to voters. Where was that brisk sense of challenge? Walking to our offices across the parking lot, Reed recalled some lines he had written for Clinton in 1991. "America was built on challenges, not promises," he said, paraphrasing JFK's "New Frontier" speech. "There isn't a program for every problem." We returned to our corner of the second-floor hall and drafted a proposed paragraph. "Challenges, not promises." Penn threw it into that night's poll. It came back off the charts. In hundreds of kitchens and living rooms across America, our fellow citizens shrugged and said, challenges, sure, that sounds fine.

The next day Morris was keyed up. "Good. Yes. Challenges. A series of challenges — not problems that can't be solved, but challenges." We would divide the speech into seven challenges — challenges that included new government initiatives, but especially ones that used the bully pulpit to encourage families to stay together, schools to impose discipline, and the television networks to impart values through programming. The consultants wrote a memo to Clinton: "We need to shape the language of the speech so that [it] talks about challenges, not insecurities; values, not class; opportunity, not inequality; community, not individualism, and shows a can-do spirit, not pessimism."

Reed slipped me a note. "When do we turn pro?"

NOW IT WAS TIME to deliver a full and polished first draft for the President.

I was determined that this speech would give Clinton a chance to develop his full, presidential voice. It would be organized and stately. I knew Clinton would resist a draft that was floated on clouds of high rhetoric. A Reaganesque paean to America's glories would sound false and fulsome coming out of his mouth. His vernacular was policies, facts, stories; they would have to provide the raw material for his eloquence. A speechwriter must write in the cadence and rhythm and voice of the President. But that doesn't merely mean miming his style, as if Rich Little were sitting behind the keyboard. It means finding the right presidential rhythm. This speech had to have vivid colors and active verbs, and move with locomotive force.

"Let me begin tonight by saying to our men and women in uniform around the world, and especially those helping peace take root in Bosnia and to their families, I thank you. America is very, very proud of you." It seemed to make sense to begin with a salute to the troops in Bosnia. The surprising success of the Dayton peace talks had been a key element in the emerging sense that Clinton was a successful foreign policy president.

Also, I reasoned, lawmakers of both parties would have no choice but to applaud the troops.

Then the speech moved into the section, common to every one of these speeches, where the President describes the State of the Union—the "morning in America" section. But Clinton couldn't simply issue superlatives. I had asked the research staff to assemble a thick binder of economic statistics and examples. I thought about the economic anxiety, free floating but real. But I also thought about the sense of renewal that could be seen in cities across the country. I remembered as well that incumbent presidents should never do their opponents' work for them. I typed, "The state of the Union is strong. Our economy is the healthiest it has been in three decades." The statistics piled on. Eight million new jobs. The lowest unemployment and inflation in twenty-seven years. America selling more cars than Japan for the first time since the 1970s.

As I worked through the draft, I asked Reed and Sperling to join me in my office.

In the Old Executive Office Building, it seemed as if the bigger the office, the smaller the influence of its occupant. My office was grand but disfigured. It had bookshelves, room for a conference table and chairs, and a view of the Washington Monument. Once, it had been the reception room for the secretary of state—so ornate that it had been named one of the most beautiful rooms in America. I liked to imagine Tojo's representatives, waiting here to deliver their ultimatum on December 7, 1941, after the Japanese bombers were already in the air. But over the years, the beauty had been hacked up, covered over. A wall was built, cutting the room in half. The gilt-edged green and gray walls were covered with coat after coat of white paint. The vaulted ceiling was painted white, too, with fluorescent lights hung on rods. The varnished wooden floor was covered with industrial style carpeting. All that remained was a magnificent marble fireplace—and the view.

Reed strolled over from his office next door. Thin, boyish, clean-cut, and nattily dressed, he looked like Christian Coalition head Ralph Reed (no relation; Bruce joked that the Republican was his "evil cousin"). He had been the policy director for the Democratic Leadership Council when Clinton was its chair, and then was traveling speechwriter and issues advisor during the campaign. Often overshadowed by flashier staff members, he was quietly confident that he understood Clinton's approach. He had been waiting to work on this speech for years.

We were joined by Sperling, a renowned workaholic. His suit, as usual, was dark and rumpled; his shirt, white and billowing. Fatigue marks smudged under his eyes. After months of staring at OMB spreadsheets, and weeks in negotiations with the Republicans, his skin had an alarming fluorescent pallor.

The speech would open with a triumphant march through good news. "Can we say 'the economy is the strongest in a generation'?" Gene checked his three-ring binders. Yes, we could.

The speech then would turn to a pugnacious discussion of the budget—as Clinton's previous two State of the Union addresses had. Now we had a chance to have the Democrats cheering for "a balanced budget that honors our values," for "Medicare, Medicaid, education, and the environment."

"What do we think, is this the right approach?" I asked. "I can't get any read on it from Clinton."

Gene shrugged. "We'll just have to see." The negotiations were so fluid, and the President's approach so mercurial, that we would have to try this approach to see if it got shot down.

We crammed the speech with values proposals, announcements, and challenges.

As Reed looked over my shoulder, he asked, "What about school uniforms?" Hillary Clinton had written about school uniforms in her book *It Takes a Village*. She believed they were a way to bring order to the schools. Morris and Penn were opposed to including them in the speech. Rahm Emanuel was nearly frantic that they be included. He called Reed at least once a day to make sure they had not been stripped from the draft.

Drugs were another issue. The Republicans had signaled that they would attack Clinton on the rise in drug use among young people. (Overall drug use was down, but drug use by teens was up.) Emanuel had worked for weeks to find a new director of the White House Office of National Drug Control Policy. He proudly whispered that he had succeeded. General Barry McCaffrey, a four-star general, would take the job—and would be willing to appear, in uniform, next to Hillary in the First Lady's box.

One of the issues was a plea for fathers to spend more time with their children. This was a constant Clinton theme, one he had even discussed in his acceptance speech. We knew that there were reams of studies showing the importance of fathers to the moral and psychological development of children—that fatherless children were more likely to commit crime, use drugs, or end up on welfare. Raising it would send a political signal as well. For years, when Democrats talked about "children," it sounded like a euphemism for government spending; when they talked about "families raising children," it sounded like a euphemism for grandmothers raising children. We would talk about parents, something like: "I challenge fathers—sending a check is not enough. You must spend more time with your children."

I stared at the screen. It was nine at night, and I was still at the office, as usual. My three-year-old and one-year-old were going to bed. I hadn't seen them in days. My fingers refused to type.

"I can't write this. I just can't do it." I stood up. "Bruce, you do it."

Bruce didn't move. He looked at the empty chair. His daughter, Julia, and son, Nelson, were born only months apart from my children. "I can't do it either."

We had to put it in. The President wanted it. It was a *challenge*. We guiltily called our wives, got their permission, and typed a desultory sentence or two.

Don Baer came in and stretched out on the couch. Soon he began to snore. At around midnight, it was time for economics. "Gene, we really need the facts about the economy." OK, OK. A few moments later, the door opened. A young man peered in and quietly entered. He wore a rumpled gray suit, a billowing white shirt; he had pale skin and mussed dark hair. He looked, in fact, strikingly like Gene. He handed Gene a draft of a fact sheet on the economy and disappeared.

We were writing about the Internet. Gene padded over to us. "I really feel strongly about this. We really need to appeal to these people. I know someone who works in educational software, and there is a huge gap. We should challenge the software makers. 'Make programming as if your own children were watching.' "

One A.M. The door opened again. It was a second young man—dark gray suit, white shirt, black hair, pale skin. He, too, looked just like Gene. He handed over a sheet of paper and left wordlessly.

"Here's my chance," I said. "Why don't I put in McCain-Feingold. That's bipartisan," I said, referring to the campaign finance reform proposal. "Sure," said Bruce.

Two A.M. The door opened again. A thin young woman entered: dark gray pants, white shirt, pale skin, black hair. Even she looked like Gene. She handed over her work and left.

We fell over laughing. "This is like *The Cat in the Hat Comes Back*," I said. "Here in the hat on the top of my head I have Little Gene A to help me, he said. And on top of his hat is Little Gene B. And on top of his hat is Little Gene C." We roared with laughter. Gene paced.

"Nooo," said Bruce. "Actually, it was the Things. That was Thing One, Thing Two, and Thing Three. 'How do you do, would you like to shake hands with Thing One and Thing Two?' "

(Sadly for them, the nickname of Gene's "things" stuck. They were described in *Time* magazine the next week. For years, Gene's many hardworking assistants tried in vain to coin nicknames for themselves, which they leaked to the press any time Sperling was profiled. The Whirling Sperlings. The Gene Machine. But the names never stuck. They were Things forever. All of them were somewhat touchy about it. The woman, in particular, has never forgiven me.)

We worked through the night. The draft was brisk and optimistic. It included an array of new proposals to help families advance their values. And it still began with a salute to the troops and a stiff rejoinder to the Republicans on the budget. The next morning, I put it in a manila envelope and walked it over to the usher's office on the first floor of the executive residence. The usher marked it in a log, rang for an elevator, and brought it up to the President.

NINE

THE ERA
OF BIG GOVERNMENT
IS OVER

CLINTON WAS SPENDING long hours negotiating with the Republicans, and with his budget team. Word came that he would squeeze in a series of meetings to discuss the speech—which was to be given less than a week later.

We filed into the Oval Office and scattered around it. The speech-writers, hunched and nervous on the alarming yellow and maroon couches. Advisors without portfolio like Stephanopoulos and Ickes lounging around the perimeter or propped against Clinton's desk. Until now, Clinton had been curiously detached. (He joked that he had seen more of House majority leader Dick Armey and Newt Gingrich than of Hillary and Chelsea.) But I sensed it was more than that. He still was wary of his White House staff, whom he regarded as too tied to Capitol Hill party orthodoxy. He was working and thinking alone, calling his friends late at night, bouncing ideas off them. Now he sat in a yellow wingback chair—the same chair, in front of the fireplace, where he was photographed meeting with a Boris Yeltsin or a Jacques Chirac. Black Sharpie pen in his left hand, he raced through the speech.

"I like this. This is good," he would say as he moved across the pages. Then he began to riff, to free associate. He liked the tone. He liked the optimism—but we needed to say more, to be more expansive. "We live in an age of possibility," he said. I scribbled, "Age of possibility."

He shook his head vigorously. The budget approach was all wrong. We should be much more conciliatory. "Regardless of the outcome of our negotiations, there is now broad, bipartisan and unshakable agreement that America will balance the budget. There was a time when both parties went

along with running a permanent deficit. Now both parties agree that the days of ever-growing deficits are over. In the past three years, my administration has cut the deficit we inherited nearly in half. Tonight, let me affirm my commitment: no matter what happens, we will balance the budget, and do it in seven years. The budget deficit is yesterday's legacy, and soon it will be history."

He focused on the drug section. He dictated a passage about the impact that a D.A.R.E. officer had on Chelsea. He told us in no uncertain terms that the description of McCaffrey was inadequate. "X years ago—I don't know how many, find out—x years ago, I sent him to command our military's campaign against drug kingpins in Latin America. His troops stormed the headquarters of the Cali cartel in Colombia, and today the seven men who ran the cartel are in prison. In the last three years, we have—then put in the details of what we've done—and that man did it. General McCaffrey convinced me through his actions that we can stop the flow of drugs."

We should put anything in that we could that was bipartisan, he said. Mention the bills' authors by name. Kennedy and Kassebaum, who wrote legislation guaranteeing that people could take their health insurance with them from job to job. McCain and Feingold on campaign reform.

The journalist Sidney Blumenthal, a writer at *The New Yorker*, had urged the President to build the speech around the theme of "One America." Clinton thought that was worth at least a sentence. Blumenthal had also suggested that the President end by saying "God bless the *United States of America*." "Good old Sidney," Clinton said, smiling. "He's always thinking."

I was charged with producing another draft. Transcribing Clinton, I wrote, "This is an age of possibility. But we know that this is also a time of great challenge and change—as profound as any we have faced. A century ago, we moved from farm to factory; today, we are moving into a new era of technology, information, and intense global competition." I added: "An era in which things certain seem to melt into air . . . and things miraculous are the daily blessings of our lives." "Melt into air," Baer nodded approvingly as he edited. "That's nice." I took the compliment but wondered. Where had I heard that phrase? Was it from something I read in college? I quietly assigned a researcher to search for it on the Internet.

ON SATURDAY, Clinton had the new draft. He was in Texas, speaking at the funeral of former congresswoman Barbara Jordan.

I thought the address was good—clean, dignified, the right mix of rhetoric and policy. Dick Morris' voice exploded over the speakerphone

from Connecticut. He didn't think so. Not all his pet policies had been included. I answered, declaiming into the air, "Dick, if we are going to keep the speech short, there is simply no room in this for more stuff."

"I don't care how long the speech is. And you can fit more into it."

He hung up. A few hours later, Kevin Moran, Baer's young assistant, brought in a fax. It was from Morris to the President. Moran had taken a copy to the Oval Office, and now was giving us ours.

Baer, Reed, and I looked at it in silence. We began to giggle. Finally, I offered, "He is out of his bloody mind."

There was no spacing between paragraphs and practically no margins. In a few hours, it seemed, Morris had frenetically typed up a new draft of the State of the Union, rewriting my draft, making it tauter and tabloidy. It was, frankly, brilliant. I still learn from it to this day. In contrast to the stately pace of my prose, Morris' was staccato, condensed. It read like a Walter Winchell column—urgent, clipped, ellipses instead of transitions. No idea was carried more than a sentence or two. Dozens of them began, "I challenge. . . ," "I challenge. . . ," "I challenge. . ."

It also read, it must be admitted, like a series of poll questions. "This reminds me of the experiment with the monkeys," I confided to Baer. "There was an experiment where an electrode was implanted in the brain of monkeys. To get a banana pellet, the monkeys pushed a lever. They got the pellet but also got a mild electric shock in the brain. The monkeys were so determined to get the banana pellets they fried themselves. These are banana pellets."

The only paragraph of any length was the plea for fathers to care for their children. What we had written was suddenly transformed into grand opera. A check was not enough, it said. Go home, fathers. Go home—your children need you. "What is all this 'daddy come home' stuff about?" Reed said. We pruned it back, not knowing about Morris' own unorthodox personal life.

One device jumped off the page. I had written: "In the last thirty years, it has become clear that government cannot solve all our problems for us. And in the last twelve months it has become equally clear that getting rid of government will not solve all our problems, either. We don't need a program for every problem; we need citizens to rise to every challenge." This was, I thought, a neat summary of the lessons of the past and of Clinton's attempt to steer a middle way.

Instead, Morris had written: "The era of big government is over. But the era of every man for himself must never begin."

It was repeated twice in the text. We agreed that was much stronger, startling in fact. Clinton sent word that he liked Morris' edits. I set about incorporating many of them into my text, making its prose less bombastic and

more Clintonian. The new version was circulated among the staff: the era of big government over, every man for himself must never begin. We waited for the explosion. We expected this sentence to cause a huge fight, a principled debate over policy and Democratic ideals.

The great debate never happened. Ann Lewis came to Baer's office. A former Democratic party official, then the vice president of Planned Parenthood, she had been supported by Hillary Clinton to be the communications director before Baer finally got the job. She went instead to the campaign office as spokesperson there. "There's a problem here," she said, frowning at the draft. The era of big government is over? Not that, she explained. The next phrase, "every man for himself." It's sexist. I wasn't even sure if she was serious. Yes, seriously, that's a problem. She left for her next meeting.

Sunday afternoon we were in the Oval Office with Clinton going over another draft. Tommy Caplan, Clinton's college roommate, told the President, "Some people have suggested that 'every man for himself' is sexist." Clinton smiled but didn't say, "Oh, that's absurd." Uh-oh, we thought. We'd better find another phrase.

We retreated downstairs to Baer's office. What about "The era of everyone for themselves must never begin"? No good—Clinton was a stickler for grammar, at least for agreements between subject and object, an odd bit of rigor for someone whose mind was frequently untidy. (I assumed it was a remnant of his Jesuit training at Georgetown.) What about "sink or swim"? Penn would poll it. What about "We must never go back to a time when you're on your own"? No, Penn shook his head. That was actually popular. For days, everyone who entered the office would be asked for a suggestion.

IN THE FINAL DAYS before a speech like this, pieces are pulled out and thrust in, proposals are discarded or revived, facts nestled in the text for draft after draft suddenly are discovered to be wrong. Trying to keep track of all its pieces is nearly impossible.

Clinton's stirring description of McCaffrey's exploits had to go. He thought he remembered it, but it hadn't happened. Scratch the Cali cartel.

We were still looking for "lift and loft." Baer and Tommy Caplan focused on finding suitable rhetoric for the speech's conclusion. Baer remembered a corporate image advertisement for Boeing that he had seen during a Sunday morning interview show. As images of the twentieth century flashed by, an unseen speaker declaimed, "Since we have come so far, who will be rash enough to set limits on our future progress? Who shall say that since we have gone so far, we can go no further?" Baer asked Boeing to

fax the script. The speaker, it turned out, was Adlai Stevenson, the Democratic presidential candidate in 1952 and 1956 who was defeated by Dwight Eisenhower. Baer and Caplan wrote an ending to the speech that was inspired by the ad.

Clinton called us up to his office. He was casually dressed, standing behind his desk, packing his briefcase and preparing to go home to the residence. He pushed the draft back at us, heavily marked with his edits. It was good; keep working at it, he said. We retreated to the basement office, now equipped with three computers, with garbage cans overflowing with coffee cups and Chinese food bins.

A nagging question got answered. The researcher came in: He had found where "all that is certain melts into air" came from. *"The Communist Manifesto.* It's by Karl Marx." That would have made for an interesting headline. ("Clinton Declares Era of Big Government Over; Quotes Marx, Engels.") And subhead. ("Speechwriter Fired, Deported.") I quietly excised the phrase. The President never knew.

The day of the speech, the press still had no idea what it would say or how. (Given a chance to ask Clinton about it the day before, during a meeting with the Israeli foreign minister, someone asked, "How long will it be?" Clinton answered, "That depends on the applause.")

Now we were ready to rehearse. The White House family theater is along a hallway at a right angle to the mansion. Tourists walk past it on the public tour. It has rows of wide movie theater–style seats and a deep stage. We had set up a presidential podium—the "blue goose"—flanked by teleprompter screens. Military personnel sat at a card table, slowly scrolling through the speech (using a joystick). A cameraman filmed the rehearsal. And a stenographer stood by. I sat next to the stage in the darkened room, typing at a desktop personal computer that had been set up. A dozen aides sprawled across the seats. They called out suggestions and answered questions. To salve bruised egos, we brought in those who had felt excluded from the process. Some senior aides were learning the content of the speech for the first time. A speech coach, Michael Sheehan, formerly with the Folger Shakespeare Company, listened for intonation. He would quietly huddle with Clinton between "takes."

"Mr. President, why don't you praise Dole for his service?" Stephanopoulos, tilted back in his chair, jackknifed forward. "Praise Dole and his generation for serving during World War II." Clinton smiled and agreed, and wrote it onto his copy. I typed it onto the computer. George chopped the air. "Bam. He's history."

Clinton read through the text again and again. By this point, he would usually stick to the paragraphs as written. Sometimes he would change a word here or there—"a" for "the," "we must" for "we should." Sometimes

he would dictate a new paragraph. I was still typing. A hand jabbed at my computer screen. "There. Change that." It was Gore—probably the most computer literate person in the room. He bent over the glowing screen, watching for words, as I entered changes.

Clinton was warming up. When he was alone, or with just an aide, he would sometimes become surly and withdrawn. Late at night, he would chew over a text, second-guessing and rewriting until it got longer and often worse. But in front of a crowd, even a small group of supportive aides, he tuned himself up. He willed himself to stand tall, keep it brisk, act the President. Remember, we were reminded by Stephanopoulos and others, our role in this final session was to cheer.

Clinton came over to the computer to look at what I was doing. (He presided over the computer revolution, but despite several attempts at training him, never managed to learn how to do even the simplest tasks until Chelsea went to college.) A White House photographer leaned in to capture the moment: Clinton, looking old in a checkered shirt; Gore beaming protons at the screen; me looking puffy and tired. The photo was released to the press to show the President working on his speech—the modern equivalent of a painting of the Great Man with a quill pen. (Or maybe of Mao swimming in the Yangtze, to show he's still alive.)

The year before, Clinton had stayed in the residence, working secretly with Morris, as staff waited in the theater below. Tonight, in command of the agenda, Clinton went upstairs to shower and dress as we prepared to print the speech to give to the press.

Ann Lewis arrived, insisting that we not endorse the McCain-Feingold campaign finance reform bill, which banned "bundling" of campaign checks by special interest groups. EMILY's List again. I argued that Clinton could hardly endorse the bipartisan campaign finance reform bill without mentioning it by name. Paul Weinstein, a member of the Domestic Policy Council staff, pointed out that we had already released a fact sheet stating that the President was endorsing McCain-Feingold. Lewis insisted that the sponsors' names be removed. I was too tired to fight. That night, the networks—which had been given an earlier draft—showed McCain and Feingold, and Clinton never mentioned them.

CLUTCHING A FLOPPY DISK, I ran through the hard corridors of the Capitol, guided by an advance man through the swinging doors, up the steps, down the hall, and up more steps past the House chamber to the cloakroom off the House floor. The word-processing disk was inserted in the teleprompter.

A few minutes later, the familiar call rang out. "Mr. Speaker, the pres-

ident of the United States." Clinton looked happy and confident. His steel hair was cut close. He handed Gingrich an envelope with a mock speech text in it—"Thank you and good night." Gingrich mimed a heartfelt laugh, but already he was off balance.

The President began with a gust of optimism. "The State of the Union is strong. Our economy is the healthiest it has been in three decades." He ran through the array of social statistics. Democrats cheered, and Republicans had to as well, or risk looking defeatist. It was the first time most voters had heard all this good news.

"We know big government does not have all the answers. We know there's not a program for every problem. We have worked to give the American people a smaller, less bureaucratic government in Washington. And we have to give the American people one that lives within its means.

"The era of big government is over." The Republicans gasped and jumped to their feet to applaud. "But"—he waved them silent—"but we cannot go back to the time when our citizens were left to fend for themselves. Instead, we must go forward as one America, one nation working together to meet the challenges we face together. Self-reliance and teamwork are not opposing virtues; we must have both." (The next day, the newspapers ran "the era of big government is over," and left out the meandering counterpoint.)

Clinton quickly dispatched with the budget. Lawmakers and viewers who were expecting an angry recapitulation of the budget war were struck by a new and soothing tone. He praised the Republicans for "the energy and determination you have brought to this task of balancing the budget." He acted as though agreement had already been reached: "The combined total of the proposed savings that are common to both [Republican and Democratic] plans is more than enough, using the numbers from your Congressional Budget Office, to balance the budget in seven years and to provide a modest tax cut."

Then Clinton turned to the new values agenda. "Our first challenge is to cherish our children and strengthen America's families." His first proposal was a challenge to the media: "To the media, I say you should create movies and CDs and television shows you would want your own children and grandchildren to enjoy." He called on Congress to pass the V-chip that would be installed in TV sets so that parents could screen violent or inappropriate programming. He invited media corporations to come to the White House to draft a ratings code.

On education, Clinton did not dwell on traditional Democratic approaches alone—more spending, support for teachers. Instead, he called for public school choice and support for public charter schools, a deft counter to the Republican push for vouchers. He paraphrased one of Gin-

grich's best lines—that every diploma should mean something. He urged character education be taught in schools. "And if it means that teenagers will stop killing each other over designer jackets, then our public schools should be able to require their students to wear school uniforms."

The Republicans realized that they had been had. With every proposal, Clinton marked off another acre of the political center ground. He was borrowing the language and style they thought they owned. TV showed them slumped in their seats, heads shaking, lips tight. It was a sight that I was to become familiar with over four more years of State of the Unions.

The government shutdown, so politically disastrous for the Republicans, had gone unmentioned in the discussion on the budget. Now, Clinton was nearing the end of the speech. He borrowed one of Ronald Reagan's bits of stagecraft. In 1982, at a time when he was under attack for his proposed budget cuts, Reagan had introduced a public employee named Lenny Skutnick who had jumped into the icy waters of the Potomac to save lives in a plane crash.

Now Clinton introduced Richard Dean, a Vietnam veteran who worked for the Social Security Administration. "Last year, he was hard at work in the federal building in Oklahoma City when the blast killed 169 people and brought the rubble down all around him. He reentered that building four times. He saved the lives of three women. He's here with us this evening, and I want to recognize Richard and applaud both his public service and his extraordinary personal heroism."

With that, every member of Congress turned toward the gallery and cheered Dean, whose eyes welled. The ovation lasted forty-five seconds, with the Republicans clapping as loudly as anyone. "I can't believe it. I can't believe they're going for it," I blurted to the woman next to me—grimacing when I realized she was a reporter. The Republicans were still on their feet when Clinton continued.

"But Richard Dean's story doesn't end there. This last November, he was forced out of his office when the government shut down. And the second time the government shut down he continued helping Social Security recipients, but he was working without pay. On behalf of Richard Dean and his family, and all the other people who are out there working every day doing a good job for the American people, I challenge all of you in this chamber: Never, ever shut the federal government down again."

Democrats roared and pounded applause. Republicans folded their arms. Gingrich looked grim. The Democrats had just "won" the shutdown, on national TV.

Clinton was aloft. He talked about the Olympics. He called for unity. He sailed into his Stevensonian conclusion. "America has always sought and always risen to every challenge. Who would say that having come so far

together, we will not go forward from here? Who would say that this age of possibility is not for all Americans?" He left the podium to the applause and hugs of his cabinet, and walked through a scrum of jubilant Democrats. The rest of us dashed through the halls of the Capitol and piled back into the motorcade; cellphones relayed the instant polls and the commentary. We gathered in the ornate Blue Room of the White House for a party. Clinton posed for a photo, grinning: the speechwriters, the policy aides, the Things.

AS WE WERE CELEBRATING the launch of our presidential campaign, Dole was destroying his own. His broadcast response to the State of the Union was harshly lit and the setting was cramped. He looked nervously at the camera, licking his lips and blinking. His tone was partisan and shrill. "It is as if we went to sleep in one America and woke up in quite another. It is as though our government, our institutions, and our culture have been hijacked by liberals and are careening dangerously off course." He clearly had not expected Clinton's conciliatory approach and made no reference to it. He looked more like the Grinch than usual.

Within days, Clinton's speech—which was pretty good—was remembered as brilliant. Dole's speech—which was pretty bad—was remembered as a colossal, perhaps irreparable blunder. Clinton's seemed vivid and in color; Dole's seemed stark and monochrome. *Time* magazine had one article entitled "What Dole Did Wrong," and another headlined "What Clinton Is Doing Right: He Seizes the Middle Ground from Congressional Republicans and Suddenly Looks Presidential": "The man written off after the 1994 elections was suddenly looking like the man to beat." Polls showed that 69 percent of the public liked what they heard, and supported Clinton's agenda over the Republicans' by a wide margin. "House Republicans are muttering that Clinton hijacked their agenda," wrote *Time*. "But to paraphrase T. S. Eliot's line about poets, good politicians borrow, great politicians steal. Now Republicans are finally learning what Bill Clinton means by common ground: your land is my land." A cartoon by Mark Alan Stamaty showed a giant Clinton, stroking the cameras.

> "How dare he?" muttered GOP lawmakers as silver-tongued Billy tickled the TV cameras Reagan style. "He sounds good, but it's all talk. He won't do the things he says like Reagan did!" "Yeh! Like balancing the budget by 1984. Um, I mean . . ."

There was at least one unintended side effect, however. The conservative *Weekly Standard* magazine blared in huge type on its cover: "WE WIN:

The Era of Big Government Is Over." The second half of the sentence —
what started as a crisp "every man for himself" — had mutated into a sentence so soggy that it simply wasn't quoted. All the public heard was the
conservative declaration of the demise of liberalism. Maybe Morris knew
what would happen all along. I said to George Stephanopoulos, "Political
correctness killed liberalism." The death was ruled accidental.

But at some level the declaration did mark a significant political wa-
tershed. The rise of markets and global free trade, spurred by Reagan and
Margaret Thatcher, was real. Clinton's brand of Democratic politics had
recognized that implicitly. With this speech, that recognition was explicit.
But Clinton didn't mean "big government" to refer specifically to the size
or even to the activism. Rather, it was meant — and it was heard by the audience — as connoting a lumbering, bureaucratic government that could
not control itself. By recognizing the market surge of the 1980s, Clinton
sought to surmount it. It was an approach soon to be emulated in England
by Tony Blair and in progressive political parties in other nations. At the
moment the *Weekly Standard* declared conservatism had "won," it had lost;
Clinton had changed the subject.

One can view the declaration, as many Republicans did, as a mere
flimflam. In the same speech, the President had proposed dozens of new
government initiatives. Spending might be going down, but regulation was
going up. It could be seen as just the latest version of a paradox long identified by political scientists: American voters are ideologically conservative
but operationally liberal. They want their leaders to denounce government
while keeping the services coming.

But this was more of a decisive political stroke than that. By saying the
era of big government is over, Clinton was really saying that the politics of
big government is over. By declaring the debate settled, he immediately
raised the question: what next? And the new series of challenges — on protecting children, on education, on small-scale health reform — were seen as
issues better addressed by Democrats than Republicans. Within a few years
of the speech, the tax-cutting, government-hating strain of the GOP had
lost its political potency.

TEN

THE PORTABLE
ROSE GARDEN

ON FEBRUARY 24, 1996, President Clinton stood before dozens of middle school students, all neatly dressed in blue-and-white school uniforms, at the Jackie Robinson Academy in Long Beach, California. He was holding a prepared text, but he was not reading from it. "One of the great hazards of our culture, with all of its wonderful opportunities, is that we can sometimes, without meaning to, teach our children to minor in the majors and major in the minors," he said. "It's tragic when young people without a balanced upbringing, without grounded values, without a secure education wind up believing that it's all right to kill somebody for a pair of sneakers or jewelry or a designer jacket." The tableau attracted national attention. But there was puzzlement, too. The President was talking about school uniforms? What was going on?

Theodore Roosevelt was the first chief executive to command the attention of national, commercial media. He said that one of the president's main jobs was to use the "bully pulpit" to challenge the country, call attention to problems, move people to action. ("Bully" was TR's adjective; the way a teen might call a pulpit "awesome.") It was a long way from Teddy Roosevelt to school uniforms.

In the winter and spring of 1996, Clinton used his bully pulpit to redefine his role as president, coloring in the themes and policies he had announced in the 1996 State of the Union. These were initiatives to help families and they emphasized "wholesome," often conservative values.

Presidents seeking reelection often rely on a "Rose Garden strategy"—rarely straying more than a few yards from the sedate trappings of power, looking fatherly, avoiding questions. But Clinton was too antsy, too

eager to campaign. His fundraising and political schedule required him to travel. So he carried with him what we called the "portable Rose Garden." It was clear that in the clamorous media environment, presidents could only get on the evening news if they made news: taking action, announcing a grant. If we were seeking to draw a contrast with a somnolent Dole, then Clinton must be seen as constantly issuing new proposals, drawing up new plans for a second term.

The "values agenda" in the State of the Union was tailor-made for such a strategy. Because so many of the initiatives did not require major spending, the President could use his pulpit to encourage communities to act. This strategy also reflected real trends in scholarship and community action. One stream, focusing on "civil society," stressed the importance of nongovernmental institutions, such as churches, unions, community groups, and small businesses, in upholding community and providing order. Another was known as the "broken windows" theory. If one window is broken and not fixed, it is more likely that hooligans will break another. Visible disorder can encourage real disorder and crime in a neighborhood. So Reed, working with Baer and Emanuel, developed a series of initiatives to advance a communitarian agenda.

Clinton's proposal for school uniforms was mocked by some as a parody of diminished vision. We believed the issue spoke to a yearning for order in the schools. A month after the State of the Union, Clinton went to Long Beach, one of the first communities to require elementary and middle school children to wear uniforms. Disorder and truancy had dropped. He urged communities to consider following Long Beach's lead. The White House had had to strain to find a governmental action to accompany the exhortation. In the end, Clinton was able to announce that the Department of Education was sending all 16,000 school districts in the country a manual on how to introduce uniforms in such a way that they would survive court challenges from civil libertarians. "When I was a governor, whenever we were the first state to do something, I was always proud of that. But I used to tell our people, I'm even more proud when we were the second state to do something, because that meant we weren't too arrogant, hardheaded, and deaf to learn from what somebody else was doing right." Within months, dozens of additional school districts around the country adopted uniforms. By decade's end, hundreds of communities had done so, including New York, Chicago, Los Angeles, Boston, Miami–Dade County, and Cleveland.

Next we turned to curfews. In May, the President spoke before the Women's International Convention of the Church of God in Christ in New Orleans, a lively gathering of several thousand African-American women. He had been handed a perfunctory speech that morning and had rejected it. We had had a few hours to pound out a new draft to send to Air

Force One. New Orleans—a city, Clinton pointed out a bit wistfully, that was "famous for its night life"—had imposed a curfew on its young people. During the first year, youth crime had dropped by a quarter during the curfew hours, auto thefts by nearly half. "I'm sure that a lot of the teenagers think this curfew is too strict. It was a long time ago, but I can still dimly remember what it was like to be that age. But they must also know that it's a dangerous world out there, and these rules are being set by people who love them and care about them and desperately want them to have good lives."

Educators complained that uniforms and curfews were not as important as truancy. Clinton told the teachers' union, "The difference between success and failure in life for our children is whether they're learning on the streets or in the school where they belong. The street is not an acceptable alternative to the classroom." It sounded a bit like Officer Krupke in *West Side Story*, lecturing the Sharks and the Jets.

Through all this, Clinton was finding a new mode. In the first two years of his presidency, he had tried to define himself by legislative victories. Now, increasingly, he was defining his presidency by actions he could take without Congress. Some involved traditional forms of executive power, such as executive orders (which have the force of law). Others tried to shine a public spotlight on promising developments at the state and local level. As Baer noted, in the manner of a pointillist painting, these pinprick events were to fill out a new portrait of presidential action. I don't believe that Clinton fully understood this until it was well under way. Some of the announcements were diminutive: announcing a plan to give cellphones to neighborhood watch community groups, announcing steps to set up new police emergency numbers. Seen up close, the dots of presidential action could seem small and puzzling. But looked at as a whole, they painted a new picture.

At the White House Correspondents Association dinner, Clinton joked about the strategy. "I took a look at those ticket prices. They seem pretty high to me. So tonight, by executive order, I am authorizing the release of one thousand additional tickets."

ON APRIL 4, I was sitting on the couch in the hallway outside the Oval Office. The President would shortly be addressing some U.S. attorneys about gang prevention. The couch was the dugout; from there we would move into the batter's circle, Betty Currie's office, where we would wait some more. Sandy Berger and other foreign policy aides rushed into the Oval Office and streaked out again. They looked grim. After a few minutes, from fragments of conversation, we realized that something was seriously wrong. A National Security Council aide rushed past, "Ron Brown's plane is missing. In Croatia."

Within a few minutes, the worst was confirmed. A military plane carrying Commerce secretary Ron Brown and thirty-two others had apparently crashed while on a mission to Bosnia and Croatia. Brown was a popular figure in the White House. Many people owed their jobs to him. Others on the flight were former campaign workers and friends of people in the White House.

The President and a few friends and aides rushed up 16th Street to Ron Brown's home in an affluent neighborhood. I was in Don Baer's office when a call came from the house. It was Alexis Herman, Ron's protégée. Her emotions were tightly controlled. The President would be going to the Commerce Department in a few minutes, she said. He needed to speak. We don't know if Ron Brown is dead. Could we put something together for the President? "Alma [Ron Brown's wife] says that Ron so loved the Commerce Department employees, and thought the world of them," she said.

"Alexis, did—does Ron have a favorite hymn or Bible passage?"

She rattled off a Bible quote in a few sentences. "I'd better go." We had a half hour. We had a Bible quote. And we had no idea if I had copied it correctly, or if it was from the Bible.

I summoned three other speechwriters. They thumbed through Bibles, called ministers and priests, logged on to the Internet to biblegateway.com, a Bible concordance site. As they searched, I typed a statement on a borrowed computer. Baer sprinted out the door with a single copy of the speech. I rushed out to West Executive Drive, but the staff caravan headed for the Commerce Department four blocks away had just left. I ran the blocks to the agency, wheezing past tourists on the Ellipse. I tried to leap over a chain link and landed spread eagle on the ground. I jumped up and kept running. Dusty and disheveled, I arrived at the Commerce Department just before the President did.

People were milling around a backstage area as the President came in. His eyes were red. Baer handed him the draft. "We have something for you to look at, Mr. President. But there's only one problem. Alexis gave us this. She said it was Ron's favorite Bible quote. But we couldn't find it. We don't know if it's real."

Clinton scanned the page. "Oh, Isaiah 40:31," he said. "This is the New English translation. I prefer the King James version myself. That's the one I'll use."

In a dingy departmental auditorium, the President's voice was scratchy. The Commerce Department workers were silent as he thanked them for what they did, and told them how much Ron Brown loved them. He blended the translations of the Bible verse: " 'They who wait upon the Lord shall have their strength renewed. They shall mount up with wings as eagles. They will run and not grow weary. They will walk and faint not.'

"Well, Ron Brown walked—and ran—and flew—through life. And he was a magnificent life force. And those of us who knew him will always be grateful for his friendship and his warmth."

Over the next few days, Clinton was called to the role of national mourner several times. There was a special poignancy to this. Presidents make choices that may cause death all the time. Caution or luck had so far mostly spared Clinton the knowledge that he had sent someone to his or her eventual death. But the Bosnia peace accord was his achievement; he had helped plan the mission; Ron Brown was his friend. At the same time, especially after the Oklahoma City bombing of a year before, he knew the purposes of public mourning. While that massacre had a far more penetrating impact on the public, Brown's death was, for Clinton and his aides, private as well. He spoke six times at services marking Brown's death.

Clinton had already committed to address the families of the victims of the Oklahoma City bombing at a memorial service marking the year that had passed. He spoke on the site of the former federal building, beneath a tree that had survived the attack, and then in a convention hall. We flew back to Washington. I rushed back to the West Wing.

The bodies of those on Brown's plane were to return to Dover Air Force Base the next day. Tony Blinken, the foreign policy speechwriter, and I had worked on a draft on Air Force One. David Shipley, one of the speechwriters, had written some beautiful passages. The President's friend Vernon Jordan called with guidance. Don Baer produced a detailed outline. He went upstairs to the chief of staff's office to help plan the logistics of the service, and I sat down at his computer. The draft struck a patriotic note. If the peace in Bosnia was to be deepened through economic means, and more broadly, if our national interest was to be advanced by economic diplomacy, then these business executives and Commerce Department officials should be treated by their president as having given their lives in battle. We suggested that Clinton read the names of the dead. (A researcher checked and rechecked the names; leaving one out, with the families sitting there, would be horrifying.)

"Today, we come to a place that has seen too many sad, silent homecomings," Clinton said before rows of flag-draped caskets in an aircraft hangar. "For this is where we in America bring home our own, those who have given their lives in the service of their country. The thirty-three fine Americans we meet today, on their last journey home, ended their lives on a hard mountain a long way from home. But in a way, they never left America. On their mission of peace and hope, they carried with them America's spirit, what our greatest martyr, Abraham Lincoln, called 'the last, best hope of Earth.' " As the sound of muffled sobs echoed through the hangar, Clinton talked about what the families had told him and Gore during their

private meetings. These lives, he said, "are a stern rebuke to the cynicism that is all too familiar today.

"The sun is going down on this day. The next time it rings it will be Easter morning, a day that marks the passage from loss and despair to hope and redemption, a day that more than any other reminds us that life is more than what we know, life is more than what we can understand, life is more than sometimes we can bear, but life is also eternal. For each of these thirty-three of our fellow Americans and the two fine Croatians that fell with them, their day on Earth was too short, but for our countrymen and -women, we must remember that what they did while the sun was out will last with us forever."

The *Washington Post*, in an editorial, called it "perhaps the best speech of his presidency and one of the finest commemorative remarks by a chief executive in memory."

EARLY ONE FRIDAY EVENING that spring, we waited in Betty Currie's office. Laura Tyson, the national economic advisor, read through her papers one more time, preparing for our meeting with the President. Sperling was taking worried calls from the Treasury Department on a courtesy phone. It was another tug-of-war, another battle for the President's ear, yet another struggle between Clinton's liberal and centrist advisors as he tried to press forward to reelection. And we were anxious, watching his closed door so that we could stage the final showdown.

After Pat Buchanan beat Bob Dole in the New Hampshire Republican primary in February, the issue of layoffs and economic anxiety had resurfaced with a vengeance. Robert Reich was arguing for an agenda that stressed corporate responsibility. He was urging that the tax code be changed to reward companies that invested in their communities, retained workers, and in other ways behaved responsibly. Dick Morris now found his interests aligned with Reich: he wanted Clinton to issue an agenda specifically challenging companies to do these things. Rubin was unhappy about the whole enterprise. It simply isn't the case, he argued, that it is always economically better for a company to do these things. He pointed to rigid European labor regulations as one reason for that continent's chronically high unemployment rate. Sperling and Tyson were supposed to mediate.

In the end, it came down to words. Reich wanted the President to talk about corporate responsibility. After all, Clinton had put "responsibility" at the center of his rhetoric. Rubin felt that word implied that business had been irresponsible and wanted, instead, to talk about corporate "citizenship," things businesses could do to improve the country. The treasury secretary was adamant. The bureaucratic struggle continued. The President

decided to devote a radio address to the topic. This was a good idea. If nothing else, once a text was before him he would have to decide.

We were editing until the final minutes. The Treasury Department sent the draft back heavily marked up. Reich worried that it was not strong enough. In the meeting minutes before the taping, we would have to fight it out once and for all. That is what had brought us to the outer office. The scheduled time for the taping slipped by; Clinton's assistant looked in through a peek hole in the door and reported that he was writing. We readied our arguments. A bustle was heard in the hall, then quiet.

Someone asked, "Where's the President?" His assistant peeked in. "He's taping the radio address." To avoid his feuding advisors, Clinton had slipped out the side door and gone into the Roosevelt Room, where an audience was waiting. We couldn't even watch, for fear of making too much noise. "Well," mused Laura Tyson, "I guess we'll have to find out what he said."

Not much, as it happened. Clinton had chosen to exhort in the least dramatic way he could. "We recognize, too, that not every business can afford to do more than worry about the bottom line—especially a lot of small businesses," he said, in a printed transcript that the press office released. "But many of America's most successful businesses have shown that you can do well by doing right by employees and their families. Let me mention five ways businesses can show good citizenship toward their employees."

The new bully pulpit strategy was employed on one of the most sensitive, politically charged issues of all: welfare reform. In 1995, as part of Gingrich's Contract With America, the Republican Congress had sent the President a welfare reform bill. It included some elements of Clinton's plan—for example, it cut people off welfare after two years—but was far more punitive than the New Democrat approach, and Clinton had vetoed it. He hoped that there would still be a chance to pass welfare reform legislation. But in the meantime, he used a novel approach to reform through executive action. Welfare was required by the national government but run by the states. (Among other things, this resulted in a wide disparity among states in how the program ran and what the benefit levels were.) Under the law, if a state applied for an exemption from federal rules, it could introduce reforms. Instead of reluctantly and quietly acceding to the waiver requests, Clinton decided to use them to put pressure on Congress. There were dozens of them. All told, as he would brag in stump speeches, 75 percent of welfare recipients were in programs subject to some form of reform—requiring welfare recipients to work, strengthening enforcement of child support laws so that fathers would help bear the cost of their children, and taking other steps. The New York Times, looking at the pattern of state waivers, concluded that a "quiet revolution" in social policy was taking place, all without benefit of congressional action on welfare reform.

The most far-reaching state welfare experiment was proposed by Wisconsin's Republican governor, Tommy Thompson. The plan had been sent to Washington for approval by the Department of Health and Human Services. Officials there—including both civil servants and political appointees—were reluctant to go along. For weeks they gave Wisconsin no answer. As Reed later joked, "they hadn't gotten around to reading it all the way through."

On Friday, May 17, White House aides used Clinton's Saturday radio address to make a lightning strike at HHS. As the taping of the speech approached, the topic was still in flux. That morning, Emanuel and Reed had had the same idea coming in to work. If the radio address was on welfare reform, they could force the bureaucrats to act on Wisconsin. With a speechwriter, they quickly drafted an address in which the President would endorse the Wisconsin plan. It was sent over to HHS. Agency officials had three hours to clear it. The President couldn't *approve* the plan—only HHS could do that. But he could *praise* it, making it awkward for HHS to resist. So Clinton called the plan "one of the boldest yet attempted in America." He crossed out a laudatory sentence that gave Wisconsin credit for replacing "a system that is based on dependency with one that is based on work." But he concluded: "All in all, Wisconsin has the makings of a solid welfare reform plan. We should get it done."

The President continued to navigate between left and right. He was no longer openly "triangulating," setting himself up between the congressional Democrats and Republicans. But he was still testing, probing how far he had to retreat, how much he had to give. He would get pressure from House Democrats to stand firm, from Senate Democrats to compromise, from White House staff to make a principled stand, from Morris to follow the polls. Sometimes it seemed to pain him—practically physically—to be caught with the Democrats on an issue where the Republican position was popular, and, he suspected, right.

For years, the Republicans had clamored to restrict the rights of consumers and others to sue corporations for harm caused by dangerous or defective products. No federal statute governed such tort lawsuits. The law was largely made in the courts, through the actions of civil juries and opinions by judges. The effort to override these state laws was one of Washington's perennial rituals, much like the Cherry Blossom festival.* As governor of Arkansas, Clinton, like nearly all Democrats, was supported by the trial

---

* For years within the White House, I quietly worked against tort reform. If a federal statute limiting these lawsuits were enacted, even a mild one, then every time a business was sued, it would hire a lobbyist, set up a PAC, and seek a loophole. Very soon the "modest" law would look like the tax code.

lawyers (the term refers to plaintiff lawyers who represent consumers and victims). But he also signed the state's liability reform bill. As a spokesperson for the Clinton campaign on the *MacNeil/Lehrer* news program during the 1992 election, I brandished a *Wall Street Journal* article to argue that Clinton was a moderate on tort reform.

Now, the Republican Congress had promised the business community it would finally achieve this long-sought goal. Clinton indicated he was not entirely opposed to such legislation, but through 1995 and 1996 he spelled out a series of conditions. He wanted pro-consumer safeguards put in the bill. In March, he had sent a letter stating that he would accept the measure with only minor changes.

The Republicans thought they had the President cornered. In December, 1995, he had vetoed a bill limiting securities lawsuits, and the Congress had surprised the White House when the Republicans mustered enough votes to override the veto. Now, they thought they had either a bill he would sign or a winning campaign issue. They passed a federal products liability bill that would for the first time override state laws and impose national limits on lawsuits. On May 1, the congressional leaders held a gala press conference. "When this bill arrives on his desk, President Clinton will choose whether he's on the side of the hardworking American consumers ... or of the smooth-talking, get-rich-quick trial lawyers," Dole said, surrounded by Gingrich, other lawmakers, and children. The next day Clinton was set to veto it.

I went to Bruce Lindsey's office to find out how to draft the presidential statement. "Just make the strong arguments against the bill," Lindsey said. Soft voice, soft eyes, soft wisps of hair, he was Clinton's liaison with the plaintiffs' attorneys. Follow the trial lawyers' arguments, he said. As long as we were vetoing it, we might as well make the strongest case.

We were planning to surround the President with victims of dangerous products who would have their rights taken away by the bill. At least we would show the human face of the issue—a diverse group of middle-class Americans—not the trial lawyers. The witnesses were carefully chosen so that their stories would match a particular objectionable provision of the bill.

The morning of the veto, I circulated the presidential statement. The comments from other offices were minimal. I stopped by the Cabinet Room, where the families were nervously waiting to meet the President. I walked down the hall, past the Oval Office, and a guard stepped on a hidden latch to let me into the President's private dining room. It was filled with staff members—Lindsey, Panetta, and a half dozen others.

The President was sitting at the polished wood table, in shirtsleeves, with glasses on. And he was yelling. "This is wrong! Just wrong!" He was

looking at me. "This reads just like it was written by the trial lawyers! This isn't my position! I'm for reform, just not this reform. This makes it sound like I'm against everything. And it doesn't go into the specific changes I would make. I like the veto statement much better," referring to the technical document prepared by the counsel's office. "Why does it read this way?"

I turned to find Bruce Lindsey. He would rescue me, explain his rationale. I frantically scanned the room. Bruce had vanished out the back door.

Panetta reassured the President. "Mr. President, you should have seen the first draft! This is much better!" I thought of explaining, "this is the only draft," but decided not to.

For a new member of the communications staff, it was the first such presidential staged event, and she was disconcerted. "Well, Mr. President, why don't you just read the veto statement prepared by the Counsel's Office!" Several people bustled off to paste the technical legal language of the veto statement onto note cards.

I finally found my voice. There's a photo of me, my eyes wide, gesticulating and pointing at the draft, showing Clinton where a few rearranged paragraphs would meet his concerns. Clinton is looking up over his glasses, skeptical. Behind me, laughing uproariously at my plight, are McCurry, Panetta, and Emanuel. "Mr. President, we can make the changes you want so that the text incorporates your concerns," I said. (In such moments, the best thing to do is speak loudly and clearly, and seem confident.) I turned to the President's personal assistant. "Can I please have a scissors and tape?"

Clinton excused himself to freshen up. I kneeled at the table, with office supplies spread out. Just a few yards away, the Oval Office was filling with reporters and cameramen. "I made very clear what I wanted in such legislation, and what I could not support," the card read. I wrote in, in neat block print, "I made my views clear, and then in the conference, it [the bill] was made worse." A passage arguing that this could hurt tobacco lawsuits was clipped from the signing statement and pasted in. Several times, we inserted that the worst provisions were added at the last minute. I shuffled the cards and wrote new page numbers at the top.

In the end, Clinton met those who had been injured by defective products, who were to stand with him. He saw that Sarah Brady, the anti-handgun crusader, was there. It seemed that in reading and rewriting the statement, he had reassured himself that he had done the right thing. In the end, the statement he read differed very little from the statement he had lacerated. After he signed the veto letter, he took questions from reporters, and parried with them on the details of the bill. "This bill would hurt families without truly improving our legal system. It would mean

more unsafe products in our homes. It would let wrongdoers off the hook. I cannot allow it to become law."

A few minutes later, I was walking down the hall with Elena Kagan, a law professor who was working as an attorney in the White House counsel's office. The door to the Oval Office swung open and Clinton looked out. "Could you come in here," he asked. This was unusual indeed. We walked in. I can't speak for Elena, but I was cringing. "That went very well, I thought," Clinton said. "Those real people were very effective. I think we really made a good case here." As Elena remarked to me later, "This is how presidents apologize."

ELEVEN

ON THE RIGHT TRACK

ON MAY 15, in Leon Panetta's office, I watched Bob Dole's announcement that he would be leaving the Senate. "I will seek the presidency with nothing to fall back on but the judgment of the people and nowhere to go but the White House or home." I had a catch in my throat, and not out of sentimentality. Dole had hired the celebrated novelist Mark Helprin as his speechwriter. Now he was reading, in his flat staccato, words that were clearly the product of a brilliant pen. "I will then stand before you without office or authority, a private citizen, a Kansan, an American, just a man."

My normal nervousness heightened dramatically, "like a prairie wind," as Dole/Helprin might say. If Dole's convention speech was anywhere near as good, a full panic attack would strike the White House. "We need a novelist to write our speech. What about Hemingway? He's dead? Norman Mailer. He's a novelist, isn't he? Let's get Norman Mailer to write our speech."

On the Fourth of July, the President was due to leave the White House for two events. First, we helicoptered to a navy base at Patuxent, Maryland, where he released a bald eagle into the wild. This was supposed to dramatize the great progress made in environmental protection; the eagle would soon be taken off the endangered species list. (The event was originally contemplated for the Rose Garden. Further inquiry revealed that the bird might peck at the President. A more woodsy setting was considered less risky.) I stood at the back of the crowd and watched as Clinton released the magnificent bird, which took wing, soaring off to the left, and was promptly attacked by some osprey. It plummeted into the bay. Fortunately, a Coast Guard boat rescued the eagle and returned it to its comfortable home indoors.

Then we moved on to Youngstown, Ohio, where the President spoke in the shadow of a large, crescent-shaped bridge. This would be a rare chance for him to deliver a formal speech in an outdoor, rally-like setting. Working in my office late the night before—surrounded by interns who wanted to "watch a speech being written"—I wrote a draft. The theme was "a bridge to the future."

All through the spring, at rallies and fundraisers, we had noticed, Clinton had toyed with the image of a bridge to the future. For audiences, the metaphor was rich with meaning. Voters were enthusiastic about the coming digital age. They recognized the benefits that technology would bring. But they feared that they, or especially their children, would lack the skills to thrive in the new era. The bridge was a way to bring everyone across. And building a bridge is a tangible, collective effort.

"Opportunity and responsibility, faith and family, freedom and community, respect for law and respect for one another: these are the bridges across which we must walk to the twenty-first century," Clinton said on Independence Day. "These are the bridges you are building here now in 1996. Our values and our visions are as sturdy as tempered steel. If we remember what it means to be Americans, how blessed we are," he said, "then the best days of America are still ahead."

The two parties shadowboxed throughout the summer. On the day he left the Senate, Dole took to the floor to reminisce, talking warmly about Hubert Humphrey and other giants he had known. It was an affecting reminder of why liberals secretly liked Dole. But it was a retirement speech—not the speech of a next president.

Dole's departure from the Senate prompted the congressional Republicans to assess his candidacy. As he dropped in the polls, his successor as majority leader, Trent Lott, decided that the only salvation for congressional Republicans was to work with the White House and pass legislation. Congress suddenly enacted a two-stage increase in the minimum wage, from $4.25 to $5.15 an hour. Then a logjam that had long blocked the Kennedy-Kassebaum bill suddenly cleared. This measure was important substantively and politically, containing some highly visible elements of the original Clinton health plan. It guaranteed the right to take a health insurance policy from job to job, thereby reflecting the mobile economy in which people no longer stayed with one company throughout an entire career. It also outlawed the current insurance company practice of denying coverage because of a "preexisting condition," such as cancer or heart disease. By choosing a health care measure to show they were a can-do Congress, the Republicans also erased one of Clinton's electoral liabilities. As was evident at the signing ceremony on the South Lawn, Hillary, beaming in the front row, felt vindicated.

The most dramatic turning came when the President decided to sign the welfare reform legislation sent to him by the Congress. The legislation was less punitive than a version he had vetoed in the previous year, though it still contained deep cuts in food stamps and would deny federal assistance to legal immigrant families. By imposing time limits, it would repeal welfare's status as an entitlement, as a benefit perpetually guaranteed to anyone who needs it. A heated debate left his advisors split. The President gathered them in the Cabinet Room to debate the matter one last time. Clinton heard the discussion—with most of his cabinet and congressional Democrats urging him to veto the measure—and retreated to the Oval Office, where he told Gore and Panetta that he had decided to sign the bill. It was flawed, he told his staff, but at its core there was constructive welfare reform, and it was his best chance to achieve it. More than any other single step, this marked his determination to change the Democratic Party and drain away the public's anger at government.

Once Clinton decided to sign the bill, it was important that his statement as he signed it be carefully framed. One person who would join Clinton was Lillie Harden, a former welfare recipient from Arkansas who figured frequently in Clinton's speeches. She had testified at a governors' meeting that the best part of being off welfare was that when her child was asked at school what his mother did, he had an answer. She was Clinton's hopeful answer to Reagan's apocryphal welfare queen.

Terry Edmonds asked to write the statement, with Bruce Reed. Edmonds, the first African-American presidential speechwriter, had been raised in a housing project in Baltimore. He was, I gathered, quietly but firmly opposed to the bill. But he wanted to make sure that the statement pointed forward—that it did not demonize welfare recipients, that it demanded a new drive to provide jobs for those who would now be forced to go to work. I suggested that he consider a quote from Robert F. Kennedy, who had pioneered the critique of the traditional welfare system. Work is "the meaning of what the country is all about," RFK said. ". . . We need to sense it in our fellow citizens; and we need it as a society and as a people." In his statement, Clinton continued that theme: "From now on, our nation's answer to this great social challenge will no longer be a never-ending cycle of welfare, it will be the dignity, the power, and the ethic of work."

But the welfare bill continued to split the Democrats. A Kennedy family member complained about the use of Robert Kennedy's words to support a bill that, in their view, ignored the concern for the poor that RFK showed in his later years. Three top officials at the Department of Health and Human Services resigned. And many delegates muttered about a floor fight at the convention, which was a week later.

In the wake of this sudden surge of legislative achievement, we began

planning in earnest for Clinton's convention speech. On August 8, Baer
and I walked a few blocks from the White House to Room 205 at the Jefferson Hotel, where Dick Morris was living. Morris was at his most grandiose.
There has been a dramatic swing in public opinion toward optimism, he
said—the result of welfare, minimum wage, and Kennedy-Kassebaum, and
the Summer Olympics. It amounted to a new consensus.

In private, Clinton grumbled that he did not get credit for his accomplishments. Undoubtedly, he would view this speech as a chance to dwell
on his record, and to compare the state of the country in 1992 and 1996. Indeed, that would be typical for an incumbent's acceptance speech. But
Morris believed Clinton was in danger of the dynamic that had led to Winston Churchill's defeat at the polls after he had led his country in World
War II. People want to know what the leader is going to do next. "There
should be no comparisons with four years ago," Morris said. "Each module
of the speech should include 20 percent vision, 25 percent accomplishments, 55 percent what is the next step." (I wondered if he had polled these
percentages.) If the State of the Union and Dole's tepid (pre-Helprin) response had served as de facto acceptance speeches, the convention speech
was "SOTU II."

At the Jefferson Hotel, Morris related a conversation he had with Clinton. The consultant had grouped all the presidents into tiers. He told Clinton that he was a third-tier figure, but might get into the second tier.
(First-tier presidents exercise great leadership in dire situations, like a war.)
Clinton could claw his way up the ladder through a series of initiatives, including a war on terrorism, balancing the budget, and ending teen smoking. We could only imagine the President's reaction to all this. This all
seemed decidedly odd. Morris was at the height of his power, but as Baer
and I walked back to the White House across Lafayette Park, we discussed
the possibility that the President's guru was becoming unhinged.

PLANNING FOR THE DEMOCRATIC CONVENTION in Chicago now consumed
an ever-larger part of the White House. It was a complex and cumbersome
operation. Dozens of advance people, security personnel, and press plan-
ners converged on a half dozen overlapping meetings. Some worked for
the campaign, others for the DNC, still others for the White House.

The President would be traveling to Chicago on a three-day train trip
through the heartland. This alone was a logistical nightmare. In the Roosevelt Room on August 15, the details were spelled out. Clinton would ride
in an antique wooden railcar like the one used by Harry Truman on his famous campaign whistle-stop tour in 1948. He would be able to stand on a
balcony and address the crowds from the back of the train.

There would be modern cars for the press and Secret Service. And most important of all, right next to the President's car would be a car for senior staff. It would be an antique as well, one actually used by Truman. There would be a parlor car for staff to sit and work in, and a separate office for speechwriting. Jordan Tamagni, our new staff director, proudly showed me the blueprint. There it was, a little office, marked "speechwriters."

Lew Merletti, the head of the presidential protection detail of the Secret Service, addressed the group about the physical dangers of a trip like this—the swarms of unknown people getting on and off the train, the crowds, the confusion. As the meeting moved on, he leaned across the table to me. "The issue is not whether there is someone out there trying to kill the President. There is. They're out there. It's when." He glowered knowingly. I knew this was a bit of Secret Service scare-the-civilians theater. But it was effective.

Then the scheduling office outlined the speaking plan. Clinton would give major policy speeches in five cities. He would make whistle-stop remarks in a dozen smaller communities. I looked at the computer printout of the President's schedule. There was little time reserved for working on the speech. I wrote an anxious note on a piece of yellow paper and shoved it over to the person who was planning the trip.

16 sets of remarks in the 3 days before the biggest speech of the year.
It's crazy.

He'll: —have no voice
        —be exhausted
        —have no time to prep & write

She nodded in agreement and moved on. In the coming days, the schedule grew more crowded.

That night, Dole addressed the Republican convention, and the nation. I stayed in the office after dark, shut my door, and turned on the TV. Dole could give a speech that would shoot him far ahead. It wouldn't be the first time. In 1988, Peggy Noonan had written a speech for George Bush that spackled together the elements of his awkwardness and reconstituted them into a Gary Cooper persona. Dole was a man of substance and grit, and Mark Helprin was very good.

Dole walked out onstage. I called Bruce Reed in his office—he, too, was nervously watching solo. We kept an open line. "This isn't so good." "Yeah, it's not so great." It was overwrought, seemingly designed to show off the writing, not to make a point. Then Dole said, "Age has its advantages. Let me be the bridge to an America that only the unknowing call myth. Let

me be the bridge to a time of tranquillity, faith, and confidence in action. And to those who say it was never so, that America has not been better, I say, you're wrong. And I know because I was there."

I leapt out of my chair. "Bruce. Did he just say he wants to build a bridge to the past? I can't believe it." Helprin had misjudged his man. Perhaps Reagan could have made the sentiment work—a bridge to our finest days . . . this is who we were and can be again. But Dole couldn't.

It was now clear what our speech had to do. Dole wants to build a bridge to the past; Clinton would build a bridge to the future. The truism in American politics is that the more optimistic candidate always wins. (That is why, after a lugubrious and sometimes hectoring speech, Dole oddly blurted that he was "the most optimistic man in America." Evidently, that note had been added by one of Dole's political aides to counteract the novelist's speech.)

The next day, a political consultant from Chicago, David Axelrod, sent a memo to Emanuel. Rahm passed it to the President, to Gore, and to the rest of us. "Clearly, people yearn for the values and comforts—and sense of control—of an earlier time. But they also recognize that we can't put the genie back in the bottle. They want a President who confidently meets the challenges of changing times, not one who curses and shrinks from them, or pretends they aren't there." Axelrod suggested some language: "We must build bridges to the future, not the past. Much as we might like to, we can't go back."

The memo was compelling, but it was one of dozens of suggestions and drafts coming in from all sides. I filed it away.

DON BAER WAS GUIDING THE THEMES for the convention and the train trip, struggling to impose some order. After Dole's speech, we were determined that *everything* would focus *on the future*. The antique train posed a bit of a dilemma. We christened it the *21st Century Express*. Our slogan was blunter. Pollsters routinely ask voters, "Do you believe the country is on the right track or the wrong track?" For months, even though times were seen to be improving—and despite Clinton's optimistic State of the Union—the "right track/wrong track" numbers were refusing to budge. So the slogan for the trip—the one that would be emblazoned on the train, on posters, and on banners draped across stages—was "ON THE RIGHT TRACK TO THE 21ST CENTURY."

Baer choreographed a coronation processional. Clinton's message, which he had repeated since 1991, was "opportunity for all; responsibility from all; a community of all." So Monday was Opportunity Day: focus on education; Tuesday was Responsibility Day: crime, cops; Wednesday was

Community Day: the environment. When the police union would not endorse Clinton in the state that the train would pass through on Tuesday but was willing to do so on Monday, it threw everyone into a tizzy. It was finally determined that—just this once—a Responsibility event could happen on Opportunity Day. (I joked at one meeting, "Opportunity Day falls on a Sunday but is usually celebrated on a Monday.")

On a train ride to Boston, where my family was vacationing, I wrote a draft on a laptop. It read more like a second State of the Union address than an acceptance speech, laying out concrete goals for the Year 2000. There were sporadic stabs at eloquence. The bridge to the future was not among them.

On August 20, nine days before the speech, Clinton met with the speechwriters and Morris in the Oval Office. Late-afternoon light streamed through the windows. Clinton seemed to tune Morris out. Morris lobbied Clinton for his vision of the speech. The President did not react. Morris said that he didn't care if Clinton spoke for a long time, it should be "packed with substance, a new idea every thirty seconds. If you can keep that up for five hours, that's fine."

Clinton kept returning to welfare reform. He had worked to change the party, but now he would be standing in front of activists, many of whom were not happy with the party's "new look." He was nervous about their reaction, even about boos from Democratic delegates, and he was set on focusing on steps to create jobs for those who would move off welfare. Most delegates polled by newspapers supported his signing, but a serious fraction did not. "Twenty percent can make a hell of a lot of noise," Clinton warned us. I pointed out that in part, it was a matter of sentence structure—if he didn't try to get applause for welfare reform, he probably wouldn't be booed. Clinton joked, "Kennedy-Kassebaum!" Then he whispered, "Welfare reform." Then shouted again, "Minimum wage!"

Signing that bill clearly weighed heavily on him. Clinton was intent, almost obsessed, with referring to welfare reform as a process, not an endpoint. He quizzed Bruce Reed about various proposals to subsidize businesses that hired welfare recipients. He was going to propose a more ambitious public works program, too.

He also thought our draft had missed the boat by not taking on Dole directly on the bridge to the past. He paused and quietly and quickly dictated a paragraph: "I am proud of America's past, and I am proud of our roots in it. And I want to preserve our values as we meet our challenges. But we don't need to build a bridge to the past—we have to build a bridge to the future."

Morris proclaimed himself pleased with the draft, but he had a few changes he wanted to make. He decamped in my office. With him was his chief of staff, his personal assistant, a speechwriter who often worked with him, and Bill Curry, who had been the Democratic nominee for governor of Connecticut and whom Morris had placed on the White House staff.

I sat at a campaign-provided keyboard as Morris declaimed in the manner of an old-style orator. He cut out Clinton's "bridge to the future" language. He doubled the length of each passage, filling paragraphs with statistics and rococo rhetoric. His associates cheered him on.

As he approached the end of the speech, his pace quickened and his voice grew louder. "To meet our challenges, to become the nation we can become, and to honor the values we must honor, to do these things, to do these things, I accept your nomination for President of the United States!" His retainers applauded. I looked up at him. He was gazing into middle distance, seeing, I suppose, the crowd of thousands of people cheering him.

"OK, gotta go, gotta see Gore," Morris announced. His retinue swept out the door with him. I later heard that the scene in the Vice President's office was odd. Morris insisted that Gore sit on a couch while he stood behind a chair and read his draft of Gore's speech. By the time he left Gore's office, he had lost a patron.

As for me, I was wondering what to do with all this Sturm und Drang, when a phone call came in. Morris had lost his handheld computer, onto which he typed constantly during meetings and which held all the campaign's polls. (It turned out it also held the notes for a book he would write.) He was frantic. We didn't have it. Eventually it was found.

On the Saturday before the convention, Baer and I met with Clinton without Morris. He discarded the consultant's draft without looking at it. "Let's use the first draft. We can put aside what you've done, we'll come back to it," he said. "The speech has got to have a little texture to it. Otherwise, I'm just reading a laundry list." He worried that the litany of accomplishments lacked a unifying thread. "I still think we're making a huge mistake, not focusing on the future," he added.

He handed us back the draft with a note scrawled across the top of the first page: "Proud of the past/bridge to future."

TWELVE

BUILDING THE BRIDGE

Sunday, August 25

We have flown to West Virginia. A rally of several thousand people crowds the *21st Century Express*. We wander around the back of the train, posing for snapshots.

It was a sunny day; spirits were soaring. Now the President would be trapped on the train. Now he would have to work on the speech.

I couldn't wait to see the speechwriters' special office—the one we had been promised. We worked our way through Clinton's dark and burnished car and into ours. There were cabins filled with electronic equipment for the cameras that were beaming the train trip back to the convention. An ample living room, with a felt-topped table and four chairs, for the senior staff. And, as the advance man led us back and to the left, there was the speechwriters' office. It was the bathroom.

I looked in. It was blue-green. We were to pile our files on the toilet and pull down a table. The window opened only a crack. A light over the door indicated whether the "office" was in use. Bruce Reed sat down across from me. There was barely enough room. "Well," I said. "It may be a bathroom. But it's *Harry Truman's* bathroom." The cell-phone trilled. It was Jordan Tamagni, calling from the White House, proud of her savvy in snagging us our own office. I told her it was the car's bathroom. She was crestfallen. "Don't worry," I said. "Actually, it's very convenient."

I snapped open my new laptop computer, provided by the campaign. It began playing Johnny Nash's "I Can See Clearly Now." I swatted at it,

pushed all the buttons, but couldn't make it stop. Every few minutes it would start to play again.

"Hey look!"

I looked up. The President of the United States, fresh from his rally and inspecting his train, was sticking his head in my door. "Waldman's in the head!" "Um, hi, Mr. President." He laughed and moved on.

I pulled Don Baer aside. "What's a 'head'?"

I was due to send the President another draft that night, based on our conversation with him. We would shear Morris' rococo language. It had to sound like Clinton again. The bridge went back in. "I love and revere the history of America as much as any other president who has ever served. I am determined to take our best traditions into the future. But with all respect, we do not need to build a bridge to the past—we need to build a bridge to the future." We sent the draft in and we waited.

Monday

The next morning, we waited. We waited some more. The tension began to build. Don Baer worked on an ending over and over. I tried to prune.

We didn't hear from the President. With every click clack of the train, we were moving closer to Chicago. We had been promised "speech prep" time. The time kept vanishing. Evelyn Lieberman, the deputy chief of staff in charge of the trip, told us to calm down. "He's working on it. He's working on it. You'll get your time."

After several hours, we began to bicker. The tension was palpable; the egos were substantial. We began to do what speechwriters do. We began to fight over credit—to fight over who had come up with what line.

Clinton was due to announce a literacy program on Tuesday in a small Michigan town. Before the speech, he would read *The Little Engine That Could* to two third graders.

Jonathan Prince, along to write the daily whistle-stop speeches, swore that it was his idea. We teased him, and he reliably erupted. "It was my idea. It was." Don Baer shook his head. *The Little Engine That Could* was his idea. "No, Don, you're wrong. I'll give you 'On the Right Track to the 21st Century.' That was your idea. *The Little Engine That Could* was mine!" Prince insisted. This continued, on and off, for an hour, absurd as it sounds.

Suddenly a Secret Service agent was posted by the wall and the President was standing among us. He was hearty, he was glad to see us. Clinton's empathy skills are legendary for good reason.

"Mr. President, we have been working on a new ending for the speech," Baer said, handing him a typed sheet. "I think this part is really good."

Clinton looked at him. "Ah. Baer must have written this line." He turned to me. "Michael, which line did you write? Jonathan, which line did you write?" He held up the text and pointed to one line. "This line from Isaiah? That one's my favorite. *God* wrote that one."

He smiled, handed back the sheet, gave a little wave, and walked back to his car. Our speech prep was over for the day.

We relocated to the modern Amtrak car halfway down the train, with a glass-domed lounge area that was set up as an office. Maybe that would help. I rewrote the speech again, not moving pieces around, but just boiling it down, trying to make it sing. For the first time, the bridge to the future was not just a good paragraph — it was the speech's leitmotif. In this draft, every section began with "I want to build a bridge to the Year 2000."

Tuesday

Tuesday was Responsibility Day. That morning, we still had not heard anything from the President. "He's working on it right now," we were told.

Static crackled over loudspeakers that had been set up throughout the train to allow reporters to hear what Clinton, using a handheld microphone, was saying to people along the tracks.

"Hi! Thank you! Nice to see you!" The soft twang. "Thank you! I like your house! Nice cat!"

"Nice cat!" I said. "Maybe we'd better put that in the speech. 'Nice cat.'"

I was growing frantic. I polished another draft and brought it up to the President's car. Bruce Lindsey came to the screen door of the kitchen that adjoined the coupling. A steward was frying a steak in a pan on a gas stove. I stood on the platform and clutched the speech, hoping the wind would not blow it out of my hands. "Here's a new draft," I said. Lindsey took it from me. "Great. Thanks." He turned. "Uh, Bruce, can I ask you? We're getting very close to Chicago, and we've had very little feedback. Is he working on it? Is it OK?"

Lindsey peered at me through the screen door. "I have one question," he said. "Does it have a lot of . . . *bridges* in it?"

"Yes. Bridges. Well, as a matter of fact it does have a lot of bridges."

Lindsey smiled. "Then you'll be fine."

Other than speculation about whether Clinton was rewriting the speech, the topic of conversation on the train was the increasingly prob-

lematic Morris. He was pictured on the cover of *Time* magazine that week, in a collage that showed him perched on Clinton's shoulder. We each posed with the cover for snapshots.

Mark Penn was angry. "We have to do something about Morris." Morris had tried to dismiss some of the other consultants. He was trying to centralize power, threatened by Penn's budding relationship with Clinton. He was losing it. Rumors of purges and counterpurges swept through the car. Media advisor Bob Squier was planning to relieve Morris of his command. No, Morris was trying to have Squier fired.

Wednesday

A woman who worked for Morris and who had been placed on the train trip as his scout came looking for Baer. It was an emergency. A half hour later, I walked past them in a glass-walled compartment in a modern car. Her eyes were red.

A few minutes later, Baer pulled me aside. "You can't tell anyone this. Anyone. But I have to tell someone! There is going to be a story in the *Star* that says that Dick has been seeing a prostitute. She listened in on calls between him and Clinton." Don was mortified.

We arrived at the hotel. That night, Vice President Gore delivered his speech. It was forceful—as his convention speeches always are—and emotional. The high point was a tearful recollection of his sister's death due to lung cancer, and a vow to fight the tobacco companies in her honor. But what was surprising to us had come earlier in the speech. "Senator Dole, we don't want to build a bridge to the past—we want to build a bridge to the future."

Later, Baer had to assure the President that Gore had simply received the same memos and had the same idea. Clinton decided not to change his speech. We would have to look as if we had planned this all along. (Many commentators would praise the consistency with which we repeated our message.)

I changed clothes and moved into a speechwriting office. Room service was brought in. Baer came back after a few hours. "Dick is gone." "What do you mean, he's 'gone'?" "He's out. Out of the campaign. He's leaving town." I had the pleasure of being able to break the news to several waves of aides who came in to kibitz on the speech.

With help from Bruce Reed, I worked all night. At nine in the morning, I slipped the draft under the doors of Panetta and Ickes, and handed it to a Secret Service agent. He put it on a table in Clinton's suite.

Thursday

Now the President was ready to dig in. I arrived at his suite later in the morning. He looked tired but happy. If he was upset about Morris, he didn't show it. In fact, I whispered to Stephanopoulos, he seemed relieved.

And I looked at the draft. Clinton had crossed out line after line. And he had begun rewriting the early pages, almost from scratch. We sat across a dining table. He moved from paragraph to paragraph, whispering to save his throat.

"TY [Thank you] for your nomination," he had written. "How about this," he said. "I can't think of a fancy way to say this, so I accept."

We didn't go through the record nearly enough, Clinton said. Liberated from Morris' insistence that he not dwell on his accomplishments, he had a whole afternoon to put them in the speech. He added a passage on the deficit, one he had been testing out on the train trip. "The only deficit we have today is the interest payment on the huge debt run up in the twelve years before this administration began. Without that, we would be in a surplus." He closed his eyes, and dictated a new applause line on the environment. "Our children should live next to parks, not poisons."

Throughout the speech, he had crossed out and refined the bridge. It wasn't a bridge to the Year 2000—it was a bridge to the twenty-first century.

He rewrote the welfare section. We had been so worried that the delegates would boo any mention of welfare reform that we had buried it. "Look at what I said in the Rose Garden," he instructed us. "Here. Listen. 'The government can only do so much; the private sector must provide most of these jobs. I challenge every business person who has ever complained about the failure of yesterday's welfare system to find a way to hire someone off the welfare rolls. There is no more who's to blame with welfare. Now it's all a question of what to do, and we all have to do our part.'" (Later he would rewrite that again. Businesses wouldn't have to "find a way" to hire someone off welfare; they should "try hard" to do so.)

Stephanopoulos suggested a contrast with Dole, who had proposed a 15 percent tax cut, but who had no way to fund it. "My proposals are paid for line by line, dime by dime."

"We've got to say something about political reform," Clinton instructed me. We could brag about having passed lobbying reform and calling for campaign finance reform. By inserting this in the accomplishments, it became one of the first policy proposals in the speech. I marked that down; that was certainly fine by me.

In all, the changes amounted to a substantial rewrite of large parts of the speech. The overstuffed sandwich was getting bigger. The accomplish-

ments were growing. I had a few hours to decipher Clinton's handwriting and prepare a new draft. I thought about Lincoln, who said, "I confess plainly not to be in control of events; events are controlling me." I was scrambling as fast as I could to produce a full draft. The delegates were already gathered at the convention hall when Baer rushed in to take the speech up to the President's suite. I followed with more copies a few minutes later.

A dozen of Clinton's friends and aides filled the suite. They were calling out changes to be incorporated into the text. Baer was marking the changes on the large-type reading copy with a thick pen. I stood with a laptop on a serving counter, trying to input the changes.

Suddenly the room emptied. I hurried after. We rode down in a freight elevator to the presidential motorcade. The President and First Lady slid into their seats. She was polished, made up, perfectly coiffed. He was still going through the speech with a pen. Baer clambered onto the jump seat opposite Hillary. I climbed in opposite the President, our knees occasionally bumping.

We began the drive through the streets of Chicago. He made changes, handed them to Baer, who would try to copy them in a wobbly hand on the large-type version. I typed them quickly, stroking the laptop's mouse and pressing the "save" key every twenty seconds or so. All I could imagine was the battery failing or the disk crashing. (I was also praying the machine would not start singing "I Can See Clearly Now.")

Hundreds lined the streets as the motorcade glided along. Clinton's attention drifted from the text. He smiled and waved. Hillary cut him short. "You work," she said. "*I'll* wave."

The car was silent. Scratch, scratch. Rustling paper. Keys clicking. The machine whirring as it saved.

The motorcade was being broadcast live to the nation. And the cameras in chase helicopters that were following the presidential limousine were showing something odd: The sleek black car; the flags flapping; the motorcycle escorts. And in the backseat, the unmistakable blue glow of a laptop.

I'm told that a network anchor narrated the scene. "Let this be a lesson for all the young people watching," he intoned. "Don't save your work for the last minute."

When we arrived at the United Center, the limousine idled as we finished our work. Secret Service agents opened the doors. I rushed through the concrete and cinderblock hallways of the center to a bunker-like room. A private company had set up a prompter system. I handed over the disk. It loaded successfully to their system. I printed out a copy of the speech for the press office. A minute later, the laptop crashed. Clinton was down the

hall. He had rehearsed for only twenty minutes before walking out to the roar of thousands of Democrats.

I watched most of the speech from a cinderblock room under the stands. The technicians—bearded contractors used to rock shows, not military men—began cursing and shouting into phones and walkie-talkies. Again, amazingly, the prompters were failing. The left and right screens were too dim to be seen. Only the one straight in front of the speaker— mounted on the platform that held photographers—was working. (News stories the next day indicated that many viewers were thrilled that Clinton was looking straight into the camera the whole time.)

THE BRIDGE TO THE TWENTY-FIRST CENTURY, repeated over and over, was a successful slogan. The press disdained it. But citizens understood. The future was promising; it was foreign, too. People wanted to get there—or they wanted their children to get there, to live in the world of technology and science that they saw—but they were nervous about whether that would happen. Though the metaphor was powerful, it was crammed in a speech full of too many specifics and not enough eloquence. Nevertheless, it worked.

A day later, Clinton came up to Terry Edmonds and me in the lobby of a hotel where we were staying. "I really like that metaphor," he said. "You can do so much with it. 'I want a bridge that is wide enough and strong enough to carry everyone across.' " He shook hands with some hotel staff. "This was a good day." The elevator door closed.

The press began to write friendly, chatty articles asking where the image had come from. I called the *New York Times* reporter from the "secure" room next to the gym in a community college in California. The mission is to give the President credit. If the reporter mentions the name of the speechwriter that would be fine, too. Then one day, word came down that no staff members were to take credit for the metaphor—or, for that matter, to give *Clinton* credit either. We weren't sure why. After the campaign was over, *Time* magazine reported that Tipper Gore believed it had been her idea.

A few months later, Don Baer waved quiet a meeting in his office. He wanted to read a passage from a Clinton convention speech. He "has spent his whole life closing the gap between what is and what might have been. He'll stand and deliver for us. He'll build a bridge to tomorrow for us. And that's why I'm so proud to say he ought to be president and to place in nomination"—Baer paused for effect—"the name of the forty-first president of the United States, Michael Dukakis from Massachusetts." Clinton had first used the line to a Democratic convention in 1988—in the worst received speech of his life.

THIRTEEN

THE VITAL CENTER

THE NEXT TWO MONTHS rushed by. A modern president running for reelection moves across the landscape like a Roman general. He carries with him political staff, presidential press secretary, campaign press secretary, and a phalanx of military aides and security personnel.

Two speechwriters who had transferred over to the campaign committee traveled with Clinton. Jonathan Prince was the most flamboyant—in fact, the most insistently *noticeable* person on the plane. If a playwright had created his character and named him Jonathan Prince, critics would sneer at the obviousness of it. Only twenty-nine, he had been given a raise and promotion earlier in the year. He promptly bought a new wardrobe of what could be described only as zoot suits. Terry Edmonds alternated with Prince. He was older, rooted, calm. I took some personal leave and traveled, as did Mark Penn. It was easy to tell where Penn had just been. He left a trail of secret polling data, loose papers, handheld electronic gizmos. Andrew Friendly, Clinton's young personal aide, had predicted that Penn would accidentally open the hatch, thinking it was the door to the restroom, and step outside the moving plane. His last words, trailing away, would be, "I forgot my cellphone!!"

Sometimes some votes are changed by debates, but the true contact with voters in a modern campaign is the paid advertisements. Even so, candidates continue to jet around the country, touching down in as many communities as they can. At nearly every stop, Clinton spoke extemporaneously, referring only to an outline handwritten in code. Prince had cracked the code, and we began to type up outlines based on the President's evolving stump speech. Δ meant "change." ↓ meant "declined"

("unemp ↓"). For each appearance, we would plug in new statistics or place-names. Once a day, we would insert a full paragraph, which was intended to be read as written. It would respond to Dole, or advance some new argument that would reinforce the ads, or address what other Democrats were saying.

Bill Clinton drew energy from these appearances, seeming to absorb it directly from the crowds. At each stop, he pressed and pressed until he found a connection, historical or emotional or substantive, that bonded him to the audience. He was at ease, seeming even to relish the chance to banter with hecklers. On these occasions, his words were fluid but rarely formally eloquent. Their power came from the intense connection with the people in front of him—that and his relaxed pride in the stream of positive indicators about the country's health.

After a speech, he would shake hands with dozens of people in the front row, as Secret Service agents scanned the periphery. The President would lean in, huddling with individuals for a half minute of conversation. Afterwards, he would come backstage and unload—recounting what he had been told by the people he had met. One had a sister who kept her job as a result of the Family and Medical Leave Act when a family member had cancer. Another got a low-interest loan to go to college. In a few seconds of conversation, he had drawn out of them a succinct lesson from their life stories. Sometimes we would discreetly go back into the hall to double-check the stories so that they could be included in subsequent speeches. Clinton's version was invariably confirmed.

AS IT BECAME INCREASINGLY CLEAR that Clinton would win, political aides could be seen scouring multicolored maps. It was possible, just possible, that the Democrats could win back the House. We believed that the odds depended upon Clinton's total.

In late September, Clinton and Gore spoke to a private meeting of the House and Senate Democratic Caucuses. It took place in the cavernous House Ways and Means Committee room in the Longworth Office Building on Capitol Hill. The congressmen sat in the seats usually occupied by the lobbyists. Staff members ringed the rostrum where the members of Congress usually sat. The Democrats were upbeat. They saw a chance to win the House. But they were still bruised by Clinton's strategy of triangulation the year before, and resentful over the voracious fundraising that they believed had consumed all the available campaign dollars.

Minority leader Gephardt welcomed Clinton and Gore and delivered a stem-winder. The lawmakers, still, after all these years, nearly all men, roared. The committee chamber had the steamy feel of a locker room.

Gephardt denounced the Republicans, predicted a Democratic win, and praised Clinton and Gore. He was followed by the Vice President, his likely rival for the Democratic presidential nomination in 2000. As his fellow congressional Democrats applauded vigorously, Gephardt returned to his seat in the front row. The whip, David Bonior, sat next to him, his arms crossed.

Gore moved to the podium and slowly read a speech, recounting how hard it was for the Democrats to pass their budget. He finished to polite applause. Then the President got up. He was in his ruminative mode. He draped himself across the podium and lowered his voice, so that the politicians would have to lean in. He explained that he very much wanted to elect a Democratic Congress. He would raise money to see it happen. Terry McAuliffe, his top fundraiser, would be detached to raise $12 million for the congressional effort. But he wouldn't overtly stress a call for a Democratic Congress. That would hurt their chances. The public hates partisanship and it doesn't want to give the Democrats too much power.

ON SEPTEMBER 21, the *Los Angeles Times* reported that the Democratic National Committee had returned an illegal $250,000 contribution given by a South Korean company. The gift had been arranged by a former Commerce Department official, John Huang, who was now a fundraiser at the DNC. Soon the press was full of stories about funds funneled from the Lippo Group, about Vice President Gore's appearance at a Buddhist temple, and about payments by Lippo to former associate attorney general Webb Hubbell.

The first debate between Clinton and Dole, in Hartford, Connecticut, went well for the President. The second debate was approaching. In contrast to the formal format of the first, this one would be a town meeting, with both candidates answering unscripted questions from the audience. This was the format that had served Clinton so well in 1992. The defining moment of that year's general election campaign had come in a town meeting–style debate. Someone asked the candidates how the debt (she meant the recession) had affected them. Bush replied, "I'm not sure I get it." Clinton strode toward her, looked in her eyes, asked about her experiences, and gave a compassionate answer. But now Clinton was rusty, cut off from regular give-and-take with voters. And with the uncertain, expanding cloud of the Asian money scandal looming, an unscripted question from an angry voter could rattle.

The campaign assembled at the Holiday Inn in Albuquerque, New Mexico—campaign consultants, policy staff, speechwriters, press aides—all told, perhaps two dozen advisors. Most of the time, most of us were cordoned off in a workroom. But a few times we trooped into a ballroom set up

as a television studio, to sit on risers and read prescripted questions. Former senator George Mitchell played Dole, a man he had jousted with on the Senate floor. Prince was given the assignment of confronting Clinton on contributions, and he warmed to it. When called on, he stood up and dramatically challenged the President on campaign finances. The debate itself was an anticlimax. Dole never raised the ethics issue forcefully. But the stories continued to pop in the press like firecrackers and Clinton had not addressed the issue.

In the last weeks of the campaign, Clinton decided to give a series of talks on the unfinished business of his presidency—a closing case to the jury. As closing speeches in a Democratic presidential campaign, they were a sign of how far he had dragged the party and himself. He addressed a university audience in Nashville on welfare reform, demanding that the private sector and government provide jobs for those who were being moved off the rolls. The next day, he spoke in front of a city hall at a suburb of St. Louis and announced that the deficit had dropped to the lowest level in fifteen years. It was an entirely over-the-top production. A chart several stories high was draped across the front of the building. The new Office of Management and Budget director, Franklin Raines, would join Clinton onstage. They would stand next to two children—representing "the future"—who would yank ropes so that sheets would fall away to reveal the rapidly shrinking deficit. At this dramatic moment, the crowd was supposed to cheer wildly and photogenically. Instead, it offered puzzled applause, as the sheets fell down prematurely.

On October 29, the President was preparing to address an enthusiastic audience at Ohio State University in Columbus. It was his third "summing-up" speech, this one on education. In a second term, he would seek higher standards for teachers and schools, public school choice through charter schools, tax cuts to cover the costs of community college, and funds for school construction and connecting classrooms to the Internet. A cavernous press center adjoined the arena. The reporters always had better food than the staff since their spread was paid for by the news organizations. I lugged my laptop through the filing center to find the buffet. Mike McCurry and Bruce Reed were briefing the press on the upcoming remarks. A reporter came up to me as I stuffed my face with muffins at the food table. "So, getting ready to write that big campaign finance reform speech? This is what you've been waiting for."

"What are you talking about?"

"McCurry announced there's going to be a big campaign finance reform speech." I tried to look nonchalant. "Oh, sure." Apparently, McCurry had come under intense questioning at the podium about foreign campaign contributions.

McCurry's gambit—he was annoyed that the campaign continued to stonewall—sent stomachs churning. Most of the President's staff hadn't wanted him to address reform because of the allegations of Asian money. Now he would do so, in a speech just days before the election.

On the flight to Las Vegas, I tapped out a draft. The campaign planned to release the text before Clinton spoke. Everyone was very nervous, and nervously looking at me. Who knew what I would write? Penn, Ann Lewis, and I sat around a gunmetal desk in a darkened government office as Clinton gave an interview down the hall. They tore up the speech until it resembled nothing Clinton had ever said on reform before.

Panetta convened a meeting in the conference room of Air Force One as we flew on to Oakland. There was a contentious argument around the table. Some didn't want the issue addressed at all. Penn argued that the focus should be on foreign contributions. I took notes and tried not to explode.

The President came in. "Hey, what's going on?"

"Mr. President, we're just working on the campaign finance reform speech," Panetta replied.

Clinton burst out, "Oh, here's what I want to say. Say it's a big priority. Say I wanted to pass it. We passed lobbying and gift reform, but that's not enough. Say we need a soft-money ban—and make sure you say spending limits and free TV." That was the argument I had used in the first draft. Clinton headed back to his cabin.

"Do you think you can get that done?" Panetta asked me.

"I already have it." If there was one thing I knew how to do, it was to whip myself into a frenzy on campaign finance reform. The President gave the speech on the morning of October 31, before thousands of students in Santa Barbara. It was the first time he addressed the issue at length in months. We were showing bruises, but political reform was once again at the forefront. Against all evidence, I was hopeful once again.

THE LAST LEG OF THE TRIP was giddy. Hillary joined us, and longtime staff members came along. Chelsea and a high school friend interviewed staff members with a handheld camcorder. In the two days before the vote, Clinton spoke at a black church in Tampa, Florida, and rallies in West Palm Beach; Union Township, New Jersey; Springfield, Massachussets; Bangor, Maine; Manchester, New Hampshire; Cleveland, Ohio; Lexington, Kentucky; and Cedar Rapids, Iowa, ending in Sioux Falls, South Dakota.

For the last rally of the campaign, Prince impishly gave Clinton a joke speech. When Clinton opened his gray documents folder at the podium,

instead of yet another identical outline, he found a page that said, "DITTO."

Speaking near midnight, Clinton was emotional. "There is no person living in this country today who has been given more gifts, who feels more humble on this night than I do. Fifty years ago, when I was born in a summer storm to a widowed mother in a little town in Arkansas, it was unthinkable that I might have ever become president. I'd like for you to believe I did it because I always worked sixty or seventy hours a week, I had an understanding and supportive and wonderful family, and I just did it. But it isn't true. I did it because at every step along the way for twenty-three years and long before, there was a Sunday school teacher, a teacher in school, a doctor, the guy running the Red Roof in my hometown who always stopped and talked to me and tried to give me encouragement when I was despondent, over and over and over. We just need to run our country the way we want to run our lives." We stood at the side of the stage, misty eyed.

The flight from South Dakota to Little Rock was a long exhale. It had seemed improbable—impossible just a year before—but Clinton was going to be comfortably reelected. The staff converged on the conference room. A boom box played the Macarena. McCurry bumped and grinded, first with Hillary's staff, then, after much coaxing, with Hillary. Stewards brought in mango ice cream in plastic cups and champagne. Panetta toasted the Clintons; Clinton thanked the staff. He got out of his chair and moved slowly around the room.

Mark Penn slipped in. He had been on the phone with his office, checking on the last night's tracking polls. A staff member called out, "Mark! Hey, Mark! Do you have the numbers? Do you?" Penn smiled and shifted uncomfortably. "I'll tell the President later."

Clinton looked intently at Penn. "No, come on," the staff member insisted. "What are the numbers?" Clinton nodded: go ahead. "Uh, you're at 49 percent, Dole is at 41 percent, Perot is at 8 percent," he said.

The President sagged slightly and was silent. The staff member who had forced Penn to tell Clinton the results in public didn't realize what he had done. He congratulated the President effusively. Clinton forced a smile. Penn looked chagrined.

Clinton had been denied his majority. In a competitive three-way race, he had gained six points over his 1992 majority, which was not insubstantial. But it would not be enough to carry in a Democratic House. On election day, the raw vote total for the Democratic congressional candidates mirrored the vote total for Clinton. His drop in the last week had been mirrored by a falloff in support for the Democrats.

At the same time, Clinton's political achievement was tremendous. He was the first Democratic President to be reelected since Roosevelt, only

the third since the Civil War. Just two years before, he had seemed finished, irrelevant. He had not only revived his own fortune, he had also succeeded in changing the way Democrats talked to the public, how they defined themselves. He had taken the steam out of the intense anti-government animus that had driven the modern Republican Party for decades. And with his stream of executive orders and announcements, he was finding a new way to be president.

The next day, lounging with Bruce Lindsey in a large, spare hotel suite, Clinton seemed spent. Baer and I were there to give him a speech draft to be delivered to the crowd that would gather that night. We urged the President to use the passage he had improvised the night before, about how far he had risen from his birth in a "summer storm." "Tonight is your night," Baer said.

A large crowd once again spread out before the Old State House. For tens of thousands, the mood was one of dull relief. In contrast to the breathless, liberal speech of four years before, Clinton spoke mostly of his personal appreciation to those who had helped him. His thanks seemed endless.

A few days before, as we had been preparing to land in San Antonio, the President had stopped in the doorway of the conference room on Air Force One to tell Baer and me to read an editorial in the New York Times. "Take a look at it," he urged. "It talks about the vital center," borrowing the title of a famous book by Arthur M. Schlesinger Jr. that defined postwar liberalism a half century earlier. "Whoever wins on Tuesday," the editorial read,

> the center has re-emerged as the pivotal place in American politics, and centrist voters, while more tough-minded, still favor a Federal role in guarding the health and security of Americans and their environment. As the center reasserts itself, the next President and Congress need to make it vital.

On election night, in Little Rock, Clinton told the nation, "Tonight we proclaim that the vital American center is alive and well. It is the common ground on which we have made our progress."

A month later, in a speech to the Democratic Leadership Council, Clinton was more explicit. (He began by announcing, "The last person clapping is my first new ambassador in the new term.") He reminded them that a year before, on the eve of the government shutdown, he had gone before the same audience to ask if the center could hold. He argued that the answer was yes. A new consensus had been formed, he said. And it was for a government that was smaller but progressive and energetic.

The ground has shifted beneath our feet, but we have clearly created a new center—not the lukewarm midpoint between overheated liberalism and chilly conservatism, but instead a place where, throughout our history, people of goodwill have tried to forge new approaches to new challenges. . . . As in every other time of profound change, we must follow Lincoln's admonition to think anew and act anew. And as in every such time, the American people must come to a common understanding about how to proceed before we can hope to succeed. Today, I believe we have come to such an understanding.

The true test would come, unexpectedly and fiercely, in the next two years.

FOURTEEN

THE POSTERITY
WAR ROOM

ON THE FIFTH DAY of the new year of 1997, the reception area outside the Oval Office was inviting and bright. Betty Currie, the President's secretary, reliably sunny herself, sat at her desk. You checked with her for news of the President's mood. Behind her were piled some of his Christmas gifts, books to be signed, knickknacks sent from Arkansas. Socks the Cat tchotchkes were scattered around the room—porcelain figures, pillows. Socks himself liked to make an appearance, walking on a leash held by a Secret Service agent and nestling in a corner chair. The television was always tuned to CNN. Baer, Reed, Penn, and I were waiting for our first meeting to work with the President on the first second-term inaugural address that would be delivered by a Democratic president in sixty years.

Don Baer was preparing to leave the White House. Bruce Reed had been elevated to domestic policy advisor. Mark Penn was the principal political advisor. I had settled into the job of chief speechwriter. We stood with studied casualness, but in fact we were steeling ourselves, reinforcing each other's nerve. In the customary drenching of advice from outside friends and advisors, one refrain was coming through clearly: it was time to decommission the bridge to the twenty-first century.

"It was an effective campaign slogan," I said. "But there's a difference between what you do in a campaign and what you do in an inaugural. We've got to be straight with him." Only Reed disagreed. "Hey, it's a good metaphor, he likes it, and it really has worked well with the public. Why should we listen to what the media says?"

The door to the Oval Office opened silently. Clinton walked out. He looked at us and without much of a hello, began, "I just don't see why we

can't use the bridge to the twenty-first century. It's the first slogan I've ever had that's resonated with the public. It's the first one that's any good. Look at this." He reached over to the credenza where the day's newspapers were laid out. He pointed at a pillow with a bridge to the twenty-first century someone had lovingly embroidered and sent him. He touched a little model bridge handcrafted out of wood. Apparently, dozens of Democrats around the country had been working on bridges for months. "It would be a terrible mistake not to use the bridge to the twenty-first century."

He looked at us.

"I agree, Mr. President. It does make sense," we all chorused. "Absolutely, sir. It's amazing how it's connected with the public." We all assured him that it was the right thing to do. Clinton ambled back in to the Oval Office. Bruce Reed was greatly amused. "Brave," he hissed.

At its best, working with Clinton as he prepared a speech was like watching Michael Jordan practice his free throws. It was a priceless opportunity to see a genius disassemble his game, practicing each part.

At its worst . . . well, at its worst it was like writing a second inaugural address.

In contrast to four years before, the President was less certain of what he wanted to say or how to say it. Though he had been reelected, his sense of mandate was tenuous. He was still testing the limits of progressive activism, as if he were prodding a sleeping animal with a stick, to see what the public would put up with. The large goals that remained from his first term—the elusive agreement to balance the budget chief among them—could be achieved only by working with congressional Republicans. That called for calm and conciliation, not drama or demands.

We were settled in our accustomed places—the President in the yellow wingback chair before the fireplace; I in the corner of the couch next to him; other staff filling out the sofas. We were all well aware of the curse of the second term. There have been thirteen of them; few had worked out well. Most were marred by scandal or war. "I'm very mindful of history's difficulties, and I'm going to try to beat them," Clinton had acknowledged at his first post-election press conference. He made the same points to us. The key was to focus, to have clear goals, continued energy. Previous presidents were felled by hubris. He would not let his political guard down. Second-term inaugural addresses had been lackluster. In fact, only two were memorable—those delivered by Lincoln and FDR. And they were stirring precisely because they addressed the same crisis of four years before.

And the President's advisors were not giving him much help. I thought he should frame his program around renewing the ideals of equal opportunity and freedom as set out in the Declaration of Independence. Since most great American speeches have used those ideals as challenges,

I argued that this would be a good way to put the information age agenda into context. Don Baer, with a more refined sense of poetry, thought that Clinton *had* restored the country's sense of self-confidence, and urged a meditation on faith. Penn thought Clinton had an opening to defend a strong, limited government. Clinton had absorbed all these ideas, and, typically, he liked aspects of all of them. He looked over a conceptual outline for the inaugural address, waved his assent at it, and set it aside. Permanently.

He was thinking about how to frame his presidency, and he was deeply influenced by a book he was reading. *The Politics Presidents Make*, by Yale political scientist Stephen Skowronek, analyzes the tenure of every president, not just those whose monuments dot the Mall. The conclusion, said Clinton, was inescapable: the best-remembered presidents are those who take bold stands to upend the existing order, who push back against their predecessors. "All kinds of presidents had significant accomplishments who never get any credit in history because they couldn't control the story line," he explained. Even those who had *acted* cautiously made bold claims. "Reagan had a story line. 'Big government's damn near screwed this country up, but there's nothing wrong with America. I'm going to return America to its basic faith, which is opposition to big government.' " He was stewing over this point because, plainly, his political circumstances dictated a different approach. He had reversed Reaganomics and ended two decades of neglect of public problems, had energized the government and redirected its efforts, he thought, but now, facing a reelected Republican Congress, his tone would be necessarily muted. The speech would have to be a call for common ground.

With these somewhat baffling injunctions in hand, I returned to my office. Soliciting suggestions and language from an array of people whose input the President wanted, I produced a first draft and sent it in.

We met with Clinton a week later. He didn't want to focus the speech around any new or dramatic set of national goals, and offhandedly asked for suggestions of what should be on the "laundry list." He seemed more taken with the idea that the speech should be "some sort of valedictory to the twentieth century," an idea he had drawn from Sidney Blumenthal, who would soon join the administration. An inaugural address, he was reasoning, was a rare opportunity to explain to the public — and mark for future readers — where the country saw itself. The President often compared this period of economic change to the time a century ago that gave rise to the Progressive Era. Then, the rise of great new industries upended old patterns of social life and demanded a new activist government, as millions moved from farms into the cities and went to work for large corporations. Now, the disruptive force, for better and worse, was the coming of the in-

formation age. Instead of rehashing this analogy, the President wanted to put an exclamation point on the twentieth century. In my draft, I included two mentions of the Internet, which had burst into public consciousness only two years before.

We met with the President nearly continually through the rest of the week. It was fascinating to watch him roll words around, contemplating their shadings and nuances. His friend, evangelical minister Tony Campolo, had suggested that he borrow the line from a hymn, "Let us be bold, for there is much to dare." Clinton thought not. "I don't want to do 'bold' again, because we said bold a lot in the last inaugural." He noted that feminist writer Betty Friedan had asked that women be specifically mentioned for the first time in any presidential inaugural (they were). He noted that saying the United States should "pay its way" was a clear signal of support for the United Nations. He crossed out securing entitlement programs for future "generations," since the longest period into the future the programs have ever been made sound is seventy-five years. And he showed his irritation with the attacks on the administration for campaign fundraising practices. My draft had referred elliptically to political reform. Clinton wanted the reference strengthened. But in the same breath, he parodied what he saw as the obsessions of editorial writers. "I see an America where McCain-Feingold is the most important thing in America—except for entitlement reform," he joked.

Clinton's calendar was cleared of most other responsibilities. With little else to tell reporters, the press office staff began to spin out ever more elaborate tales of how the President was working on the speech, the poetry he was reading, the history he was pondering. The *Boston Globe* reported that, according to White House aides, Clinton was "obsessed" with the speech.

Every morning, the President picked up the newspaper, or shuffled through the photocopied news clippings that were flagged for his attention, filled with stories about how hard he was working. As the days went by, I sensed an increasing pressure on him. He had a rhythm, a method of preparing for these speeches. Often he procrastinated as a way of finding his "zone." And this time, that method wasn't working. Clinton's great gift was his connection with the audience, and this kind of abstract ceremonial speech could wind up sounding forced.

Clinton wanted to find a way to avoid the bitter partisanship that had marked the previous term. I had written that the voters had chosen a president of one party and a Congress of another, "with eyes wide open." "I really like that," he said, but he had his own version of the same thought. "Now. What do you think about this: 'The American people put us all in the same boat, handed us oars, and told us to start rowing'?" It was a deft

metaphor. The image of Clinton and Gingrich crammed into a boat, each straining at their oars, and the boat going in circles, was somewhat delicious. But it was too political. We agreed it would work better in the State of the Union. "The dial meters will go off the chart," he chortled, referring to the devices that pollsters use to gauge reactions to different passages of a speech.

As one meeting broke up, Clinton read aloud a new passage he wanted included. "America demands and deserves big things from us, and nothing big ever came from being small," the President said. "What do you think?" he asked. It sounded good at the time.

As the inaugural day approached, and the capital filled with revelers and friends, Clinton kept rewriting. The day before he was due to take the oath, he had planned to start rehearsing in the family theater. Instead, he sat at his desk in the Oval Office, working. Baer and I felt besieged. Clinton's extended circle of advisors, arriving to watch the rehearsal, one by one sat down and began helping with the redraft.

Soon twelve people had gathered to work on the speech, hovering around three word processors and a laptop computer in two basement offices in the West Wing. Penn, Reed, Sperling, Ann Lewis, and senior advisor Rahm Emanuel. Michael Sheehan, the speech coach, and Tommy Caplan. Paul Begala, the political consultant who worked on the first campaign and who had since returned to Texas. Henry Cisneros, the outgoing HUD secretary.

Taylor Branch arrived, his face flushed from the cold. He had been thinking while driving in from his home in Baltimore, he said. The speech needed a unifying image. What about the New Freedom? After all, Clinton's program sought to find a new meaning of freedom in the information age. No go: that had been Woodrow Wilson's slogan. Still, he thought, the speech did not do enough to point toward the destination, did not summon a picture of the future. The bridge was nice, but what was on the other side? Martin Luther King, and the Pilgrims, echoing Moses, had seen the Promised Land. That would be a bit much. It couldn't be the Promised Land, but what about a land of New Promise? A new, lofty opening to the speech was written in.

The morning of the inaugural, as Clinton looked over his reading copy in the marble grand foyer of the residence one more time, Jordan Tamagni took a White House car up to the Capitol with a computer disk for the final transfer to the teleprompters.

In contrast to four years before, the drill was familiar. She would never think of simply leaving the disk for the operators, as I had naively done. Tamagni found the tiny wooden room under the inaugural stands where the operator waited. The space wasn't high enough to stand comfortably, and

the teleprompter team shared it with two soldiers carrying forbidding auto-
matic weapons. Jimmy Van Keuren—the military aide whom she called
"iron man" for his imperturbability in the face of teleprompter glitches—
gingerly inserted the disk. Gibberish came up on the screen. Somehow, despite all the testing, the formatting on the computer disk had gone awry,
probably saved in the wrong version of WordPerfect. And the Secret Service was reporting that the President's motorcade was about to leave the
White House. Drive time to the Capitol: five minutes.

Tamagni had ordered a printer and computer set up in the Speaker
of the House's private office off the House floor—what was called the
"POTUS Hold" for today. Tottering on high heels, leaping over mink coats
and pushing past members of Congress filing out to their seats, she dashed
up the inaugural stand into the Capitol. She found the Speaker's office and
reformatted the disk, and ran back to the teleprompter compartment. Once
again, they inserted the disk into the teleprompter and held their breath.
The speech appeared. Seconds later, the President's motorcade left the
White House for the Capitol.

Clinton looked grave as he took the oath of office. Delivering his address, he spoke very slowly—sometimes decelerating to half his normal
speaking rate. In one of our meetings, he had observed that other inaugurals had fewer words than his first one, but his somehow had been shorter in
delivery. We had pointed out that they had lacked a microphone, and he
talked faster. At the last rehearsal he said he intended to slow things down.

Sixteen years earlier, Ronald Reagan had declared that "Government
is not the solution; government is the problem." Now Clinton answered:
"Once again, we have resolved for our time a great debate over the role of
government. Today we can declare: Government is not the problem, and
government is not the solution. . . . As times change, so government must
change. We need a new government for a new century—humble enough
not to try to solve all our problems for us, but strong enough to give us the
tools to solve our problems for ourselves; a government that is smaller, lives
within its means, and does more with less. Yet where it can stand up for our
values and interests in the world, and where it can give Americans the
power to make a real difference in their everyday lives, government should
do more, not less."

He picked up speed and showed passion in the section, which he had
written almost entirely by hand, on race. "Our greatest responsibility is to
embrace a new spirit of community for a new century. For any one of us to
succeed we must succeed as one America. The challenge of our past remains the challenge of our future. Will we be one nation, one people, with
one common destiny, or not? Will we all come together or come apart?
The divide of race has been America's constant curse. And each new wave

of immigrants gives new targets to old prejudices—prejudice and contempt in the pretense of religious or political convictions are no different. These forces have nearly destroyed our nation in the past. They plague us still. They fuel the fanaticism of terror, and they torment the lives of millions in fractured nations all around the world. These obsessions cripple both those who hate and, of course, those who are hated, robbing both of what they might become. We cannot, we will not succumb to the dark impulses that lurk in the far regions of the soul everywhere. We shall overcome them." Not since Lincoln had a president's inaugural speech dealt at such length and with such force on the nation's oldest, most divisive dilemma.

In his most pointed political moment, Clinton implored the Republicans in the Congress to drop their partisan pose and work with him. The morning of the speech, John Hilley, the new legislative director, had warned me that describing the public as having chosen a Democratic president and a Republican Congress "with eyes wide open" would risk a severe backlash from our own legislative caucus. I had made the cut. Still, Clinton's meaning was clear as he said, "The American people returned to office a president of one party and a Congress of another. Surely, they did not do this to advance the politics of petty bickering and extreme partisanship they plainly deplore. No, they call on us instead to be repairers of the breach," a line he drew from Scripture.

The reaction of those in the public who saw it was positive. The reaction from the crowd was polite applause. The reaction from the press and talking heads was scalding criticism.

I tuned in to watch a panel of historians on *The NewsHour with Jim Lehrer*. Stephen Ambrose grumbled, "It was so general and so full of platitudes, it reminded me of what [Senator] William Gibbs McAdoo once said of Warren Harding's speeches. 'It's an army of pompous praises marching over the landscape in search of an idea.' " In the next day's *New York Times*, Reagan's speechwriter Peggy Noonan sneered that the speech was "the worst Inaugural Address of our lifetime, and I think the only controversy will be between those who say it was completely and utterly banal and those who say, 'Well, not completely and utterly.' " (William Safire wrote generously about it in the newspaper, one saving grace.)

This was, in fact, an exaggerated version of the derision that Clinton's speeches often drew from commentators. For other big speeches, say, a convention address, the networks then poll the public—and anchors read, with a tone of surprise, that the speech was a boffo hit. This time there were no public polls. Our private surveys showed that the public rather liked the speech, especially the passages on reconciliation and race. But I have to say, this time, I had a sinking feeling the pundits may have been more right than the polls.

Later on inaugural day, the President called me at home to offer thanks and a bit of consolation. When a president calls, the house—full of visitors and relatives—is suddenly full of eavesdroppers, straining to hear my end of the conversation. I hid on a landing between floors. "I was happy with it," Clinton said generously. "And I think the public got it. Did you see, Bob Shrum said nice things about it. I appreciated that." Shrum—the legendary Democratic speechwriter who had penned George McGovern's and Ted Kennedy's best speeches—had told the *New York Times*, "I'm very pro the speech." (Shrum later told me that Clinton had sent him the speech the morning it was to be delivered for his comments. He had no choice but to praise it, and then felt constrained to be positive in his public comments as well.)

Don Baer worried, half seriously, that gossiping former colleagues in the press were crediting him with the greeting card–like "nothing big comes from being small." One night, a week after the speech, Baer lamented the unfairness of it all to Sperling and me in my office. "They're blaming me," he moaned. "And I didn't even write it!" As we chatted, I turned to my computer, and quietly typed a sheet, in big bold letters, reading "NOTHING BIG EVER COMES FROM BEING SMALL." I nonchalantly printed it out and affixed tape. As Don was leaving, I patted him on the back. "Don't worry about it. Nobody blames you." He walked down the hall, back toward the West Wing, with the sign taped to his back. Sperling and I laughed so hard our sides hurt. Baer, finally noticing, just smiled and shook his head.

A few days later, the White House correspondence office sent me a note. A mother had called in, distraught, the day after the speech. "My ten-year-old daughter loves President Clinton. She is also very small for her age. She has great difficulty dealing with this. Hearing the President say 'nothing big ever came from being small' devastated her. The speechwriters really let the President down." Fortunately, a letter had been drafted for the President apologizing to the girl, and explaining that he meant "small in mind and spirit."

After the buildup, letdown, and self-reproach of the inaugural address, it was a relief to turn to the State of the Union address, only two weeks after the inaugural.

The theme was straightforward enough. The evening that Clinton had called to commiserate after the first speech, I suggested that the congressional appearance be framed as the answer to a rhetorical question: what must America do to get ready for the twenty-first century? Clinton liked it, and we were off. The next morning, I had the small pleasure of being able to mention to the chief of staff and others that we had discussed the theme, that Clinton liked it, and here's what it was. We then sent in a

memorandum with an outline of the speech, the possible policies, and a summary line offered by Baer: "The enemy of our time is inaction."

Each State of the Union has a central thrust or prominent proposal. Shortly before the election, the President had told Bruce Reed to begin developing a major education proposal for the 1997 address. Education was rarely a central topic in national politics. But now Clinton would make it a signature issue for his second term. It had been at the core of his economic arguments in 1992. Government should not try to stop economic change. That would be futile and counterproductive. Instead, the mission should be to build an educated workforce with constantly tuned skills—"giving people the tools," as he would say, "to make the most of their own lives." In practice, during the first term, the issue had been shunted to the side. School reform had been Clinton's greatest avocation as governor of Arkansas. He had battled the teachers' union to impose competency tests on teachers, while also pushing for higher salaries. He had led the effort to set national education goals, working with President Bush in a meeting at Williamsburg. School reform was Hillary's expertise as well. Early in the first term, Congress passed the Goals 2000 law that set those education benchmarks as national policy. But, largely because elementary and secondary schools were controlled at the local level, education had never before achieved the attention that health care or crime or the budget held.

Long afterwards, I wondered why, if education was to be proclaimed the principal goal, it could not have been the centerpiece of the inaugural address. But Clinton did not settle on education as the goal until he drafted the State of the Union. It was the act of putting the plan on paper that elevated and shaped it.

The form of the program was very much guided by the fact that both Clinton and his education secretary, Richard Riley, were former governors. A few days into the new term, the two of them, along with Reed, the speechwriters, and a cohort of Education Department staff and domestic policy aides convened in the Oval Office. Plainly, Clinton revered Riley, leaning in to decipher his soft mumble (which must have been hard even for a southerner). Bent over and prematurely aged as the victim of a degenerative spinal disease, Riley had refused even to take aspirin during fifteen years of pain. He had willed himself into being a formidable politician and had served two terms as governor.

Both were suspicious of mandatory federal action. They rejected out of hand the idea of removing federal funds from states that failed to meet tough new standards, or using some other sharp stick. They knew that the Republican Congress would block any such effort. Instead, the national government would help devise a test in reading and math by which students would be judged. The President's principal role was to use the bully

pulpit, encouraging states to sign on to the standards. Don Baer proposed that Clinton commit to speaking at state legislatures for the program. After all, if much of the action of government was now at the state level, that meant the President's role had changed, not disappeared.

It was an interesting approach. Standards are not only sound education policy—they send a message that we have high expectations of all students, and we insist that they be met. But after loading up the rhetorical cannons for an assault on the education citadel, this program was rather muffled. If it worked, after all, it would amount to jawboning about voluntary standards.

Days later, the education plan was largely complete. It included a call for states to follow national education standards, financial support so that 100,000 educators could receive additional training as "master teachers," public school choice through funding of innovative charter schools, and tax cuts to help pay for college tuition. But the staff was split over a matter of both substance and philosophy that disguised itself as aesthetics. The heart of the proposal was to be included in a booklet that the President might hold aloft during the speech. Jonathan Prince, who was writing the speech with me, wanted the education focus to just be standards and public education reform, a New Democrat thrust that involved little expenditure of federal dollars. Gene Sperling insisted that the broader education agenda should be advanced as well, including student aid for college, computers in classrooms, and worker training. These were programs that cost more money; they also fell under Gene's jurisdiction. "We know we're going to be able to get some of these," he pointed out.

On a Saturday morning, as we waited to meet with the President, a large number of aides, casually dressed, sat at a table in the Roosevelt Room haggling over the proposal. I agreed with Gene's approach. But even more, I wanted us to stop bickering about it. I figured there had to be some Solomon-like way to split the baby. I went to the corner and stood among the multihued battle flags that line one wall of the room.

Eureka! "Folks, listen up!" I stood over the table like a camp counselor. "If you count these proposals, there are nine of them. If we add another one—or just split one of the existing ones into two—there are ten."

"Wow, a ten-point plan!" Several people nodded at the sagacity of it all. Jonathan threw up his hands in defeat.

"So that's what we'll do." At different ends of the table, various aides busied themselves finding a tenth plank.

We had produced a taut first draft, and despite revisions, it remained recognizable as Clinton worked through it, line by line. In one meeting, he explained that while he wanted to find a way to deal with entitlements, he thought it was a problem that got harder to solve the more you talked about

it. He had consulted Lott and Gingrich, and they wanted to do something—*after* they all reached a balanced budget agreement. Free trade, on the other hand, was something he wanted to address head-on, even if it angered Democrats. He wanted to press for fast track legislation that would give him a free hand to negotiate trade deals. "I do not believe it will appreciably increase the chances of passing fast track to weenie out on it," he said, his country boy drawl thickening as it often did when he was advancing positions that were more frequently heard in a faculty club than a trailer park. "I *do* believe it *will* appreciably increase the chances of doing something on these big Social Security and Medicare issues if we *don't* get specific. So I don't mind having the elitists dump on me on that, because they don't have a responsibility to get anything done."

The President began dropping increasingly broad hints that we should widen the circle of those we were consulting with. At his prodding, Baer invited Shrum to come to the Oval Office. At first, I was resentful: just what we needed, another helper, especially one who is larger-than-life. In fact, Shrum was unfailingly helpful, especially as a speech doctor. He was a true professional at crafting things like applause lines that the more literary, or literal, writers on Clinton's staff didn't "get."

The day of the State of the Union, all of America was transfixed. Some 85 million people in homes across the country watched television that night. Unfortunately, they weren't waiting for the President to introduce the heroes in the First Lady's box. They were waiting to hear about the O. J. Simpson verdict.

By an odd quirk of timing, the jury was returning in the civil trial of O. J. Simpson, a case brought by the families of his murdered ex-wife and her friend. Network producers watched their video feeds from Santa Monica, trying to decide whether to skip the President's speech altogether or offer a split screen of the address and the verdict.

I wasn't worried about that. I was worried that the teleprompter wouldn't work.

After the convention speech nearly failed, after the near catastrophe at the inaugural ceremony, Jordan Tamagni had run through the procedures repeatedly with the White House Communications Agency. Over and over, they checked the formatting of the files to make sure that a regular WordPerfect disk could be loaded onto the teleprompter. Everything worked fine.

As the presidential motorcade rumbled from the White House up Pennsylvania Avenue, I had reason to feel pleased. We had finished the speech early. It was good. I flipped open my laptop, popped in the floppy disk and made one final change. (I think it was a comma.) As the motorcade pulled up, an advance man waited for the speechwriters. Prince and I

dashed up the marble steps and back toward the speakers' lobby. The disk was inserted into the machine. The file was called up. There is was—the right speech, "STATE OF THE UNION ADDRESS." There was only one problem—the speech had become one long paragraph.

Somehow, the insertion of the comma had erased all the paragraph returns from the computer file. Clinton would not know where to pause, he would lose his place. We stared at the screen in horror. There was no choice but to reenter the paragraph returns, by hand. Jimmy Van Keuren, crew cut, military posture, a fighter pilot's cool, gripped the dial of the prompter. Jonathan Prince and I crowded over him, jabbing our fingers at the screen. "There!" "Put a paragraph return in there!" "There!"

"Mr. Speaker!" We heard the stentorian voice of the House sergeant at arms: "The President of the United States!" A television monitor showed Clinton strolling down the aisle, pumping the outstretched hands of the members of Congress. "There! Not there, one sentence earlier!" As Clinton rounded past the members of the Supreme Court and his cabinet, and climbed the stairs to the rostrum, Van Keuren scrolled to the last paragraph. "Done," he said. A rivulet of sweat trickled down his forehead. Jordan Tamagni sighed in admiration. "Iron man," she said.

The speech began by laying out the unfinished business of the Congress: finishing the job of balancing the budget, fixing the flaws in welfare reform, passing campaign reform. Then it moved to the call to action on education. (A reporter friend wandered over from where journalists were watching on a TV just off the House floor. When Clinton got to the education section, she exclaimed, "A ten-point plan! This is really well organized!" I beamed.)

The ending was drawn from an article in an undergraduate newspaper written by a college student Baer had met. Baer had showed it to Clinton, who loved it. "This is the best summary I have seen yet of what we are trying to do," he told us, handing it back with favorite passages about the role of government circled. The student's article had ended with the image Clinton used to conclude the speech. "A child born tonight will have almost no memory of the twentieth century. Everything that child will know about America will be because of what we do now to build a new century."

The doors of the House floor opened and lawmakers, staff, reporters, and spectators poured out. We joined up with Penn and Baer and made our way to the reception room that the President would be passing through. Hillary was standing there, smiling broadly. She confided that the idea for "politics must stop at the schoolhouse door" was hers. Originally, Bob Shrum had suggested "classroom door." "This turns George Wallace on his head," she explained mischievously.

On the motorcade back up Pennsylvania Avenue, everyone was chat-

tering into their cellphone, finding out poll results, talking to reporters, taking the pulse. We were all eager for the reaction, and eager to be the ones to convey it. As I walked in to the White House, a member of the press office staff called out after me, "CBS said that not since Reagan's inaugural in 1981 has there been a speech like that!" I sprinted upstairs to the grand Blue Room, where a small reception was being held. I found the President and told him. He lifted his eyebrows and grunted soulfully. "That's great, man."

(Later, I asked someone who had watched CBS if their reporters had really said that. Yes, it was explained. Not since Reagan's 1981 inaugural — when the country was really waiting for the hostages to be released by Iran — had there been a speech like this, as the country waited for the real news from O.J.'s courtroom. I chose not to correct the record with the President.)

There is a feeling of great exultation after a successful speech. Researchers and cabinet secretaries hug. The heroes from the First Lady's box wander, eyes wide at being inside the White House. The Reverend Robert Schuller was standing alone. I had enjoyed watching his televised ministry for years, and had admired his eulogy at Hubert Humphrey's funeral. He had suggested the Scripture passage that Clinton used in his inaugural — "repairers of the breach." I pulled Prince over to talk to the televangelist.

Clinton came over to Jonathan and me. "This is Jonathan," he told Schuller. He draped his arm around me. "And this — is Michael." I swelled with pride. "They're the guys who typed my speech."

IN THE FIRST DAYS of the new term, a big change came over the White House staff. The kids — the thirty-two-year-old deputies who had made the place run for years — one by one found themselves elevated to top jobs. Just a few months before, on election night, Gene Sperling, Bruce Reed and his wife, Bonnie, my wife, Liz, and I walked the streets of Little Rock, anonymously. Now Gene and Bruce had the paneled corner offices on the second floor of the West Wing.

And with Stephanopoulos' departure, Rahm Emanuel took his job and office, and became our go-to person on message. What should be the sound bite, the killer political paragraph?

Rahm was an energetic former ballet dancer who had volunteered to serve in the Israeli Army during the Gulf war. He had been Clinton's chief fundraiser in 1992 and was a ferociously effective organizer, the best in the White House. Rahm's speech was somewhat fractured, like the comedian Norm Crosby. Terry Edmonds had dubbed it Rahmbonics. The speechwriters began posting examples, clipped from the newspapers, on the office

bulletin board. One *New York Times* article read, " 'Trade,' " Emanuel said, 'is the one issue that still runs down the canyon between those who want to walk forward into the future confidently . . . and [those] who want to pull up the drawbridge and hunker down.' " Another read, "We have to slam shut the revolving door between drugs and crime." A later specimen read, " 'It reeks of politics from beginning to end,' said Emanuel. 'It seethes politics out of every pore of the office of independent counsel.' " By the time he left the White House two years later, the "Rahm Wall" was full.

But Rahm had a sharp ear for other people's cant. He squirmed in almost physical agony at having to endure dreamy rhetoric or political correctness. He called it "singing Kumbaya." One day in 1997, an event to mark the millennium and the White House's newly minted "Millennium Program" to "honor the past, imagine the future" was added to the schedule. Rahm summoned the speechwriter to his office. "I don't care what you write about this thing," he said sternly. She waited for her instruction. Finally he burst out, "But whatever you do, just don't use the word 'millennium.' "

One day, just outside the Oval Office, he charged up to Terry Edmonds and me. Terry was writing the remarks for a ceremony at Independence Hall where the President would join General Colin Powell and Presidents Bush, Carter, and Ford to encourage citizen service. Rahm was nervous.

"Guys, this should be poetry. Poetry," he said.

I responded. "You know, Rahm, that's really a misconception. Speeches aren't poetry. We make a real mistake when we aim for that, it comes off sounding stilted. Speeches aren't poetry, they're rhetoric. Rhetoric and arguments. What we need is some good rhetoric."

He nodded. "You're right, you're right," he said, turning on his heels and stalking away. "Just make it something that can be chiseled in marble on the wall."

I turned to Terry. "Got that? Chiseled on the wall."

In the State of the Union address, the President had agreed to call for Congress to pass campaign finance reform by July 1. Senator John McCain had sprung to his feet, pugnaciously clapping, while his fellow Republicans sat smiling faintly around him.

Three days after the address, Clinton met with the reform groups and the House sponsors of reform, Republican congressman Chris Shays and Democrat Marty Meehan. He cautioned the reformers that the White House would play a major role, when the time was right—when a bill was actually ready for a vote on the floor of Congress. When that happens, we will mount a full-throated effort, Clinton said. He pointed down the Cabinet Room table to where staff was sitting, and announced that he had chosen Emanuel to head the drive. I was thrilled. Finally, a presidential

confidant would have a stake in the issue. I looked at Rahm. He had slumped down in his chair, scowling. His foot jiggled angrily.

In his office afterwards, I congratulated him. "Don't you see?" he demanded. John Podesta, the new deputy chief of staff, had maneuvered for Rahm to be assigned the topic as a way of sidelining him, keeping him busy with a losing issue.

This time, I was clear-eyed about the chances of forcing reform through a Republican Congress. Trent Lott, the majority leader, cornered by reporters at a retreat that brought together donors and senators, defended the practice of unlimited soft-money contributions as "the American way." But after four years, Clinton had finally learned not simply to tether himself to the legislative process, and he was pressing his staff for things he could do without waiting for Congress. Emanuel and I devised a series of executive actions designed to show commitment and movement on the key elements of reform. So Clinton asked the Federal Communications Commission to provide free airtime to candidates. Rahm arranged for the Justice Department to leak that it would argue that mandatory spending limits—struck down by the Supreme Court a quarter century before in *Buckley* v. *Valeo*—were in fact constitutional.

There was a third step. Soft money had not been thought exempt from federal law in the original campaign reforms passed in the 1970s. So why couldn't the Federal Election Commission ban it under the existing statute? Working with staff from the Domestic Policy Council and counsel's office, I prepared a letter to the agency from the President proposing that it ban soft money without waiting for legislation. Clinton had approved the proposal. It was going to be announced in a radio address. At the end of a presidential press conference, we returned to Rahm's office to discover that he had left—his wife was having a baby. Five minutes later John Podesta came in. This was a ridiculous proposal, he said. It hadn't been cleared with the Democratic leaders on the Hill. Let's postpone it. And it was put off for another month.

Indeed, every time we tried to schedule an event to call for passage of campaign reform, it seemed, something intervened. A big ceremony was planned in the grand foyer of the residence to announce that former vice president Walter Mondale and former Republican senator Nancy Kassebaum would lead a citizens' group at the behest of the White House, when Clinton fell down some steps in Florida and blew out his knee. Vice President Gore spoke instead. On another occasion, the advocacy group Common Cause was scheduled to come to the White House to present a petition for reform, and to have the President sign it. They had been pressing for the session for weeks. A few days before the event, Common Cause officials told me that the group would not attend, evidently because they

did not want to be associated with the administration while campaign finance irregularities continued to emerge. Republicans, in turn, warned that our vocal support would hurt legislative efforts.

The newspapers were filled with stories about campaign fundraising: calls for a special prosecutor, sleepovers in the Lincoln Bedroom by contributors, preparation for congressional hearings. The endless revelations disturbed me deeply. Though I knew we had to raise the money to compete with the Republicans, the reality of the system was still dismaying.

For me, the lowest point came during a press conference that the President held at the height of the controversy. It was a chance to channel the negative energy of scandal into a positive crusade for change. What Clinton offered instead was an honest defense of the current system. "This business of money takes too much time, and if you have to do too much of it, it will take too much time and raise too many questions," he said. "But I do not agree with the inherent premise that some have advanced that there is somehow something intrinsically wrong with a person that wants to give money to a person running for office and that if you accept it, that something bad has happened. . . . But the system is out of whack, and I think we all know it and we all know it's not going to get better until and unless we pass a reasonable campaign finance reform law." To my surprise, the President's remarks were described by the press not as a betrayal, but as an unusually effective argument for reform. Maybe I was being hotheaded. I, too, was annoyed with columnists and investigators who never cared about reform until Bill Clinton had come into the viewfinder, then had declared a holy war. Once again, I persuaded myself that staying and fighting for reform from within was better than leaving—and that, in any case, the broader work of the Clinton administration was of importance to me.

The White House settled into a rat-a-tat-tat of announcements and statements. A "message event" of the day. Each one with an element of news—issuing an executive order, announcing the results of a study, setting a regulation, passing out grants. In previous administrations, many of these had been the province of cabinet secretaries or their underlings.

In part, this was the strategy that had first been implemented during the Morris Regency. It was a way of showing the public that Bill Clinton was working on issues that counted, issues that might be derided in Washington as "small" but that mattered a lot to ordinary citizens. It was a way of showing that the era of big government might have ended, but the era of activist government had not.

It was also a way of holding controversy at bay. Ronald Reagan's administration had found it could manipulate the media by repeating a carefully honed message, over and over, in front of constantly varying and stirring backdrops. A flag. Schoolchildren. A really big flag. The repeti-

tion—and the striking visual imagery—conveyed a powerful message as surely as a Madison Avenue advertising strategy could. That would not work in the competitive, overheated media environment of the 1990s. I would constantly ask speechwriters, "What's the AP lead?" Hard news, no matter how minuscule, would force the press to cover the thrust of the President's remarks. We had to commit news or news would be done to us.

And the real work was going on in the budget negotiations with the Congress. Immediately after the inauguration, the White House had sent word that our position on Medicare would shift—that we would be willing to accept deeper cuts than would have been anticipated during the government shutdown or election campaign. This risked confirming the charge that the "Mediscare" tactics of the year before had been mere demagoguery. But maneuvering was beginning in earnest that could lead to a balanced budget. That required signals, conciliation, and secrecy. And a host of administration priorities—including education funding, health care, and other matters—would be folded into the talks.

Mark Katz was a joke writer from New York who was paid by the DNC to write humorous material for the President. He had been a researcher for Michael Dukakis (well known for his light touch!), and had then set up shop as the Soundbite Institute, writing jokes for politicians. With large, sad eyes, he looked a bit like Fozzie Bear, the comedian on *The Muppet Show*. Managing Katz, keeping him happy, keeping his name out of the newspaper, was one of my jobs. In the spring of 1997, as was the case every year, Clinton was due to be the guest of honor at so-called humor dinners held in hotel ballrooms in Washington. Members of the media would gather to give each other awards and be entertained by the President and other politicians. Once, these dinners were clubby affairs, reflecting the capital of "protocol, alcohol, and Geritol." Though Presidents spoke, they were not expected to be particularly funny. (It was in a speech to the Alfalfa Club that President Theodore Roosevelt had denounced scandal-seeking journalists as "the man with the muckrake"—and the name "muckraker" entered the lexicon.) Now, as with everything else, presidents were expected to perform: to do comedy, Borscht Belt routines satirizing themselves and everyone around them. In the first year, Clinton had ad-libbed at the dinners and had come off sounding bitter. After that, he worked diligently with Katz and the speechwriters, writing jokes and polishing and memorizing his routine.

These dinners were a useful moment to defuse with humor whatever controversy was festering. That spring, we tried to "lance the boil" of the fundraising scandals with humor. "The bad news is, our only child is going off to college," Clinton told the White House Correspondents Dinner. "The good news is, it opens up another bedroom." At another dinner, we

recruited Darrell Hammond, the actor from *Saturday Night Live* who regularly parodied Clinton, to play his "clone." Hammond arrived the afternoon of the dinner, made up and dressed as Clinton. Apparently, he had spent endless hours watching Clinton's every move. More exciting than meeting Clinton was meeting Clinton's speech coach, Michael Sheehan, and all of us. "I love it when he does this!" he said, chopping the air. "And this!" He made some other hand gesture. "And remember, during the '94 State of the Union, when he did this thing?" He pouted and waved his arms in some fashion memorable to him but indistinguishable to the rest of us. "I have a question. Does he do this?" He slapped the podium in a particular way. We were staring at him, dumbfounded. Finally, Sheehan realized that he was supposed to answer. "Um, sure. Sure, he does that." Hammond practically exploded with joy. "I *knew* it!"

But Clinton's favorite routine of the whole year—one of his favorites during all the years he delivered these speeches—mocked his own obsession with history, with the train of presidents and his place in it. In the first read-through, when a script was presented to him in the Oval Office, he laughed silently to himself, as a half dozen aides looked on anxiously, then laughed louder and louder. "This is goooood," he said.

"It is hard to ignore the deliberations of history's jury," he told the Alfalfa Dinner—an off-the-record, white-tie gathering of self-styled power brokers. "So we're going to be more proactive about managing our place in history. This week at the White House, we operationalized something called the Posterity War Room. . . . My media team is busy putting together spots that will go negative on James Buchanan and Warren Harding. Bring 'em down a peg."

A fact sheet had been faxed to supporters, he told them. "Bill Clinton reduced crime on our streets; Thomas Jefferson's vice president shot a guy! Bill Clinton signed more nuclear disarmament agreements than James Madison, Andrew Jackson, and James K. Polk, combined. Bill and Hillary Clinton have made more of an effort than FDR to seek the counsel of Eleanor Roosevelt."

For all the self-mockery, Clinton believed that his place in history would in part be measured by a subject that had absorbed him from his first days in politics: race. And in the spring of 1997, he prepared to launch a full-throated effort to bridge racial divides—a presidential initiative on race. It would demonstrate how hard it was to tackle massive problems at a placid moment.

FIFTEEN

RACE:
BACKGROUND MUSIC

ONE DAY THAT SPRING, I slipped into a meeting in the Cabinet Room that had been called to discuss themes for the launching of the President's race initiative. Clinton was talking about stereotyping. He ran through the stereotypes applied to Hispanics and Asian-Americans. Hillary interjected that poor whites face stereotyping as well. The President agreed. "Truth and reconciliation are about more than race. We have all kinds of prejudices we haven't thought about. It's not just race. It's not just race. There are other kinds of cancers eating away at our society."

It was earnest though not exactly focused. I was relieved that my services appeared unneeded.

The one thing everybody knew was that Bill Clinton was at his most eloquent, most persuasive, most morally commanding when it came to race. He had been shaped, growing up, by the civil rights struggle around him. In 1992, on the eve of the Democratic convention, Bill Moyers asked him in a PBS interview, is there any issue on which he would never compromise? "Racial justice," he had answered.

Clinton also knew that racial division, more than any other single factor, had kept Democrats from the White House. He knew what Lyndon Johnson had said to Moyers the night he signed the Civil Rights Act: "I think we just delivered the South to the Republican Party for a long time to come." LBJ was right. Beginning with Richard Nixon's Southern Strategy in 1968, the national Republican Party had pounded away at race, sometimes openly, sometimes with code words, seeking to put a black face on social problems. Over a quarter century, first the White House, and then

ultimately the Congress, became Republican as southerners switched en masse.*

Clinton did not shrink from condemning racism or discrimination. But he was influenced by the sociologist William Julius Wilson, an African-American academic who argued that the most important issues of race were no longer principally those of raw prejudice, that they were issues of opportunity, of jobs and education and health care — of class more than color. Broad programs such as national health care, which helped the white middle class while helping poor minorities even more, could unite people across economic and racial lines. Clinton was determined to show he could speak the same language of responsibility to working-class whites and to blacks. During the Michigan primary campaign in 1992, he had spoken in Macomb County, the home of the Reagan Democrats who had fled Detroit and their ancestral political party, and in inner-city Detroit on the same day. To the white suburbanites, he scolded: you must cleanse yourselves of the racist attitudes of the 1980s. To the inner-city audience, he said: you can not simply blame racism for the cultural problems of the inner city. This was more than a political parlor trick. This language re-wove the cross-racial coalition that had been the heart of the Democratic Party.

It was widely recognized that Clinton's single most powerful speech as president had been delivered in November 1993 from the pulpit in Memphis where Martin Luther King Jr. had told parishioners he had "been to the mountaintop" in April 1968, the night before he was assassinated. He imagined what King might say in 1993. " 'You did a good job,' he would say, 'voting and electing people who formerly were not electable because of the color of their skin. . . . You did a good job in opening opportunity.'

> But, he would say, I did not live and die to see the American fam-
> ily destroyed. I did not live and die to see thirteen-year-old boys
> get automatic weapons and gun down nine-year-olds just for the
> kick of it. I did not live and die to see young people destroy their
> own lives with drugs and then build fortunes destroying the lives
> of others. That is not what I came here to do. I fought for free-
> dom, he would say, but not for the freedom of people to kill each
> other with reckless abandon, not for the freedom of children to
> have children and the fathers of the children walk away from
> them and abandon them as if they don't amount to anything. . . .
> My fellow Americans, he would say, I fought to stop white people

* During that time the only two Democrats to win the White House were southerners: Carter and Clinton.

from being so filled with hate that they would wreak violence on black people. I did not fight for the right of black people to murder other black people with reckless abandon.

Clinton had returned to the subject sporadically during his presidency. In 1995, his speech on affirmative action at the National Archives, calling on Congress to "mend it, don't end it," was credited with helping to save it. In October of that year, he gave a brilliant speech in Austin, Texas, on the same day as the self-help Million Man March organized by Louis Farrakhan, calling on whites and blacks alike to take responsibility and shun racism.

As his second term approached, Clinton was clearly eager to say more, to do more. Repeatedly, he noted that within fifty years, the United States would no longer have a single majority race. Indeed, during Clinton's first term immigration was at the highest level it had been in a century, the highest since the days Europeans thronged Ellis Island and changed the country. "Entitlements aren't our biggest challenge," he said impatiently in the Oval Office one day as we prepared for the inaugural address. "Managing our diverse culture is."

One evening, at the weekly strategy session in the residence, Clinton mulled a proposal to appoint a panel, modeled on the Kerner Commission, that would look at the problems of diversity and race relations.* Politically, one goal was to cement the support of Hispanics and Asians, who had swung to the Democrats decisively in the last election. Clinton seized on it, and the race initiative was born. Of course, it would be announced in a speech—a commencement address at the University of California at San Diego, on June 14.

The preparation for this address was a formal and massive affair, reflecting the literal-minded approach of the new chief of staff, Erskine Bowles, a former business executive. The prospect of presidential attention to the subject had energized many of the administration's supporters, and the White House was deluged with suggestions and warnings. A variety of overlapping committees—for outreach, for planning, for communications—met regularly. Each was plotted with exquisite attention to the sensitivities of staff members and constituency groups. Civil rights leaders met with Clinton to offer their advice. Reporters were invited for long inter-

---

* The Kerner Commission was appointed by President Johnson to look into the causes of the riots that tore through American cities in 1967. It was filled with prominent current officeholders, starting with Governor Otto Kerner of Illinois. It memorably declared that America was "moving toward two societies, one black, one white—separate but unequal," and urged an ambitious series of programs to address race and poverty. Three decades later, few of its recommendations have been implemented.

views. Throughout, the press was told that the speech would be a land-mark, a breakthrough, a signal moment for Clinton and his legacy.

But while Clinton's speeches on race had spoken in a fresh voice, the emerging race initiative took a far more lumbering, traditional route. Much of the policy and speechwriting staff was excluded from the preparation for the speech. I was not invited to the meetings. Neither was Bruce Reed, the domestic policy advisor. Two speechwriters were included and were eager to work on the speech. Carolyn Curiel, the first Latino speech-writer, had been on the White House staff since the early days and had worked on the Memphis speech and the affirmative action address. She would soon be nominated as the United States ambassador to Belize. She and Terry Edmonds worked arduously on a draft.

From a distance, though, I sensed things were not going well. Edmonds and Curiel were confronting vexing issues. Was the core issue still the oldest one—the history of racism against African-Americans? Or did Hispanics, Asians, and other minorities face similar discrimina-tion? Was the glass half empty or half full? A few days before the speech, I received an urgent summons to Rahm Emanuel's office. A group of senior staff members were there. "You have to get involved in this," came a stern instruction from Hillary Clinton's chief of staff, Melanne Verveer. "Uh-uh, I haven't been involved up to now, how can I be expected to jump in now?" I knew they were right—especially since Edmonds was going to have to leave on a longstanding commitment to move his daughter into college.

The President asked me to come over to the residence for a quiet chat. He was having his hair cut in a tiny barbershop off a stairwell halfway be-tween the first and second floors. It is an odd thing to see that famous face with the bouffant of hair suddenly slicked back and flat. He didn't really like the draft, he said, which I recognized was his ritualistic way of saying, it's time to get started. As a razor buzzed and a barber snipped, he went through the draft. "It's almost as if the longer it is, the worse it is," he said. (I wasn't sure if he meant the speech or his hair.) For this speech, there would be no triangulation. He wanted to say how America's promise had been constantly undercut by racism. "We were born with a Declaration of Inde-pendence proclaiming that it is self-evident that we are all created equal— and a Constitution that enshrined slavery. We fought in a bloody civil war to abolish that slavery, preserved the union, but remained a house unequal and divided for another century. We pushed the Native Americans off their lands and into reservations, often crushing their culture and destroying their livelihoods." And so on. As he read his notes so that they could be typed into a speech draft, I thought that it was a good thing, a remarkable thing, in fact, that the President of the United States understood these

thoughts, let alone wanted to express them. I also worried that it risked sounding like a tiresome guilt trip.

The speech was scheduled for Saturday. I began to work on a draft on Friday morning, as my assistant packed up my files and laptop. I carried them into a minivan, loaded with staff and dignitaries, and typed on the drive through Maryland to Andrews Air Force Base. I switched to the on-board office for the five-hour flight to California, feeding sections to Clinton in his office at the front of the plane, receiving his extensive edits, and trying to put them together. I worked in the motorcade to the hotel in San Diego. And I kept typing all night. By the time of the speech, I had been typing for nearly twenty-four hours straight.

We worked at the sprawling, shingled Hotel Del Coronado on the Pacific Ocean, where Marilyn Monroe had cavorted on the beach in *Some Like It Hot*. Sylvia Mathews, coordinating the trip and determined to squeeze the last ounce of input from every possible source, proposed that all the advisors and cabinet members who had traveled with Clinton systematically edit the speech, line by line. Harvard Law School professor Chris Edley, who was guiding the race initiative's policy, transportation secretary Rodney Slater, labor secretary Alexis Herman, White House aides Bob Nash, Janice Kearney, and Minyon Moore, and I sat around a hotel room. I squatted on the floor, trying to keep up with their proposed changes.

Then, mercifully, word came that the President wanted to see us. Slater, Edley, Curiel, Mathews, and I bolted for his room. On yellow paper, in tight, unreadable scrawl, he had written out a dozen or so new pages. A new speech. (At least it short-circuited the editing session.)

I walked back to the workroom. I struggled to transcribe Clinton's text, page by page, banging on the mouse on my balky laptop. Edley sat with me. Chris was brainy, ebullient, and openly scornful of New Democrat politics. More important to me at this moment, he was willing to stay up late. We sat and tried to read Clinton's handwriting. Whenever my eyes began to close, Chris would poke me in the ribs. By three in the morning, we had mostly entered Clinton's new draft, a first draft, wordy and repetitive. I began to worry seriously that nobody would be alert enough to edit it and polish the prose.

There was a tap on my shoulder. The President had come down from his room in shorts and a T-shirt. "You know, I thought about it, and our earlier draft is better. Forget this stuff. Just stick with the other draft." I was vastly relieved. Edley and I finished as the sun came up.

In the event, the speech posed a series of questions. "We know what we will look like, but what will we be like? Can we be one America respecting, even celebrating our differences, but embracing even more what

we have in common?" The only policy passage of any heft came on the topic of affirmative action. The previous year, California voters had enacted a referendum ending state government affirmative action. The State Regents had ended affirmative action at the state university system, and as a result, African-American admissions at Boalt Law School at Berkeley were down 80 percent. Clinton said, "I know that the people of California voted to repeal affirmative action without any ill motive. The vast majority of them simply did it with a conviction that discrimination and isolation are no longer barriers to achievement. But consider the results," he concluded. "We must not resegregate higher education."

"Honest dialogue will not be easy at first," Clinton told the large crowd on a low flat field. "We'll all have to get past defensiveness and fear and political correctness and other barriers to honesty. Emotions may be rubbed raw, but we must begin."

He announced the formation of a new advisory board—One America in the 21st Century: The President's Initiative on Race. (Even this locution was fraught. The "race initiative" referred to the problems of black and white, in apposition to "One America," with its broad sense of ethnic diversity.) To lead it, he chose John Hope Franklin, one of America's most esteemed historians. Franklin's signal work on race had been completed a *half century* before.

Within minutes after the commencement speech, answering a reporter's question, Clinton became mired in the sticky issue of whether or not the United States should issue an apology for slavery. He said he needed time to study it. The initiative itself, housed several blocks from the White House, got off to a slow start, and was staffed with people who had never worked for Clinton (and didn't seem particularly familiar with his views). The panel pointedly excluded critics of affirmative action, such as University of California regent Ward Connerly, from its early fact-finding sessions. When Clinton himself moderated a town meeting, the room was so filled with supportive people that he had to ask for other views. The enterprise was at risk of suffocating in its own pillow of political correctness.

Ronald Brownstein, a columnist for the *Los Angeles Times* who has always been one of the most perceptive chroniclers of Clinton, wrote a regretful article, saying that the race initiative marked Clinton's "journey toward convention on race."

The desegregation of Little Rock Central High School, when Bill Clinton was eleven years old, had been one of the shattering experiences of his youth. In September 1957, nine black schoolchildren, seeking to attend the imposing brick high school, were turned away by a jeering, spitting mob. President Dwight Eisenhower was forced to send in the army to conduct the children to school. Clinton had agreed to attend the anniversary of

the school's desegregation. It was never at question. He was friends with some of the former students, when he was governor. Ernie Green, one of the children who were turned away, was an investment banker and a pivotal supporter.

Terry Edmonds, whom I had appointed my deputy, was looking forward to working on the speech Clinton would give at that occasion. It was the speech he had been waiting to write his entire life, he told me. A product of the projects in Baltimore, an alumnus of an all-black college, Terry had a breadth of experience very rare for the more pampered speechwriters with whom he worked. The President loved his writing. "Every time you write something for me, it makes me want to sing," Clinton told him one day.

Terry traveled to Little Rock, met with students at the high school, talked to officials and got a sense of the physical surroundings. He was gathering his thoughts for a burst of writing—what would undoubtedly have been an eloquent and passionate speech. Four days before the ceremony, the unthinkable happened. Terry's wife, Angie, developed a serious illness. He abruptly stopped working on the speech (and soon left the White House, though he returned, and when I left he became my successor).

We had little written and no sense from the President of what he wanted to say. I began to write. June Shih, our newest speechwriter, was eager to help. She was twenty-five, first-generation Chinese-American, a product of sheltered schools and Harvard. June wrote beautiful, crystal prose, but I had been reluctant to hire her because she seemed so shy, so terrified of me and other authority figures. Now, she burrowed with files on the Little Rock incident, borrowed from a reporter friend. She handed me some paragraphs she had written, paragraphs that could begin the speech. They were breathtaking. "Forty years ago, a single image first seared the heart and stirred the conscience of our nation; so powerful most of us who saw it then recall it still. A fifteen-year-old girl wearing a crisp black-and-white dress, carrying only a notebook, surrounded by large crowds of boys and girls, men and women, soldiers and police officers, her head held high, her eyes fixed straight ahead.

"And she is utterly alone."

I wove those lines into a fabric of America's struggle for its own ideals. It touched down at Independence Hall and Gettysburg. "Like them, Little Rock is historic ground. For, surely it was here at Central High that we took another giant step close to the idea of America." We churned away and sent a draft in after a few hours' work.

The afternoon before the speech, in the conference room of Air Force One, an ad hoc committee of staff and advisors picked at the speech as we flew away from Washington toward Little Rock.

"This, here," said one staff member. "Where it says, we are all Americans, 'whether we came here in a ship to Ellis Island or on a 747 to LAX.' We can't say that. It feeds the image of rich Asians."

"That's how you get here from China," June sputtered. "That's how my father came here from China! He wasn't rich."

Line by line, individuals identified words that might offend, lines that might actually challenge the listener. June began to breathe heavily. "Just look at my pen," I whispered to her. "Look at my pen." She glanced sideways. "The cap is on. Just 'cause they're saying it, doesn't mean that I'm writing it."

Meanwhile, in his office at the front of the plane, Clinton was already back in Arkansas. He was relaxing with Rodney Slater, Bob Nash, and Carroll Willis, a DNC official—three African-American aides from Arkansas. He was growing visibly more comfortable, teasing, reminiscing, avoiding serious discussion of the speech. With every mile, his accent deepened and he relaxed.

Across the street from the Excelsior Hotel is Arkansas' tallest building, the TCBY Tower. The state Democratic Party rented an office for the President there. It had sat forlornly for four years. This was the first time Clinton had set foot in it. Elderly volunteers stood proud as he came through. We met in the conference room to discuss the speech. Clinton had invited Ernie Green, John Hope Franklin, Secretaries Herman and Slater, and a host of other friends and advisors. "Speak from the heart." "Just put your heart into it." "Tell your story." Clinton drank in their affirmation. "Do you really think so?"

Franklin reminisced about growing up in West Virginia. It was growing late, and we still had not spoken to the President about the speech. Nancy Hernreich and Alexis Herman exchanged pointed glances as they tried to figure out—through raised eyebrows and slight tilts of the head—how to extract the President from the room. At Nancy's signal, I excused myself and went into an adjoining office. A minute later Clinton came in. He wanted to make sure that the former student, whose dramatic story was recounted at the beginning of the speech, would not mind being singled out. Alexis Herman volunteered to find out. "Look," he said to me. "Just take what the people here said tonight, take the best stuff. Type them up as bullet points. I'll figure out what to do with them."

June and I went back to the hotel room that was being used as a staff office, and began working at about 10 P.M. Bullet points? We couldn't believe that was actually what the President wanted us to do. Instead, we set about incorporating the best one-liners and arguments into the speech. At eleven, one of the guards where the President was staying called. Where were the talking points? "He actually wants talking points," I moaned to

June. We scrambled to organize them on paper. We faxed them to Clinton but told him that we would have a new draft for him when he awoke. By 2 A.M., we were done—drowsy but exultant. The phone rang.

"Please hold for the President."

"Hi, Mike. I couldn't sleep. So I did a lot of work on it. Can you come over?" *Can I come over? Nah, I'm tired.*

"Certainly, Mr. President. We'll be right there."

Right *where?* He was staying, I knew, at his mother-in-law's house, somewhere in West Little Rock. We called the room of the advance person who should know and got no answer. June ran down and knocked on his door frantically. With June on one extension and me on another, we dialed to the military, to the Secret Service, to the hotel front desk. We took the glass elevator down to the empty lobby. Our choice was painful: wait for a police car or grab a cab.

In front of the hotel there was an old yellow jalopy. We leapt into the backseat, breathless. "We need to go to Mrs. Rodham's house. The President's mother-in-law. Where the President is. Do you know where that is?" The cabdriver thought for a moment. "Naw."

June hopped out, dashed into the hotel. She returned a minute later with directions.

I pulled out a twenty-dollar bill and held it aloft, doing my best arrogant city-slicker routine. "Mrs. Rodham's house. And there's $20 in it for you if you get there *fast!*" The driver looked at me. The cab jolted forward and settled into an uneven crawl, apparently the fastest it could go, stopping for yellow lights. I aged in the backseat as it wended its way through suburban streets. At one point the driver pulled over and consulted a road map. Finally, he pulled up near the Secret Service checkpoints that blocked off a cul-de-sac. He seemed alarmed by all the police presence. I gave him the $20 and he sped off.

Inside the small condominium, which Clinton had bought for his mother-in-law, the President, in a lavender Hope Watermelon Festival T-shirt, was at the kitchen table. Books about the Little Rock Nine and photocopied magazine articles were spread out. He had just talked to his daughter, Chelsea, who was in her first weeks at Stanford two time zones earlier. "She said she knew I would be up," he said proudly. He had borrowed a passage from a newspaper article. He showed us the circled paragraph and instructed, "Let the reporter know." We had left a gap for him to fill in with a first-person account of his memories of the crisis. He read to us.

> As Melba [Patillo Beals] said years later in her wonderful memoir, *Warriors Don't Cry,* "My friends and I paid for the integration of Little Rock Central High with our innocence."

Folks, in 1957, I was eleven years old, living fifty miles away in Hot Springs, when the eyes of the world were fixed here. Like almost all southerners then, I never attended school with a person of another race until I went to college. But as a young boy in my grandfather's small grocery store, I learned lessons that nobody bothered to teach me in my segregated school. My grandfather had a sixth-grade education from a tiny rural school. He never made a bit of money. But in that store, in the way he treated his customers and encouraged me to play with their children, I learned America's most profound lessons: We really are all equal. We really do have the right to live in dignity. We really do have the right to be treated with respect. We do have the right to be heard.

I never knew how he and my grandmother came to those convictions, but I'll never forget how they lived them. Ironically, my grandfather died in 1957. He never lived to see America come around to his way of thinking. But I know he's smiling down today not on his grandson, but on the Little Rock Nine, who gave up their innocence so all good people could have a chance to live their dreams.

But let me tell you something else that was true about that time. Before Little Rock, for me and other white children, the struggles of black people, whether we were sympathetic or hostile to them, were mostly background music in our normal, self-absorbed lives. We were all, like you, more concerned about our friends and our lives, day in and day out. But then we saw what was happening in our own backyard, and we all had to deal with it. Where did we stand? What did we believe? How did we want to live? It was Little Rock that made racial equality a driving obsession in my life.

"Background music." It was a beautiful image in a powerful passage. Our enthusiasm was unfeigned. We retreated as quickly as we could and incorporated his revisions into the draft.

A few hours later, we waited for the President at the foot of the driveway, an incongruous sight of a full presidential motorcade snaking around a suburban cul-de-sac, with agents talking into their sleeves and staff members striking casual poses. He continued to work on the speech in the car.

"What do you think of this line—'Nothing that must be, can be, for free.' Do you think I should say that?"

"No, I don't," I said. "It's the kind of thing that might look good on

paper, but you'll regret it later. Like 'Nothing big ever came from being small.' " Oops. Clinton glowered at me and returned to his editing.

The last session was in the principal's office at Little Rock Central High School—surely one of the more striking locales to watch a president prepare a challenge on racism. The most controversial part of the speech was a strong denunciation of "voluntary segregation," the common tendency of white and black students to separate themselves from one another. Now Clinton was chewing it over one more time. "I'm not comfortable with this." He pointed at a key passage. "Today children of every race walk through the same door, but then they often walk down different halls. Not only in this school but across America, they sit in different classrooms, they eat at different tables. They even sit in different parts of the bleachers at the football game. . . . We retreat into the comfortable enclaves of ethnic isolation. Segregation is no longer the law, but too often, separation is still the rule." The idea had been suggested by Edley, but I had run it past centrist Democrats as well. I reported to him that I thought it would be fine.

Clinton returned to the text. He wrote in, "And we cannot forget one stubborn fact that has not yet been said as clearly as it should. There is still discrimination in America."

The ceremony was remarkably moving. The huge, fortress-like high school must have been frightening to those young boys and girls, now middle aged. As he spoke, Clinton was interrupted by hecklers who were protesting local policies. The Republican governor, a minister, denounced segregation as a sin. A parade of officials thanked the civil rights veterans. A crowd of black and white high school students looked on. Then, in a bit of ceremony that seems hokey on paper but was thrilling to watch, the Little Rock Nine walked up the steps to the front door of the high school. This time, the door was held for them by a Democratic president and a conservative Republican governor. Several of them buckled with emotion as they reached the portal. I was crying, too.

In November, Clinton convened another meeting on race in the Cabinet Room. The initiative was dragging on. He was unhappy that he had not been presented with more aggressive policy initiatives to match the rhetoric.

To prepare for the meeting, all sides had readied their arguments. Bruce Reed had sent a memo citing William Julius Wilson to urge a return to Clinton's original cross-racial approach. "The best hope for improving race relations and reducing racial disparities over the long term is a set of policies that extend opportunities across race lines and, in doing so, force the recognition of shared interests. These policies—for example, educa-

tion opportunity zones, university-school mentoring programs, housing vouchers, and community policing and prosecuting initiatives—address the concerns of working people of all races at the same time as they provide especial benefits to racial minorities." Chris Edley's memo argued instead for a sharper focus on race, especially the cultural issues of racism and racial separation. "The greatest obstacles we face in creating One America are the fault lines of color that in many ways still divide our communities, minds and hearts. . . . We cannot move forward without addressing the *separation and exclusion* that weaken us."

The first part of the meeting devolved into an endless discussion of scheduling and media opportunities. Then Clinton steered it to policy. "I really liked Chris' memo," he said. "I agreed with it." He summarized it, reciting the arguments of the memo submitted by Reed. "That clears everything up," the person next to me muttered. The meeting broke up.

The President continued to soar above his own race initiative, speaking out repeatedly and clearly on race. By facing America's hardest issue at a placid time, his words would have the effect of making presidential talk on race seem the norm. Bearing witness against racism now seems like part of the job. The initiative itself finally closed up shop in September 1998. Plainly, it had not sparked a transforming national conversation on race— probably, it never could have.

The letdown—and lack of clarity—of the race initiative was a symptom of a deeper malady. The project of restoring confidence in government, of working with the Republicans to achieve a balanced budget, was drawing to a close. And in the closing months of 1997, in a little-noted moment of indecision, the Democratic Party faced severe split.

SIXTEEN

DEMOCRATS DIVIDED

On May 2, 1997, the President spoke at the dedication of the new memorial to Franklin Delano Roosevelt, on the Mall in Washington. Surrounded by members of the Roosevelt family, historians, and veterans of the New Deal and World War II, Clinton honored the man who launched the federal government's massive efforts to improve the lives of the majority of Americans.

I couldn't go to the ceremony. I was scrambling to write an announcement, due in a few hours, that a balanced budget agreement had been reached with the Republicans—an emphatic exclamation point on the end of the era of big government, as had been proclaimed in 1996. A seemingly glum Clinton made his statement at a Democratic Party retreat in Maryland, surrounded by glum senators.

In fact, the agreement was a win for his strategy of co-opting the Republicans on the matter of the budget. The anguish over backing the principle of a balanced budget only two years before now seemed quaint. In a stroke, the 1997 agreement wrote into law many of the major goals he had set out in the previous year's campaign. It boosted education spending dramatically, including a tax cut that would pay for nearly all community college tuition, in effect using the tax code to create a new entitlement to a college education. It was the biggest single federal investment in higher education since the GI Bill after World War II. The agreement fixed many of the flaws that Clinton had criticized in the welfare reform bill, restoring disability and health benefits to legal immigrants, and spending $3 billion to encourage companies to hire those who move off the relief rolls. It sharply expanded health insurance for poor children, the first significant

widening of health care coverage to pass the Congress during Clinton's term, with a new program, run by the states, that provides health care for children in families with incomes too high to qualify for Medicaid and too low to afford private insurance.* At the same time, the Republicans won an array of tax cuts. Both sides quietly agreed to Medicare reductions as well. At the same time all this was being done, the job of eliminating the deficit, which Clinton had begun at such political cost in 1993 was being finished. Most Democrats voted for the measure, as did most Republicans. This was the culmination of his strategy of reaching out, of being a "repairer of the breach." By August, when Clinton signed the final bill into law, his mood was far more expansive. "The sun is rising on America," he proclaimed.

The second-term White House had settled into a rather placid middle age. Meetings were orderly, lines of authority were clear, decisions were made on time. The bracing liberal-centrist quarrels of earlier years were over. The President asked two old friends to join the staff as all-purpose advisors: Paul Begala, the ebullient political consultant; and Sidney Blumenthal, the journalist. Both were talented writers, so they could be called on to help on big speeches. The campaign finance hearings on Capitol Hill had closed down when the spotlight turned to abuses by Republican groups as well as Democrats, and now the call from the press and Republicans was for a special prosecutor to probe campaign violations. The Whitewater investigation, having dragged on for nearly four years, seemed somnolent.

But the effort to deflect the Republican thrust and rebuild the Democratic Party that had begun after the 1994 election had run its course. The budget was balanced. So what next? Erskine Bowles launched an elaborate business school–style endeavor known as the Pillars project. The policies of the administration would be clustered into "pillars," categories with a dozen or more priorities hung on each. (Campaign finance was not among them. I complained. It became number 15.)

In the meantime, the President was scheduled to give a speech at American University about the need to get back to work after summer vacation. He outlined his goals for the coming months—a series of educational, trade, and environmental initiatives. (And, yes, campaign reform.) A few days later, we gathered in the residence in the Yellow Oval Room with Clinton and Gore.

Erskine Bowles opened. "This meeting is to discuss choices, and to get your reaction to the pillars. Do we do a little of a lot, or a lot of a little?"

Clinton thanked everyone for their efforts, then discarded them. He had

---

* The limits of minimalist government are evident, too. Many states balked, fearing that they would be caught without enough funds in the next recession. As of spring 2000, 2 million children nationwide had been enrolled in that plan.

some specific goals. Above all else he wanted to concentrate carefully on economic stewardship. "There may be something that happens, there may be a recession, but it ought not be our fault. I don't want to be asleep at the switch." We needed to recognize that the economy was being remade by technology. "And as in all paradigm shifts, power has shifted from labor to capital."

On social policy, Clinton asked for a continued focus on health care, in part an effort to reclaim the political high ground that had been lost in 1994. "Every single step we take removes the stain of having tried to do what we did," and failed. We had to move forward on child care: we have a higher percentage of women working than in Europe, but with "a piss-poor child-care system. The most vivid memory I have of campaigning as governor," he said, "is going, early in the morning, to plants, and seeing one parent drop off the children with another."

He was looking forward to the 2000 elections, he told us. "Anything that has to be done on entitlements has to be done in a bipartisan process—set it up, make sure it gets you the result you want," Clinton said with relish. "On Social Security, it doesn't matter for the integrity of the program if the solution comes in '99, 2000, 2001. But strategically, I want to remove all divisive issues for a conservative candidate, so all the issues are on progressive terrain."

Eventually on to campaign finance. "We all know that this—at least, McCain-Feingold in a broad form—is going to die of a Republican filibuster." We had to make sure people knew it was the GOP's doing. "Now when it dies, then we have to devote our energy to what we can get done." Clinton turned to me. "I just can't understand why the Federal Communications Commission can't just move forward and provide free airtime." (As I had explained to him repeatedly, the chairman of the commission, Reed Hundt, lacked a majority. We were stalling for time until the Senate confirmed new commissioners.)

Now Al Gore cleared his throat. The Vice President was carefully dressed in casual clothes—cowboy boots, olive pants, a brown shirt. "One word that doesn't jump at me in these documents is 'values.' And if you were in a room full of Republicans doing the same thing, that would be number one on their list." That's what campaign reform is about, he noted, as well as all the proposals on culture. He thought also that we were further along than we realized toward a "New Economy" transformed by computers. There is now a realization of the new importance of markets and the international economy—"a new maturity for progressives. If government is going to play a progressive role, it cannot try to manhandle reality and wrestle it to the ground."

It was striking to see the differences between Clinton and Gore. Both were committed wonks who enjoyed the arcana of policy. The President would often leap to the political consequences, doing a mental "cross-tabs"

of demographic trends, polls, electoral votes, and congressional committee jurisdictions. One might cringe at first, but soon one realized that his dexterity was so sure that he could squeeze issues into the modeling clay of a practicing politician without losing them. Gore's approach was more formal, more professorial, more linear. Here he was talking about how globalization was pulling power to the global level and the local level, threatening the central role of the nation-state.

When my turn came, I said, "I urge you to consider the possibility of speaking less. You would have a greater chance of being heard more if you spoke less. FDR spoke only eight times during the first hundred days of the New Deal. They didn't try to make message events out of Rose Garden events." Bowles seconded. "You can't imagine the strain on the policy staff of these events." "I strongly agree," added Gore.

Clinton leaned forward. The years of controversy and investigations clearly rankling, his eyes were flashing. "We live in a *crazy* environment!" He spoke slowly, emphasizing each syllable. "FDR did *not* have someone trying to put him in *jail*. If someone could find a way to come to me and say, you don't have to do *one more mind-numbing event*, I would jump at it. But it's like fundraising. Sometimes you just have to do it."

Podesta changed the subject. Presumably, 1998 was to be peaceful, productive, and scandal-free. We could tamp down the volume of public appearances then. "Let's try this next year."

As THE ADMINISTRATION groped toward priorities and pondered how to articulate them, the congressional Democrats were getting and staying mad. After "triangulation," welfare reform, the 1996 elections, and the balanced budget agreement, the rank and file of Democratic members of Congress were fed up. Now they would take out their wrath in a fight with the administration over international trade. By late fall, an open break between the congressional Democrats and the White House threatened.

At issue was the President's request that Congress grant him "fast track" authority for trade agreements. Fast track, in effect, gives presidents the ability to negotiate trade pacts, especially multilateral agreements that bind many products and many nations, and then send them to Congress for an up or down vote. No amendments are possible, the argument goes, because other nations will not negotiate with the United States if Congress can then rewrite the pact. Presidents have been given the authority for decades. Usually, Congress granted it in anticipation of a specific trade deal. This time, though, Clinton's advisors persuaded him to request it without its being tied to a specific pact. He needed fast track, they argued. It was an insult to his executive authority not to have it.

The fact is that Clinton had been drifting toward this particular confrontation with the Democratic Party for four years. When he endorsed
NAFTA in 1992, he had done so only on the condition that side agreements protecting labor and the environment be appended to the agreement. He had hoped that this compromise would win the support of
Richard Gephardt and other lawmakers sympathetic to labor. But
Gephardt had led the fight against. And after the Republicans won control
of Congress, Clinton had appeared to calculate that the only way to win
trade fights was to discard the liberal approach and fight on the grounds of
pure free trade. He needed Republican votes. To get them, he made Republican arguments. In the years since NAFTA, as the economy had
grown, trade had played an increasingly central role. By 1997, it accounted
for fully one third of the country's economic expansion.

Fast track was in trouble. A patchy schedule of public appearances was
arranged, a mini–war room was set up, exemptions and projects were offered to wavering lawmakers. Since there was no specific trade agreement,
few corporations caught the scent of profit—and did little lobbying. Some
of the promises that had been made in 1993 to pass NAFTA had not been
kept. My staff wrote speeches that the President on the whole discarded. He
was increasingly annoyed that he was being asked to make orthodox arguments for free trade. He handed Bowles a heavily marked up copy of a book
by the economist Dani Rodrik, *Has Globalization Gone Too Far?*

A critical moment came when Clinton went up to the Democratic
Caucus in the House of Representatives to try to persuade skeptical lawmakers. This one, I wanted to see. I wrote some talking points largely so
that I could go along for the ride.

The Democrats were reminded of their minority status in Congress as
they crowded into a low-ceilinged, fluorescent-lit room. Clinton looked
like a college president facing an angry janitorial staff. He gave a meandering, almost apologetic pitch for fast track. He understood why some of
them would be against it, he said. He understood why it was difficult. But
they had to give him this tool to create jobs. This time, the famous Clinton
soft sell wasn't working.

Congresswoman Marcy Kaptur, representing an industrial district in
Ohio and fiercely opposed to free trade, was one of the first to rise. Fast
track is a constitutional issue, she rapped out flatly. The trade deficit over
the past year was the largest in the country's history. In fact, the gross domestic product would be one point greater if there were no trade deficit.
Clinton could brag about creating jobs. Sure, there were jobs. But what
were the jobs? "My neighbor works at Kmart, then sweeps the floor, then
sells boat covers down at the lake on weekends." They don't care about the
multinational corporations at Geneva writing trade rules through the

World Trade Organization. "I'm speaking on behalf of a woman named Wanda," she concluded. Wanda had written to the White House and hadn't gotten an answer. "Why should I believe you?"

Clinton's face hardened. "Every week I sign dozens of letters to people who write me. I could show you the letters we get and the letters we sent. I have kinfolk who are still working two jobs, too." It seemed almost impossible to him to have to explain this—at a time when a Democratic administration had produced real prosperity, when their legislative fortunes rose or fell by the perceived success of the President. His voice rose. "We have a big trade deficit because Ronald Reagan bankrupted the country!" He was almost shouting. "Most countries in the world would give anything to have"—and his voice made quote marks—"the 'terrible problems' we have had over the past four years."

A few weeks later, fast track was withdrawn. Few Democrats supported it, and Gingrich could not—or would not—persuade enough Republicans to give Clinton the victory.

A week after that, Gephardt spoke at the John F. Kennedy School of Government at Harvard. He had voted against the balanced budget and had led the fight against fast track. At the time it was clear that he was itching to run against Gore for the Democratic nomination (the two had been rivals since they faced off in the 1988 presidential campaign). Gephardt assaulted the President in barely disguised terms. "Our people have not failed, but our politics is failing our people. Today, the political process has largely become an echo chamber of petty charges, a parade ground for poll-driven maneuvers. Too often, our leaders seem enamored with small ideas that nibble around the edges of big problems. . . . This will be an era of small issues in our politics only if fearful and calculating politicians make it so."

Clinton and Gore had gotten good news earlier in the day, when Attorney General Janet Reno announced she would not appoint a special prosecutor to probe alleged campaign law violations. Now Gephardt said, "We need a Democratic Party that is a movement of change and a movement for values—and not a money machine." (This was especially galling, given the role the House Democrats played in scuttling reform in 1993.)

As I walked into Rahm Emanuel's office that day, CNN's *Inside Politics* was airing Gephardt's comments. Rahm was concluding a phone call with a *New York Times* political reporter during which he had blasted the Democratic leader. He slammed down the phone, then looked sheepish. "I think I screwed up," he said.

Paul Begala was furious. Deeply loyal to Clinton, he could not understand a party leader like Gephardt turning his fire on his own. Begala had worked for Gephardt. Bob Shrum was Gephardt's chief consultant and political advisor. Begala and Shrum had an angry exchange.

I walked back to my office, slightly bemused by all the snorting and pawing. Then I realized we had a problem. The annual Kennedy Center honors were to take place in a few days. This was a project for the First Lady's office. The First Lady especially fond of Shrum. The producers of the honors program had hired him to write a script for the President's remarks. Usually, we would edit a submission from an outside group a bit, but stick to it when possible. I asked Begala what we should do. I was instructed to tell the Kennedy Center that we were not interested in using their script.

A few minutes later, Shrum called. Did we get the script, how did we like it, did we want any changes? Trying to make clear with my tone that I was acting under instructions, I told him no thanks. "Frankly, Bob, after that speech, I don't think a draft from you would be particularly welcome here right now, among the higher-ups." (I tried to make it sound as if I were a POW reading a statement drafted for me by my captors.) Shrum said that he had not written the speech.

I explained the power game to June Shih. The script was carefully constructed to introduce the film clips of each of the artists being honored. So she needed to rewrite each sentence. "You know how when you were in sixth grade, you rewrote the *World Book Encyclopedia* to write a report on Mexico? That way. Just change every sentence. E-mail it to me, and boldface anything that's still from Shrum." She shot me a look that said, *Men!* and returned to her keyboard.

On Sunday morning, I opened my e-mail, but the boldface had been wiped out. I called June at home. "Look, my computer didn't read the boldface. So can we go, line by line, and you tell me what came from you and what came from Shrum?" "Oh, come on." "Please, just do it." We had gotten halfway through Bob Dylan's introduction when my call waiting beeped. "Hold on."

"Mr. Waldman? This is the White House operator calling. We have the President calling for you."

"Mike?"

"Yes, Mr. President."

"Mike, somebody told me that you told Bob Shrum we didn't want his speech for the Kennedy Center honors."

Do I fudge? Do I risk presidential wrath? "Yes, Mr. President. I was instructed to do so. You know, because of that speech by Gephardt." I waited. Clinton seemed to ponder this for a bit.

"You know, I appreciate that. But Shrum's been good to us, he helped us a lot with the State of the Union and all that. I think we should give him another bite at the apple. If it all blows up, I want to make sure it's Gephardt's fault, not ours."

"Let me make sure I understand. You want me to use Bob's stuff?"

"Yeah. Use as much of it as you can. Thanks. Sorry to bother you on a weekend." Clinton hung up. I clicked back to June, who was on hold.

"Hi, June, are you there? You won't believe this, but . . . that was the President. You need to put back in all of Shrum's stuff and take out all of your stuff." She shrieked. Line by line, we went through the speech again. We took care that the first paragraph was all Shrum.

A few days later, I sat across from the President in a large meeting in the Cabinet Room. Begala, Emanuel, all the boys were there.

"Michael, I just want to say, those Kennedy Center honors remarks were *great*. Your people did a terrific job on them. If the State of the Union is anything like that, we'll be in great shape." Did he realize what he was saying? Did he remember? Only a practiced eye would detect the twinkle. To his political advisors, he was saying: *See, I'm praising what Shrum wrote. Back off.* To me, he was saying: *I know that I'm lauding you in front of everyone for something you didn't write—thanks for playing ball with me.* He was also saying: *Keep Shrum in the loop for the State of the Union.*

Fast track's failure, the fight with Gephardt, the fading of the race initiative—the first year of Clinton's second term was drooping to a close. The balanced budget agreement was a real accomplishment. But the politics of the vital center were tepid. Staff members were planning their departures. There was a *New Yorker* article about all the top aides who were planning to leave (including me). Throughout the year, the President seemed subdued, his normal ebullience tamped down. Perhaps the effort of clawing back from the political ledge over the previous two years had left him exhausted. Certainly he was frustrated by the effort to reach accord with a Republican Congress that hated him and was determined to see him fail.

Clinton roused himself. He had struck out ahead of his fellow party members; now it was time to bring them back together. He was determined to repair the rifts with the congressional Democrats, he was set on forging a common agenda toward the 1998 elections. Now that the budget was balanced, now that welfare was reformed, now that taxes had been cut, he was determined to press for a new and more aggressive role for government. This, at last, was the time to restate the case for progressive government. Clinton was ready to step up to entitlements. And he was determined to speak plainly about the international economy, to build a consensus on trade that pressed both for liberalization and the legitimate fears of Democrats and their constituencies. All of this would be included in the State of the Union address, now scheduled for late January.

The only bump along the way was the deposition that the President was scheduled to give in a civil lawsuit for sexual harassment brought by Paula Corbin Jones.

SEVENTEEN

SAVE
SOCIAL SECURITY
FIRST

THE CABINET ROOM is the grandest stage set in the West Wing—high-backed leather chairs surround a long polished table, light streams in from the Rose Garden, portraits of presidents peer down. For three decades, presidents had sat there with their budget advisors and pondered massive deficits—"deficits," as David Stockman told Ronald Reagan, "as far as the eye can see."

On December 1, 1997, President Clinton and his team settled in to our places to begin shaping the agenda for 1998. It was two months before the plan would be unveiled to the country in the State of the Union. I was there to capture the nuances of the proposals that were taking shape. At one level, this first meeting was routine, acronyms and jargon flowing freely. Clinton worked through the budget decisions attentively, making political asides and cracking jokes, as budget director Frank Raines reported on months of haggling that had pitted OMB against the federal agencies.

But this meeting was anything but routine. As Raines and Gene Sperling made their presentations, it was clear that a new era had arrived with surprising, if pleasant, suddenness. OMB's computers had begun to churn out startling projections: the budget had been balanced, and there would soon be massive surpluses. The balanced budget agreement had been law for only a few months. The economy was still growing at a pace far faster than anyone had imagined. The upper-income tax increase, forced through at such political cost in 1993, was now producing revenue well above projections.

For Clinton, it was another chance for a new beginning. After three years of treading lightly, seeking to rebuild confidence in government, he could propose a more ambitious program. The 1998 State of the Union would be a far-reaching attempt to persuade the public that government could do big things again.

At stake was the fiscal policy that Clinton had advanced in 1993. With rumors that the government would soon be in the black, a massive tax cut had Mack truck momentum on Capitol Hill. The Republican members had made it clear that they would seek to spend the surplus, when it materialized, on tax relief. It would be gone before it arrived. We were worried that Democrats—terrified to vote against a tax cut—would crumble. Already, members of Congress of both parties had attempted to break free of the budget agreement by passing a huge and expensive transportation bill that would be exempt from the budget caps. The President would probably have little choice but to sign it. If that happened, he worried, "We'd be a little bit pregnant," discarding the principle of fiscal discipline just months after the balanced budget.

It was clear that the policy choices were in fact the key decisions for the State of the Union. "You're asking me to write my State of the Union, right here, before I've had a chance to absorb all this," Clinton complained. "Next to a recession, a major foreign screwup, or the discovery of my Swiss bank account [this budget is] one of the major things that could affect the legacy of this administration."

A couple of weeks later, we returned to the Cabinet Room. This was the first formal meeting on the speech itself—the first plumbing of themes. "Mr. President," I began, "we wanted to get your reaction to the memo we've sent you, and to hear your thoughts on the themes for the State of the Union."

Clinton sat across the big table from me. His sharp blue eyes met mine. This would be our moment of intellectual communion. The President. Me. And about fifteen other aides. Seeing the large crowd and realizing that little of substance could be done in such a setting, Clinton began a monologue—an elegant filibuster, really. For much of an hour, he traced the country's history and the role of the presidency and the Democratic Party. He had just read a 700-page biography of John Marshall, the Chief Justice of the United States who established judicial supremacy. *Definer of a Nation*, it called him. Throughout the country's history, Clinton said, one of the parties has been dominant—and it has been the one that stood most strongly for the nation. He was circling around the issue of government and its role.

"Most people are conservative most of the time," he began. "They turn to the progressive party in a time of crisis. Then, that party becomes

less progressive, or people turn to the other party." Throughout history two things mark the progressive party. "First, the importance of the nation, as opposed to its parts. Second, extending the Constitution and the Bill of Rights to meet the challenge of the moment."

Jefferson's words are remembered for their elevation of the individual. "But while in office, he acted like the Federalists." Lincoln, especially, was obsessed with strengthening the nation above all else. "He entered office saying, 'I'll preserve the union if it kills me.' First, union. Only second, slavery. That's why no one quotes his first inaugural address, only his second. This formula was so successful that basically for forty years the Republicans stayed in power, from 1860 through to TR.

"I've been reading about all these presidents in the backwaters of American history," he added. "You know, for a while after the Civil War, if you were a Republican, and from Ohio, and had served in the army, you got to be president." That unbroken string was interrupted only by Democrat Grover Cleveland, an anomaly, and only because he was such a good politician.

"Ever since Wilson, the Democrats have been the party of the nation and the party of the extension of the Constitution." He offered a revealing insight into how he himself had run and won. "JFK was a conservative liberal, the only way a liberal can be elected in America. The people who win are conservative liberals or liberal conservatives. Nixon was a liberal conservative. He played to the right wing, but he was a liberal conservative, passing EPA, OSHA, and so on.

"Then, Reagan was able to cloak a reactionary social agenda with national terms. . . . He did stick up for the nation—he did it in external terms," with a strong foreign policy. In fact, Clinton went on, when the Republicans tried finally to implement Reagan's domestic policies through the Contract With America, they were repudiated by the public—"unmasked," he said.

Clinton had tried to make the Democrats the party of the strong nation again—a restoration he traced back to Robert Kennedy's presidential run in 1968. "From RFK in Indiana [where he appealed both to working-class whites and blacks] to Carter to Gary Hart to me, there has been a constant attempt to redefine the party. We took what Bobby Kennedy was trying to do in Indiana in 1968, and we pulled it off."

With the budget in balance, Clinton was now ready to draw a clear line between Democrats and Republicans. The Republicans, he said, with their radically individualist notions, no longer talked about strengthening the nation, as they had even when Ronald Reagan was president. "We have to make it clear. There was a meaningful break in 1992. If we don't do it here, we will never get it done. If the GOP gets back in, if they control the presidency, the Congress, the courts, all three branches—they will dramat-

ically erode the ability of this nation to hold together. Global corporate interests that don't give a damn about America will run the country."

As the year drew to a close, Clinton fished around for possible themes, only to throw them back in the water. In a speech before the Democratic Leadership Council, he called for a "new social contract" for the information age. In the industrial economy, he argued, an implicit bargain had been made: working people would keep their jobs and have health care and pensions provided through their company and the government. Now, a mobile economy demanded new guarantees and new ways to provide them. That theme seemed a bit clunky, though; among other things, "social contract" may have meaning to students of Rousseau, but nobody else. He committed to giving a speech on the new economy—the idea that technological change had fundamentally altered the way the economy functioned. But Rubin and Sperling balked at such sweeping claims. Minutes before the speech, the stock market plunged. The news was relayed via pager to Paul Begala, riding in the limousine with the President. Clinton largely discarded the ambitious text and pulled back from proclaiming a new economy.*

These themes would inevitably be focused in the opening minutes of the State of the Union. I collected suggestions from the advisors, batting away the bad ones and framing an initial approach. The President always wrote and rewrote the beginning—and would undoubtedly do so again. Bruce Reed wisely warned me early on, "I wouldn't spend too much time on that stuff. The first few pages come out of his word count, not yours." The bulk of the speech would be the policy.

BY NOW, REED, SPERLING, AND I were like a basketball team: I could throw the ball to a precise spot down the court, without even looking, and know that one of them would be there to catch it. Sperling was focusing on the big budget items. At the same time he was working to fashion a few key programs for the poor. In particular, he worked with Congressman Chaka Fattah of Philadelphia to develop a program modeled after Eugene Lang's "I Have a Dream" Foundation, in which wealthy individuals adopt an individual elementary school class in a poor school and offer to provide college scholarships for any child who gets that far.

---

* In fact, every time the President wanted to talk about the new economy, the market would coincidentally swoon. This continued for years. In April 2000, the White House held a full-day conference on the subject. I joked to a friend that it was time to sell. Two days later, the Nasdaq, heavily high tech, plunged, wiping out 40 percent of its value in two months.

Reed shepherded the big social issues of crime and welfare reform—new incentives for companies to hire former welfare recipients, transportation aid so that poor people could get from the inner city to their jobs in the suburbs. His deputy, Elena Kagan, was a University of Chicago law professor whom Bowles had dubbed "the smartest person in the White House." Reed and Kagan churned out an array of initiatives and executive actions that broke the policy into manageable pieces.

The speech would have several significant initiatives, any one of which would cost more money and was larger in scope than the offerings of the previous two years. Clinton would propose a hefty child-care program, costing $40 billion. Expanding health coverage step by step, he would propose allowing middle-aged people to buy health insurance from Medicare.

Emanuel and Begala argued that the policy proposals should not wait until the State of the Union speech itself. With Congress out of session in January, a president can dominate the news by announcing them one at a time—getting more attention than if he waited to blurt them out all at once. "The State of the Union used to be a speech," Emanuel said. "Now it's a month." It was unstated but obvious that, this particular month, there was an added reason for trying to get as much good press early in the month as possible. The press would obviously obsess about the President giving a deposition in the Paula Jones civil suit, scheduled for a week and a half before the address.

My job was to keep the pieces in perspective, to make sure that there were one or two big proposals that would define the speech. To make sure that the tilt was not unduly liberal. To make sure that the budget process—which ground mindlessly on, turning everything into a spending initiative—did not alone determine the agenda. I kept prodding Sperling and Reed to think about the significant, demonstrably important policy "mountain" that would rise above the "molehills." Before fast track was defeated, for example, it had seemed that a new "Clinton Round" of global trade talks could be dramatically proposed—but that was now impossible to imagine. In the Roosevelt Room one morning after the senior staff meeting, Sperling pulled me aside. I knew that he had been holding meetings in his office for months on "special issues." His assistant had turned away questions by explaining that they were "technical sessions." In fact, they were a series of secret, delicate deliberations on entitlements and the budget surplus. "Look, I do think we'll have something big," he whispered. "On Social Security."

Social Security was the "third rail" of American politics—touch it and be crisped. Word that the administration was even contemplating a discussion of the subject in the State of the Union would send the capital

into an uproar. Secrecy was essential. Every morning, Sperling checked the newspapers to make sure nothing had been divulged. My outlines for the speech, circulated among the staff, omitted any mention of Social Security.

Finally, the Social Security proposal was ready for an airing. A tightly controlled manifest of budget experts sat around the Cabinet Room table on January 5, 1998. The press wasn't told of the meeting; most of the other political and communications advisors were excluded, too. Sitting across the table from Clinton, Sperling no longer looked permanently wrinkled. He had long been intellectually ready for his job; now he looked the part. "Now that we've balanced the budget. . . ," he began, with a Woody Allen intonation. The other aides laughed. Clinton provided the punch line. "Now, let's spend some money?"

Social Security was facing a crisis—several decades away. Everybody knew that as the baby boomers aged, with fewer active workers supporting an ever larger group of retirees, the program would become financially unsupportable. It would be technically insolvent in the year 2030. Any proposal for the surplus would be the first move in a chess game with the Republicans. Vice President Gore said, "Just recognize that the decisions we make are going to affect the future of progressive government for decades into the future." Agreeing to a tax cut, say, could mean that if the economy slipped into recession and the surplus vanished, spending programs would be curtailed. If the surplus was committed solely to entitlements, that, too, could starve other programs.

Sperling outlined several options. Clinton could demand that the entire surplus—100 percent—be used for Social Security. That was simple and it packed the most powerful political punch. The second option would be to announce that 75 percent of the surplus should go to Social Security, while asking for a national dialogue on how the other quarter would be allocated among further spending for the elderly, children and education, science, and tax cuts. Sperling had included this convoluted option at the pleading of Gore's staff, to preserve for the Vice President the option of proposing more social spending in his presidential run. A third choice would be to say that all of a conservative, current estimate of the surplus would go to Social Security, but that if the surplus grew, the extra money could be used for other purposes.

Gore weighed in with surprising force. The Republicans want to take money from Social Security to replay the massive tax cuts of the 1980s. "We're not saying no tax cuts. We are saying: Let's do Social Security first. Then we can do tax cuts, whatever. But let's make sure it doesn't mess up the system in 2030." Gore saw immediately the strength of posing Social Security against a tax cut. He was acutely aware of the power of the big play,

the strength that comes from drawing an unwavering line on the ground—in many ways, more so than Clinton.

There was still another option, a variant on the first option, that Sperling had also presented. The conversation turned to it with increasing frequency: "An alternative would be that none of the projected surpluses should be spent until Social Security has been adequately addressed." Set aside the surplus until Social Security had been saved. This would imply that most of the surplus would be needed for Social Security, but not necessarily all of it. In effect, it would hold hostage the Republicans' pet proposal: I'll veto your tax cut until you agree to fix Social Security. Then you can have a (small) tax cut. This option depended upon how forcefully the speech issued the challenge—and how carefully, since we did not want to falsely pretend that we would spend the entire surplus on Social Security.

If Clinton committed to reserving the surplus until Social Security was reformed, he would be doing several things, all of them big. The first purpose was tactical: to block the Republicans from using the surplus as an excuse to pass a gigantic tax cut. It would also put the perilous state of the big entitlement programs, Social Security and Medicare, at the center of political debate. It was a gamble. If surpluses shrank, or turned into deficits, any new government spending or even a return to Keynesian-style deficits would be said to come out of Social Security. It could hamstring fiscal policy for a generation.

By Christmas, I had compiled a book of submissions from outside authors, focusing on the new economy and globalization for the President. Memos by the novelist Amy Tan, historians Alan Brinkley and Joseph Ellis, Internet guru Esther Dyson. Speeches by Václav Havel and Tony Blair. FDR's proposal for an "economic bill of rights." Clinton especially liked an article by *New York Times* columnist Thomas Friedman. It divided political leaders into three categories: those who supported globalization but didn't care what happened to people in it ("Let Them Eat Cakers," which included Newt Gingrich), those who opposed globalization from the right and left, and those who supported globalization but wanted a safety net (lead among them Clinton). He treated the notebook dutifully, periodically reporting how much of it he had read.

On January 7, the Clintons again hosted an intellectuals' dinner. In previous years, the sociologist Bill Galston, on the White House staff, had organized them. Now Sidney Blumenthal was the moderator and convener, and the focus was on globalization and the role of government. As the professors dined on a carefully composed lobster and shrimp appetizer,

with wineglasses refilled regularly, the President explained that he believed the current period to be most like the beginning of the industrial age a century ago. During that time, a new, strong national government had to be created to deal with the problems created by a national market.

"In many ways, the challenge today is harder than the one faced by the Progressives," said Michael Sandel, the Harvard political philosopher who was regarded as a leading "communitarian." "Their solution was simpler. Build a national government and build up a national community." Now, the challenge is globalization. "If we follow their logic, we would build transnational institutions"—world government. "But the terms of the political community cannot be stretched to that extent." So the challenge is how to build democratic institutions without undermining national sovereignty.

Dani Rodrik, the economist, argued that the scope of globalization was not really any greater than it had been in the late nineteenth century, when the British pound sterling was as powerful a currency as the dollar is today. Governments were not powerless, now or then, he said. The Vice President, who had arrived late with Clinton, pressed the professor to back up his point. Several others pointed out that what had changed was the speed with which money, ideas, and jobs moved around the world. "When we talk about economic dynamism, it's a double whammy," said social critic Barbara Whitehead. Economic change can undermine family stability. "Family must be certain, permanent, strong, enduring bonds—or family life will start to resemble the global economy."

Time and again, the talk—which had begun as a seminar on globalization—returned to the theme of finding a role for nationalism and a strong government. Gore pointed out that the administration had tried to do concrete things to build confidence in government—reinventing agencies, balancing the budget, and increasing efforts to collect funds from deadbeat dads. The writers spoke about Theodore Roosevelt, Herbert Croly (who had founded The New Republic), the lost nationalist strain of American liberalism—the belief in social solidarity that had often been overshadowed by the quest for individual rights. The founding father whose name came up most often was Alexander Hamilton, who wanted a strong government. The writer Michael Lind pointed out that while liberals revered Thomas Jefferson, in fact their policies were descended from his rival Hamilton.

Sandel raised his hand to inject one note of caution. "If we look out this window here, there is a memorial to Thomas Jefferson. There is no memorial to Alexander Hamilton. And the reason for that is he didn't need one." We build memorials to ideals that are under siege—and Hamilton's commercial society is triumphant. The goal has to be to find a way to make the market the servant of democratic values, not the other way around.

Afterwards, the professors and writers surrounded Clinton. In "Superman Comes to the Supermarket," Norman Mailer writes that he was thrilled to find that John Kennedy knew an obscure book of his and not just *The Naked and the Dead.* These writers, too, appeared a bit dazzled by a president who seemed to have read their works and who respected ideas. I edged toward the circle. They were discussing the changing South, books, and the onslaught that the presidency faces. Clinton was running through his reading on nineteenth-century presidents. He was up to the 1870s. "You know, Ulysses Grant was really misunderstood," he was telling them. "He wasn't a drunk. He was just a little guy who couldn't hold his liquor. And he wasn't corrupt. His brother was corrupt, and others in his administration."

DURING THIS TIME, I was invited to attend the weekly political strategy sessions with the President upstairs in the White House residence. These meetings had begun in 1995 as private meetings between Dick Morris and the President. By now, they were a ritual involving twenty political and policy aides, as well as cabinet secretaries and party officials. The right to attend was a prize symbol of status within the White House. Most who did made a great show of how much they hated the meetings, found them useless, resented pollster Penn's role—but would have ripped down the drapes if they had been disinvited. For me, attendance had the added value of actually being useful: a one-hour session, each week, where I could join in discussions with Clinton on how he wanted issues framed. The sessions were held in the Yellow Oval Room, an ellipse that opens onto the Truman Balcony and a spectacular view of the Washington Monument.

The meetings would begin with a slide show presentation by Douglas Schoen, the New York–based pollster who was Penn's partner. Schoen would run through the overall ratings—the popularity of Democrats and Republicans, approval ratings for Clinton and Gingrich, whether people had heard of Tom Daschle (they haven't), and so on. Then Penn would make a presentation, interpreting poll results on issues (for example, which Republican tax cut proposals were most popular) and themes. I began to e-mail Penn things to include in his presentations. After that, the policy and legislative staff would hold the floor and discuss the intersection of issues and strategy.

After the meeting on the evening of January 14, Clinton stayed behind with a few of us. He was joined by Al From, the head of the Democratic Leadership Council. From had sent in a memo urging a few priorities (such as saving the cities), but the President was in a more ruminative mood.

Sitting in his easy chair in the half-darkened room, he said that he

thought we were now in a position, finally, to devote ample time in one of these speeches to the theory—to the argument for our philosophy. After balancing the budget and signing welfare reform, after the country had finally begun to win victories against crime, after the dysfunctions of a generation of public policy seemed finally to be receding, Clinton believed that the most poisonous anti-government venom had been drained. The public hadn't realized it yet, but it was now, instinctively, trusting government more than it had in years.

As he talked I thought about the room itself. Franklin Roosevelt used it as his office throughout his term. In May 1935, he had summoned the leading progressives in the Congress and his administration to tell them he would press for liberal social legislation. They berated him for his timidity and indecision. He pledged that he would act boldly. Within weeks, he signed Social Security and let loose the torrent of social legislation that still shaped the government. This was the room, perhaps this was the very spot, where the decisions were made that extended government's help into the lives of ordinary citizens.

The President leaned forward in his chair. "You know, FDR saved capitalism from itself," he mused, echoing a common analysis of the New Deal. "Our mission has been to save government from its own excesses. So it can again be a progressive force."

RAHM EMANUEL had instructed me to produce a draft early in January. I had quickly written it, consulting with others in the White House. (The draft was held up for a day while I incorporated the edits of Begala and Blumenthal. Paul called in on a cellphone from a hunting trip; Sidney was preparing to go to the opera.)

The early draft was necessary because Clinton's mind would soon turn elsewhere: he was scheduled to give a deposition to Paula Jones' lawyers. The previous year, the Supreme Court had ruled that the civil lawsuit could continue against the sitting president because it would not take a great deal of his time or energy. In the days before the deposition, Clinton did not focus much on the speech. But we knew that once it was over, he would want to return to the task with a vengeance.

At one session in the Roosevelt Room, we recognized that we needed a line summing up the progress on the budget that was as compelling as the one Ronald Reagan used in 1981, denouncing the national debt as he first proposed his tax cuts to Congress. Then, he had said, "If you had stack of $1000 bills in your hand only four inches high you'd be a millionaire. A trillion dollars would be a stack of $1000 bills sixty-seven miles high." Begala and Sperling went off together to huddle. Fifteen minutes later they re-

turned. Begala read to the group: "The federal budget deficit, once so large that it contained eleven zeroes, is now simply zero." Bull's-eye.

At another, we showed the draft to the "outreach offices." In a White House, the speechwriters are charged with thinking "presidentially"—with propounding a public philosophy and speaking to the nation as a whole. Others are supposed to tend to specific interests and constituencies. Bit by bit, they picked at the speech. Recycling a favorite Clinton line, I had written that while American universities are the best in the world, plainly American public schools are not. The person from the Office of Public Liaison objected strongly. That was too harsh a slap at the schools, at a time we were trying to defend teachers and public education. I groaned but took it out. (Later, Clinton dictated a passage that reverted to the way we had it.)

When the President was finished with his deposition, I was instructed, there was to be a new draft waiting for him. Shortly before he returned to the White House on January 17, I handed it to Erskine Bowles and went home.

The next morning, as I was working at my house, I logged on to the Internet. The Web is catnip for procrastinators. I regularly checked the newswires and other sites, especially to see if any of the State of the Union policies had leaked. I checked the *New York Times*, and the *Washington Post*, and looked at the AP wire. Then I clicked on the Drudge Report. I had first begun to use it earlier in the year; it was a quick way to get gossip. The Web site had printed a scurrilous and false rumor about Sidney Blumenthal his first day on the job. Now Sidney was suing Matt Drudge, in what promised to be a key test case for libel law on the Internet.

Now, on Drudge, I was alarmed to read that *Newsweek* had "killed" a story about a White House affair that was "destined to shake official Washington to its foundation."

Hmmm, I thought. That doesn't sound very good. There's always something. That morning, on ABC's *This Week*, the pundits' roundtable discussed the rumor. William Kristol reported the rumor that *Newsweek* had scotched a story about the President and an intern. George Stephanopoulos scoffed at it. "Where did it come from? The Drudge Report. You know, we've all seen how discredited . . ." Sam Donaldson cut off the discussion.

I put it out of my mind. The mood among most White House staff was one of relief: the deposition was over, the speech was coming up, Clinton would finally be able to clear the decks and make his case to the country. On Monday, the government was closed to celebrate the birthday of Dr. Martin Luther King Jr., and the White House was largely empty. We met with the President that afternoon. In the two days since the deposition, he had rewritten furiously, crossing out nearly the whole of the first three pages and writing a new opening. He toughened the language, tightened

the structure, and was clearly working through in his own mind how this speech fit in with the previous 209 annual messages. He had written a long paragraph, tracing the country's history starting with George Washington, Alexander Hamilton, and John Marshall, all the way down to Martin Luther King Jr., on how each had strengthened the nation. It was a paragraph destined to drop from the final draft, but it helped focus his thinking. Now he read it out loud, line by line, soliciting comments. He was in an expansive, animated mood.

In previous years, he said, the speeches had been too disjointed, spewing out policies without a guiding philosophical theme. He had a well-developed governing philosophy, he said, far more than most presidents. "It's consistent with what I've done for ten years as governor, and what I've done for five years as president, and what I've said I was going to do in 1991—and people still act surprised that there's any coherence to it. 'Because after all,' " he mimicked, " 'it's poll-driven.' "

Clinton told me to write a description of the positive future that could come if the right policies were followed. This was a perennial question: whether to warn of danger or keep calm and confident. The President also read from a speech by Tony Blair, commenting on how good it was. "In London," Emanuel reminded him, "they sit around going, why can't we be as good as Clinton?"

This speech, in any case, was going to make the case more clearly than its predecessors for the "Third Way" approach to politics. The Third Way was a description that Clinton had begun using in 1992 to distinguish himself from what he called "the brain-dead politics of both parties." Now Blair and other Social Democrats in Europe had borrowed it to describe their efforts to modernize their parties and move them to the center. American observers, who had scorned Clinton's political shift as merely tactical, saw Blair's moves as a more fundamental transformation of the left-of-center parties. (In England, on the other hand, they called Blair "Tony Blur.") He would argue for a lean but active government, for an economic policy that did not try to stop technological change and trade, but that gave people education and health care so that they could thrive in the global economy.

The next morning, Clinton had yet another version of the opening, one he had written—indecipherably—on a small White House notepad. He told a handful of us standing around his desk that he had stayed up late writing, perhaps there wasn't much worth using, but we should see—and he would go over it later. As we filed out of the office, I noticed that Blumenthal had stayed behind to chat.

An hour later, Blumenthal's assistant called. They were having a hard time reading Clinton's handwriting. I asked for a photocopy. I knew I could read the handwriting better than anyone except for the Oval Office staff. I

was sitting at my desk, transcribing the notes (as Blumenthal did the same, in his office), when the phone rang. Come to the Oval Office immediately for a discussion on the global economy.

When I slipped in the door, the President was in his chair by the fireplace. A sizable group of senior economic advisors from the Treasury and State Departments were sitting and standing around him. "This is not what I want to say," he said, with a draft on his lap. "This is not adequate."

Clinton and his team were facing a frightening financial crisis that was brewing, largely out of sight of the American people, halfway around the world in Korea. For years, the economies of nations in Asia had grown at spectacular rates. Free market policies seemed to be allowing modern economies, with large and thriving middle classes, to spring up overnight. Billions of dollars in foreign capital had flooded into these markets to finance the expansion. But first in Thailand and now in Korea, the currency had collapsed, and foreign money that had flooded in was just as quickly rushing out. Treasury secretary Rubin had spent days calling bankers and asking them to roll over Korea's debt rather than calling it in. It was a near miss.

We were convinced that the Asian financial crisis would hurt the U.S. economy in the coming year. Because the Asian economies were in recession, indeed in depression, they would buy fewer American products. And they, in turn, were seeking to save their own economies by cheapening the value of their currencies. That let them export goods to the United States at lower prices, thereby undercutting our domestic manufacturers. Clinton was determined to speak directly to the public, to explain the need for action. Gene Sperling and I supported tough, even alarmist language that would shake people out of their complacency. The President wanted to put the warning high up in the speech, even though it would be unpopular. Paul Begala had drafted an evocative passage. "Preparing for a far-off storm that may reach our shores is far wiser than ignoring the thunder until the clouds are just overhead." After the failure to pass fast track four months before, it had become clear that Clinton's brand of aggressive internationalism was in deep political trouble. He constantly expressed frustration that he had not been more successful at persuading the country to embrace the global economy, even at a time of rising plenty.

The economists filed out as the writers filed in. Clinton searched for his notes. In triumph, I showed him the typed version. He read it out loud and marked it up, describing some of what he had written as middle-of-the-night "psychobabble": "Just as we, as individuals, must always strive to grow through success and failure, pain and joy, so must the nation grow in wisdom and spirit."

That night, I reworked the day's revisions to the opening section. It

was getting better. It began strongly, with a paragraph written by the President: "For 209 years, it has been the President's duty to report to you on the state of the Union. Tonight, it is a duty any citizen would cherish. Thanks to the hard work and strong values of the American people, these are good times for America. With our economy growing, our incomes rising, our social fabric mending, and our leadership in the world unrivaled, the state of our union is strong."

Normally, a speech or other document that goes to the President must be sent through the staff secretary's office, which routes the hundreds of documents a week that go to him for his review or signature: memoranda, letters to members of Congress, decisions that he has to make, bills to sign, as well as speeches. All of it is photocopied, with duplicates sent to the National Archives. In the late hours, people who had worked at the White House for years, nonpartisan professionals who knew how the institution worked, staffed the office. But when they went home, speechwriters brought a speech draft over to the residence itself.

That night, I stuffed the speech into a manila envelope and walked past the guards, down the colonnade that links the West Wing and the residence, and up the steps to the usher's office. There, the guards and staff of the mansion waited for the President or First Lady to summon them. I left the envelope and headed back to the West Wing. Tonight, the press office was full; reporters lounged around, waiting for any results of the private meeting with Israeli prime minister Benjamin Netanyahu that Clinton was hosting. I headed home.

When I got there, I switched on the computer and logged on again to Drudge. It was even more ominous. Increasingly lurid details were pouring out.

The next morning, I rose early and opened the front door. The *Washington Post* was lying on the doormat. I rubbed sleep from my eyes as I fumbled to pull the paper out of its shrink wrapper. There it lay, with the implausible clarity of a bad novel, four columns of black type on the front page: "CLINTON ACCUSED OF URGING AIDE TO LIE; STARR PROBES WHETHER PRESIDENT TOLD WOMAN TO DENY ALLEGED AFFAIR TO JONES'S LAWYERS."

EIGHTEEN

ONE WEEK

Wednesday, January 21

My head was spinning as I barreled down the Rock Creek Parkway toward the White House. There had been scandals before, allegations, explosions, but it was obvious that this would be different.

At the Southwest Gate, where I drove my car through two security checkpoints, the German shepherd sniffed under the chassis and pawed through my trunk, searching for explosives as usual. Then I saw a handful of television camera crews huddled on the sidewalk next to the gate that led to the parking lot. They sprang into action as my battered red Honda drove by, peering in the cab to see if I was anyone, looking disappointed when I wasn't.

The morning meeting in the Roosevelt Room was packed. I squeezed in and stood in my accustomed place near the door. (By rank, as an assistant to the President, I was entitled to sit at the table. But I was habitually so late that I had staked out a place to stand, where my tardy arrival would be less noticeable. Twenty years of formal education gave me a formidable talent for evading the teacher's glance.)

Erskine Bowles sat down at the center of the table and began to talk. He was miming unconcern and not fully succeeding. He had been trying to leave after a year—his heart was in balancing the budget, and after that he was more interested in returning home to North Carolina—but Clinton had just persuaded him to stay.

He noted that there was some news in the paper. "I've been here for a while. These things come and these things go." He pointed out that ABC

News crews were filming everyone who came and left the complex. They are staking out the staff, looking for your reactions. "Get about your business." Some aides obviously had not yet read the paper that morning. They began to thumb through the thick collection of news clippings stapled and delivered to each senior staffer. One after another they turned to the *Washington Post* and stared. One of Clinton's longtime aides from Arkansas apparently hadn't seen it; her eyes widened to saucers when she reached the page.

The meeting continued, rolling around the room. Gene Sperling talked about the Republicans' tax plans. Dan Tarullo, the expert on the international economy, fretted about the Asian financial crisis. "Overnight, the Asian markets were mixed, except for the Indonesian rupiah, which was down." Other staff members droned on about meetings, reports, budget levels, and plans.

One of Hillary's aides turned and said, half to me and half to herself, "Sometimes it feels like a dreamland."

As soon as the session ended, the senior communications, political and policy advisors reconvened across the hall in John Podesta's office. For me, on a typical day, this was the most important meeting—a re-creation in spirit of the Little Rock War Room. Mike McCurry would grill Sperling and Reed on the policy questions he might get. Rahm Emanuel would fume and curse and demand that the afternoon's speech be rewritten to take account of the morning's newspaper. Press aides and schedulers would keep track of the rapidly changing calendar. Usually, the air hummed with wisecracks and Rahm's nervous energy.

Today, it was numb. Nobody knew quite what to do, except that nobody should say that to the press. Someone made a feeble joke about *Wag the Dog*, a current movie in which presidential aides concocted a war to divert attention from a sex scandal. There was some discussion of the State of the Union. "Now the speech has to be *really* poetic," I said. "Yeah," Podesta cracked. "Now it's going to have to be in iambic pentameter." The White House had planned to let Clinton be interviewed by Jim Lehrer for the *NewsHour* on PBS and by Mara Liasson for National Public Radio. We couldn't cancel the interviews, we agreed. Also, we were kind of wondering what the President might say.

I walked dully back to the Old Executive Office Building. As I opened the carved wooden doors, Lanny Breuer ran past me. He was a special counsel to the President, a former high-powered partner in a Washington law firm now charged with responding to the various investigations. The day before, looking forward to the big speech, I had said to him jovially, "This is the only week my job is harder than your job." Now, as he sprinted past me toward the West Wing, I called after him, "That's what I call one-upsmanship."

That day, the White House was aswirl with questions and rumors. Gradually, as the reality sunk in that this was not just a spate of bad headlines but a fiercely determined criminal investigation closing in, staff members clammed up. Those of us who had been through Whitewater and other investigations knew that even a casual conversation could be interpreted as part of some complex conspiracy. I did wonder: did I know Monica Lewinsky? I didn't think so. Undoubtedly I had been in the same room with her; if she, in fact, sat outside Leon Panetta's office, then I should have known her by sight. I had never really paid that much attention to the interns.

Walking over to the West Wing, I saw a burly figure charging up the front driveway, chased by photographers and a news crew. It looked like Bob Bennett, one of Clinton's private lawyers—but he wouldn't really choose to enter by the most visible possible route, would he? I arrived in Rahm Emanuel's office. He and Begala had been pulled into an endless round of worried phone calls—with reporters, friends, with anyone who might know anything.

Emanuel looked at me darkly. "You're not going to get any help on this one," he said; what he meant was that my army of kibitzers on the State of the Union were now going to be otherwise occupied. "You're going to have to do this alone," he said. I tried to look dismayed about that prospect.

In the late afternoon, the President sat in the Oval Office for his first press interviews since the *Post*'s headlines. He was passive and soft-spoken in his defense. "There is no improper relationship," he told Lehrer. But it seemed obvious that something heavy was weighing on him; he did not react with the fury that would have been natural had the charge been entirely false.

While the President was on the rack, a handful of us sat in an empty Cabinet Room. As soon as his interview with Lehrer was over, he came in. Everyone stood and greeted him heartily. But we were all studying him closely as he sagged into his seat. If he had been wearing pancake makeup for his interview, it didn't show. He looked shrunken, tired. As he absently discussed the speech, he clutched a coffee cup. He talked about the structure of the speech, the number of policies, made a few desultory comments. "I'll work on it some more tonight," he said, and left.

"I have known Bill Clinton for decades, and I have never seen him like that," said Bob Shrum quietly. We stayed in our seats as the twilight darkened through the French windows, having a frustrating discussion of whether to tear up the structure of the speech and rework it. After forty-five minutes the Oval Office staff peeked in and suggested we vacate the room, which only the President was supposed to use for meetings. We picked up our files and briefcases and took them twenty feet away to the less grand Roosevelt Room.

Afterwards, Elena Kagan and I sat in a deserted Roosevelt Room, surrounded by Frederic Remington sculptures and paintings of the West. It was one of those days where energy is best spent with endless talking. "Here's the interesting thing," I said. "There is no middle ground. Either it happened or it didn't."

Thursday, January 22

The morning papers were awful. "THE LEGAL IMPLICATIONS; Allegations Against Clinton Could Lead to Impeachment, Prosecution," reported the *Washington Post*. "Subpoenas Sent," headlined the *Times*. I came in to my office after the morning meetings. One of the interns was blithely showing his colleagues a copy of Monica Lewinsky's business card from the Pentagon, which she had given him at a party. I scowled at him. "This is a criminal investigation. You should not be showing this around like this. If you have something to say, you should say it to the Counsel's Office — not other staff. By showing this card to everyone here, you are putting them at risk."

Still seething, I summoned the speechwriting staff and took out my frustration on them. "This is serious business. You must comport yourselves as the staff of the President of the United States." They looked downcast and backed out the door. One stayed behind. "You have to understand," he said. "Morale is really low." I thought about the people who were about to get pulled into the whirlpool. I thought about the President. "You have to understand that real people, people with whom we work, are facing serious criminal jeopardy," I said evenly. "This is not some abstract matter."

That afternoon, I wandered around the West Wing to see what was going on. The halls, usually filled with scurrying aides, were empty. Every office door was open, and staff — top officials and secretaries and interns — stood watching Mike McCurry's briefing on television. He was being pummeled. What was the nature of the President's relationship with the intern? When would they get answers? This was thrilling for the reporters: a scandal, sex, the chance to get on the news, a constitutional crisis in the making.

In the middle of McCurry's ordeal, my pager vibrated: call the Oval Office. I grabbed Ann Lewis' courtesy phone, and the President came on the line. "Michael, that memo that you sent me from Stephen Carter. Did you read it?" I had passed on to Clinton a memorandum from the Yale law professor, a leading African-American scholar. In truth, I barely remembered the memo — and I had just seen it a few hours before. "Yes, I did. It was very good." "What did you think of his ideas? I thought it was very well written. Look at the language on page two, about the 'idea of America.' "

"OK, we'll incorporate it." "I think you should use it. I'll send it out to you." We hung up. I looked at the television: McCurry was still being flayed.

My mind reeled. Around the West Wing, two dozen television sets were tuned to McCurry—a session that was broadcast live on the television networks—and Clinton was chatting about a memo. Was this his way of avoiding, of denying? Was he consciously calling people during the press briefing so that we would see—and repeat to others—that he was focusing on the speech?

Reed, Sperling, and I stood in a tired huddle blocking the doorway to Rahm Emanuel's office. We were speculating, sotto voce, about what would happen, as people were in thousands of hallways that afternoon. From around the corner, past the Vice President's office, we sensed a silent commotion, as the First Lady briskly strode toward us. She was svelte, smiling, and composed. For days, we had debated whether the President should propose an expansion of the Family and Medical Leave Act in the speech—and if so, whether to broaden it to cover a larger number of firms, or to allow leave for a wider array of purposes. Reed explained the choice to her. "Oh, that's really important," she said, perhaps a bit faster than usual. It was important that employees of smaller companies get family leave— and it was important that the categories of leave be expanded. Both.

We watched her disappear. "Well, I guess it's both!" We burst into laughter. "Well, she's had a harder day than we have," Reed said. "Today," I concluded, "she could have said, 'Everyone gets two years off from work,' and we would have agreed."

Early in the evening, the "economic principals" were meeting to hash out, one more time, the trade section of the speech. Each of them had a cardboard placard in front of his or her name. A deputy secretary was droning on when my pager began to vibrate. It was a message from my assistant, Paul Tuchman: "SID, ANN, SHRUM AND PENN ARE IN YOUR OF-FICE, PLOTTING YOUR OVERTHROW NO DOUBT." Alarmed, I excused myself from the conference and bolted back to my office.

I felt like a peasant whose quiet country had suddenly been filled with "advisors" "invited in" to help. Blumenthal was pacing, speculating about the impact the Starr probe would have on the Paula Jones case. Someone else was trying to talk him down. This was going to be a long night.

It was clear what was needed: reinforcements. "We really need Gene here to discuss the policy," I said to protests from the helpers. Sperling could be counted on to talk—at length—about the substantive issues in the speech. He arrived about an hour later. After a while, as he held the floor, the helpers began to fade. Some of them left.

I sat at my keyboard with my back to them, my feet on the desk and keyboard at my lap. I made the type even larger so that everyone could see.

We worked into the night on a new draft, with Shrum's theatrical baritone booming out eloquent language.

Friday, January 23

The siege deepened with each day. The papers were full of lurid stories about a supposedly saved dress. Some old friends in the press called solicitously, also to see if I would say anything. Several journalists—who knew I was thinking of leaving the White House anyway—offered to let me "resign in protest" in their pages.

In the morning, there was a cabinet meeting—ostensibly to discuss the speech. I arrived a few minutes late. Cabinet meetings are rare, but even so, secretaries sometimes send a substitute: not today. Whether practiced politicians or technocratic administrators, every one of them was a student of power. Every eye in the room was focused on Clinton, all looking for the same clues: was he collapsing, would he make it? And one topic was extensively discussed: the end of the world. Not the sense of the administration slipping away—the havoc expected to result from the so-called Y2K computer bug that was to strike at midnight on New Year's Eve two years hence.

It has been imagined that the President pounded the table, looked at his top appointees, and demanded their support. Maybe he did, and I missed it by arriving late. In fact, he was genial, turning the floor over to OMB director Raines for a lengthy warning about Y2K and its impact. Clinton joked, "I've put the Vice President in charge of this problem," and everyone laughed too hard. Clinton warned the agency heads that breakdowns would be held against them, and would hurt Gore's presidential prospects. He turned to the imminent State of the Union. As the secretaries earnestly proposed topics—Rubin suggesting Y2K, Agriculture's Dan Glickman food safety—Clinton would turn theatrically to Paul Begala, sitting in the corner. "Paul, did you get that?" I jabbed the pen into my notepad. *Me! I'm the speechwriter!* Begala looked at me sympathetically and rolled his eyes. Donna Shalala recounted a visit to a school. "I spoke to a class of students, and here are two things they said you should tell the country. 'Wash your hands.' 'Don't smoke—anything.' " Clinton nodded. "Paul, did you get that?"

Afterwards I went to see Rahm Emanuel in his small office next to the President's dining room. "Get him at the podium. Now." Emanuel practically spat out the words. He knew that Clinton would edit effectively only when he was planted at the podium. Otherwise, he would endlessly rewrite the first few pages.

Thus far, the drafts had made no mention of the scandal. I handed Rahm photocopies of two speeches. One was Nixon's 1974 State of the

Union, in which he declared, "One year of Watergate is enough." The other was Ronald Reagan's 1987 address, in which he admitted mistakes on Iran-Contra and pledged a full investigation. I said, "I know that there may be discussions of what to say about this. Please let me know when those discussions are taking place." Emanuel nodded. "If I have anything to do with it," he said, "he won't say a word."

The family theater was readied; the teleprompter operators sat at their posts. But the President didn't feel prepared. He still wanted to sift through the policy sections again. We met in the Oval Office a few hours after the cabinet meeting. He was matter of fact, cool, joking.

He continued to wrestle with the section on international economics. Sperling expected the impact of the Asian financial crisis to hit the U.S. economy soon. He and I wanted language that was uncharacteristically foreboding, even a bit frightening, to prepare the public. Penn and Begala were aghast. Why suddenly proclaim the glass half empty and, above all, why now? The draft read, "The turmoil in Asia will have an effect on our economy." Clinton asked Penn if he agreed with that phrasing. He didn't. Clinton rewrote it. " 'I want to minimize the impact of the turmoil in Asia on our economy.' There, Gene, you admit it will have an impact—but you say your policy wants to minimize it. 'It will have an impact on all the world's economies, including ours. Our job is to make the negative impact as small as possible.' "

The speech ended with a series of proposals on science and technology. Clinton had been reading widely about biology. ("You know, if the twentieth century is the century of physics, then in a lot of ways the twenty-first century will be the century of biology," he explained.) We had a section on Gifts to the Future, leading into the discussion of the millennium. But he found it drab. "Paint a picture," he said. "Excitement. The twenty-first century. The age of biology, of technology. Paint the picture."

Saturday, January 24

The next day, we began to rehearse in the family theater.

The President was dressed in a coat and tie. He had pulled himself together; the mask of command was now firmly and fully back in place. He was concentrated. An observer would not know that anything was amiss.

He read the section on the budget and Social Security. It said, "What should we do with our surplus? Social Security first." He stopped, wrote on his draft, and looked up. "What should we do with our surplus? I have a simple four-word answer. *Save* Social Security first!" He smiled and flung his arms wide. "See? I haven't totally lost it."

He reached the education paragraphs and stopped. Rather than merely proposing new aid to college students, he wanted to brag about what had been accomplished in the previous year's balanced budget agreement, which included a huge increase in college aid. And because the Hope Scholarship tax cut in essence made community college free, it focused new aid to working-class people who attended those two-year schools, often years after graduating from high school.

"I'm not sure I like it the way it is," he mused. "How about this? Because of these actions, I have something to say to every family listening to us tonight: Your children can go on to college. If you know a child from a poor family, tell her not to give up—she can go on to college. If you know a young couple struggling with bills, worried they won't be able to send their children to college, tell them not to give up—their children can go on to college." A dozen aides shouted, "That was great!" "What's wrong with that?" Clinton pointed at me: put it in. I smiled silently. I had heard the exact same paragraph before—at the other end of a phone line. Dick Morris had dictated it for a commencement address in 1996. *Hmm. Dick's back Wonder what else they have been talking about.* (As we later learned, they were, in fact, also talking about how Clinton should handle the scandal.)

Clinton read through the speech, changing words, striking out sentences, dictating new passages. Advisors passed on suggestions. Every paragraph was tweaked, as he called out questions about phrasing or factual accuracy. Line by line, he was making the speech his own. He reworked the sections on the international economy and on race.

Shortly after Clinton left, Nancy Hernreich paged me. I called her back from a phone in the family theater. "Michael," she drawled, "the President wants to know if he left behind any . . . papers." She paused. "Uh, any speech drafts that weren't yours." Dick Morris again. I found this very funny. "What are you giggling about?" she said, slightly alarmed. "No, Nancy, I have not found any other speech drafts." She started giggling, too.

After the session, we moved to the Roosevelt Room. A few speechwriters, Reed and Sperling, and the consultants sat around the long table, trying to reconstruct all the changes that had been made. We were shaky. The draft had said, "As our government is smaller, our nation is stronger." Sperling heatedly objected. Reagan could have said that, he insisted. It was too conservative, too old guard Republican. As Sperling and Shrum debated, I scrolled through the draft, trying to reconstruct all of Clinton's changes. Pizza from Domino's and McDonald's french fries were spread out across the table.

The President wandered in, trailed by his dog, Buddy, and looking pensive. He was heading to his office and brightened when he saw the cor-

nucopia of junk food. "You know, I haven't had McDonald's since I was elected," he said as he speared some french fries. He looked around at the same people who had filled the Roosevelt Room each year, now older and paunchier. Less chaos. He marveled at how far ahead of schedule we were. Reed cheerfully offered to work all night. Clinton smiled. "Yeah, you should work all night, just for old times' sake."

(Later, I leaked this detail to the press to show Clinton's continued good humor. The *New York Times* used it, instead, to paint a picture of him wistfully wandering the halls of the West Wing, pining for the past. Leaking should be left to the professionals.)

Gene Sperling pulled me aside. ABC News had decided to tape a story on how those who were writing the State of the Union were keeping their noses to the grindstone in the face of the controversy. The story would profile him. He was generous as usual: come to his office, we would stage a work session for the cameras.

For a half hour, we toiled over the paragraphs on economic development in the cities. The President frequently asserted that he had a "stealth urban policy," citing a newspaper article that pointed out the varying strands of his approach. The administration had focused on providing capital for economic development in inner-city areas, through devices such as empowerment zones that cut taxes for businesses willing to invest in poor neighborhoods. It had also strengthened the Community Reinvestment Act, which required commercial banks to make loans in poor neighborhoods. And incomes for the working poor had been boosted significantly with the expansion in 1993 of the Earned Income Tax Credit. It was a good example of Clinton's updated liberalism: by not talking about it, and by rooting the policy in an ethos of work and responsibility, he had been able to channel funds to cities with little political controversy.

The camera crew readied its equipment in Sperling's reception area. CNN, playing nonstop on a TV in Gene's inner office, announced, "Breaking News." I quickly shut the door. Wolf Blitzer stood on the White House lawn. Apparently, minutes before, he had reported that Clinton was considering resigning. Now, he reported, he had been harangued by White House staff, insisting it was not so. Gene hit the mute button as the ABC crew came in. We furrowed our brows and looked at the drafts. The paragraph grew and grews as we "edited" it. After a few minutes the crew left, and we deflated. We speculated morosely about what might happen, then shook ourselves out of it.

Sunday, January 25

Another morning of mounting pressure and crushing speculation. On ABC's *This Week*, Sam Donaldson declared that "if he's not telling the truth, I think his presidency is numbered in days." I wondered. Would the speech be canceled? Would he resign? If he did, would I work on the announcement?

Another day of rehearsals, too. The family theater was to be used for a Super Bowl viewing party later in the day, so we moved the session to the Map Room. The President entered, standing about five feet in front of the computer, his aides and friends filling out the room on either side. He held up the hefty manuscript, worrying about length. "How about I just say this," he suggested. " 'Turn to page thirty-three.' "

Clinton was also starting to focus on the reaction from Congress—a lot. He asked for a count of how many times he "challenged" Congress, instead of "asking." Clinton delivered the speech as I sat at the keyboard, with staff members and consultants whispering changes. John Podesta wanted some language about the diffusion of technology into the economy as one reason for sustained growth. Sperling relayed factual corrections fed to him by his researchers. All the while I tried to listen to the President, catching every tick of his speech. Did he say "a" or "the"? Did he turn two sentences into one? Did he dictate a new paragraph? A gaggle looked over my shoulder, calling out changes that I might have missed. The session lasted two hours.

Monday, January 26

That morning, Hillary Clinton and Vice President Gore were scheduled to host a polite Roosevelt Room session announcing a proposal to increase funding for after-school programs. At the beginning of the morning meeting in John Podesta's office, we were told that there would be a change of plans. The President would join them. (It was unstated, but obvious, that the purpose was to give him a chance to say something about the Lewinsky affair.) We were asked to prepare a statement—on education, not on the scandal.

Reed and I huffed upstairs to his office. This would be on live national television, before a huge audience, perhaps larger than for the State of the Union itself. "They want a statement," Bruce said dryly, "we'll give them a statement." We sat at his word processor and spliced the entire education section straight out of the State of the Union address and turned it into a statement. Within twenty minutes, we were finished.

The Roosevelt Room was harshly lit, crowded with cameras and reporters, a few rows of education experts and lawmakers in front. I decided not to stand in back to watch (to my eternal regret, I must admit). An hour later, I sat at my desk, editing, watching on network TV as Clinton read the education section of the State of the Union. Then, as expected, as the reporters shouted a cacophony of questions on the scandal, Clinton crooked his finger in a gesture that was familiar to any staff member facing presidential anger, and uttered the line about "that woman, Miss Lewinsky," that will live as long as anything I ever wrote for him.

There was a sense of finality, of relief. *Well. That answers that. I guess we're not resigning. I guess the speech is on . . .*

I stopped by Rahm Emanuel's office. He and Begala had been working the phones for days. I offered my sympathy. "How's it going?"

Emanuel looked unhappily up at me. "These lawyers. They get paid $500 an hour, and they say to us, 'We can't talk in public — we don't have all the facts. So *you* go out and destroy your credibility.' "

I told him the story of the man who fell off the top of the Empire State Building. About halfway down, someone learned out the window and shouted at him as he dropped, "How do you feel?" "So far, so good," shouted the man. Rahm didn't smile.

I understood why Rahm felt that way. I was lucky. I never had to confront the issues directly, never had to declare my support publicly. Worrying about it, this week, was a luxury. I was being counted on for the address.

That afternoon, we gathered to rehearse again. Clinton was steady, pouring his energy into the speech, treating his problems as a tactical and strategic challenge to be mastered. In the hallway outside the family theater, the President told Tommy Caplan and me, "You know, I got a phone call from Newt. Did you hear about my phone call from Newt? He strongly suggested putting some bipartisan applause lines right at the top." It seemed that the Speaker was generously trying to make sure that the atmosphere did not curdle in the House chamber. Perhaps he was also worried that the Republicans would once again be seen as disgruntled on national television.

In the family theater, Clinton stood at the lectern reading, asking questions, prodding Sperling or Reed or me for a fuller explanation of the policy. In the first and second rows of seats, the staff quietly scanned the text with a different goal: searching for any possible double entendres or lines that could seem to refer to the President's own predicament. Now, between drafts, we cut them out, hoping Clinton wouldn't notice what we were doing or figure out why. Reference to economic change producing a "quiet crisis." Gone. "We confront another decisive moment in our destiny."

Gone. Even lines as innocuous as, "We have experienced more change more suddenly than ever before." Gone.

For weeks, the draft of the speech had read, "Let us say to everyone listening tonight—whether you are seventy or fifty or twenty years old—Social Security will be there when you need it." I had changed it to "seventy or fifty or thirty years old." Clinton stopped and looked up. "Why does this say thirty?" He knew that demographically, the youngest workers were at the greatest risk of not receiving Social Security. Penn called out, "Yes, twenty years old is better." I half turned around and whispered, "We cannot have the President say 'twenty years old' in the speech. Do you want it replayed on David Letterman, over and over?"

After wavering in the first days of the scandal, Clinton seemed in complete command—of his speech, of himself, of the situation.

"What should we do with the surplus? I have a simple, four-word answer: Save Social Security first." Clinton squinted into the teleprompter, stopped, and looked up. "Yea! Boo! Hiss! The silence is deafening." He was worried that the Republicans would hold fast to their tax cut. He tossed out other options for the surplus. "Buy a football team? Extend Michael Jordan's contract?"

The strategy would succeed only if the Democrats in Congress backed Clinton instead of stampeding to a popular tax cut. The President looked to Shrum, who was Gephardt's close advisor. "You think the Democrats will clap for that?" Shrum called out reassurance. We also assured Clinton that support for a minimum wage hike should come early in the speech, even if it was logically out of sequence, again to stir the Democrats to applause.

Clinton moved into education. He began with a long and growing list of accomplishments: a tax cut to pay for college tuition, cheaper student loans, an influx of high technology in the classroom. I had been stripping items out, trying to pare the section back. "You talk about something average people want to hear about—they want to hear about this," Clinton argued. From behind me came a loud chorus, as everyone jokingly sided with the President. "Yeah! Yeah!" "I stand my ground," I replied with mock seriousness. Clinton threatened to hold a student aid form aloft to explain in detail how it worked. "I will be stunned, when they do the analysis of this, if this isn't one that registers most." He picked through the section, line by line, asking Sperling to find out how many schools or classrooms would be modernized. School construction appealed to liberals: with 40 percent of the nation's schools needing repair or replacement, it helped the most run-down inner-city schools. Clinton continued: " 'It is time to end social promotion in America's schools.' Now Republicans cheer, Democrats sit on their hands."

The section on the Patients' Bill of Rights came next. The legislation was a menu of items designed to address the worst abuses committed by Health Maintenance Organizations. (In 1993, Clinton's health plan was criticized because it would herd people into these large groups. Now, over half the public received their health care through managed care plans, with few rights if their coverage was denied.) Clinton had insisted on spelling out the details of the plan in the speech. "You have the right to know all your medical options, not just the cheapest. You have the right to choose the doctor you want for the care you need. You have the right to emergency room care, whenever and wherever you need it." He punched the air for emphasis. "This is a rockin' sucker! I wish they all had this kind of rhythm."

Mark Penn urged that Clinton move the rousing health care section into a position before the downcast discussion of the Asian financial crisis. "Mark is worried that everyone will kick in their TV sets," I explained. The President was amused by the debate. "How about this. 'Everybody, tune out.' " He waved his arms. "Wonks: IMF! Everybody else: back to health care!" No, he said, the International Monetary Fund needed to be near the top of the speech.

We got to campaign finance reform. He would now be formally asking the Federal Communications Commission to provide free airtime for candidates. But the proposal did not—could not—link that free airtime to spending limits, a provision that would require legislation. "You mean Michael Huffington [the millionaire who had spent $29.4 million on a Senate run in California] would get free time? That would just make it worse!"

At his moment of maximum peril, Clinton was trying to lose himself in what he loved best: the details of policy. But it was more than that. We were seeing what kept him aloft—and what would save him in the months to come. His popularity wasn't just a product of the good economy, like a stock market index fund. The public approved his leadership, liked the approach to government and even to the presidency. That connection would prove to be potent, more than we could imagine that day.

Tuesday, January 27

State of the Union day is typically filled with frenetic and chaotic rewriting, but not this one. Clinton wanted to rehearse quietly with Michael Sheehan and me. He showed me yet another new first paragraph. "Tonight it is my honor and our duty to focus our minds and join our wills on the work of strengthening our nation at this defining moment in our his-

tory—and that is what we will do." I looked around for reinforcements. There were none. As gently as I could, I pointed out that his original impulse not to talk about the controversy was the right one. This would only invite a headline, "Clinton Urges Congress to Focus on Policy, Not Controversy." He agreed.

Throughout that week, as I had watched Clinton will himself to do his job, I pondered the layers of his personality: the bonhomie, the anger, the calculation, the earnestness. I wondered whether he really put his troubles in a box, as his mother reportedly said. Or did they gnaw at him, as they would at anyone, and he pressed on anyway? I got a bit of an answer that morning. He pointed to an innocuous line in the speech, worrying that it could possibly be seen as a comment on his situation. So he wasn't oblivious. That made his composure all the more impressive.

By late in the afternoon, the speech was finished. It was the smoothest, earliest draft we had ever done. We would even release it early to the press, partly to show how well things were going. After Clinton went back to the residence to shower and change, we readied the file for final release.

The speech would end with a patriotic tribute to Senator John Glenn, who would soon be returning to space as a member of the space shuttle crew. Clinton asked the Congress to join in tribute, and would receive bipartisan applause. But we wanted Glenn to be surprised, and we wanted the Republicans to be surprised as well, so we had chopped off the speech, marking the end with three asterisks: "Ending to come."

Ending to come. "Wait a minute!" I shouted after I'd turned over the disk. The press would read "ending to come" as a red alert. Shrum intoned, "Fox News has just learned there will be a surprise ending to the President's speech!" "They'll stop trading on the stock markets," I moaned. The Internet will scream, "Clinton to confess," "Clinton to resign."

"DON'T RELEASE IT!" I shouted. Someone ran after the press aide, while I dialed McCurry's office. The draft was pulled back.

7 P.M. An urgent page: Call Begala at Rahm's office. "The line at the beginning of the foreign policy section. 'We must exercise responsibility not only at home but abroad.' " "We can't say 'abroad.' " "Say 'around the world,' " Begala replied.

8:30 P.M. The presidential motorcade was idling, enveloped in steam as sheets of rain pelted the South Lawn of the White House. Aides, too nervous to pace, stood in silent clusters. Outside the Diplomatic Reception Room on the ground floor of the mansion, I held tight the last copy of the speech, seventy-two pages, still warm from the laser printer. Clinton walked out of the elevator from upstairs and strode into the Map Room. He looked grim, glancing neither left nor right.

"Well, here's what I think," Mark Penn said. "If this speech is a success, the presidency is saved. If it's a failure, the presidency is over." I gasped. "You haven't told *him* that, have you?" "No. Are you crazy?"

As I stood waiting in the hall, temporarily at rest for the first time in days, the enormity of the stakes hit me. After six years, I was finally where I wanted to be. The crisis had made my job easier; the army of advisors who normally parachute into a speech in the last days were mostly distracted. The President seemed comfortable trusting me with this responsibility. I felt proud that I had risen to the task. But like everyone else in America at that moment, I was holding my breath. Could the President do it?

The motorcade slowly, silently moved up Pennsylvania Avenue. We rode in the "control" van, with the most sophisticated electronic equipment. In the front seat, the military aide, carrying the "football." In the middle row, the NSC advisor and deputy chief of staff. Wedged in the back, the speechwriter. I murmured into a cellphone, checking to see that the last changes had been entered into the teleprompter on Capitol Hill.

The red lights of the motorcycle escort winked on and off, refracted in the raindrops on the windshield. The Capitol glowed straight ahead. And on the left, a half dozen TV satellite trucks stood sentry outside the Federal Courthouse, where the Lewinsky grand jury met every day.

The House chamber was jammed and tense as Clinton entered. Lawmakers applauded as usual, but were also craning their necks, watching him as he moved down the aisle.

"For 209 years, it has been the President's duty to report to you on the state of the Union," he began. "Because of the hard work and high purpose of the American people, these are good times for America. We have more than 14 million new jobs; the lowest unemployment in twenty-four years; the lowest core inflation in thirty years." Each fact was a small concussion.

"Incomes are rising; and we have the highest homeownership in history. Crime has dropped for a record five years in a row. And the welfare rolls are at their lowest levels in twenty-seven years. Our leadership in the world is unrivaled.

"Ladies and gentlemen," he said, lowering his voice and raising the volume for emphasis, "the state of our Union is *strong*."

The litany of facts was persuasive; the country *was* in good shape. Lawmakers of both parties had no choice but to rise and applaud. Penn and I stood just below the rostrum. He poked me in the ribs. "The Republicans are toast!"

Clinton proclaimed a "Third Way." "We have moved past the sterile debate between those who say government is the enemy and those who say government is the answer." He announced an imminent balanced budget. "For three decades, six presidents have come before you to warn of the

damage deficits pose to our nation. Tonight, I come before you to announce that the federal deficit—once so incomprehensibly large that it
had eleven zeroes—will be, simply, zero. I will submit to Congress for 1999
the first balanced budget in thirty years. And if we hold fast to fiscal discipline, we may balance the budget this year—four years ahead of schedule."

By now, the Democrats were cheering the semicolons. The Republicans were slack jawed. On a purely personal level, measured solely by grace
under pressure, it was a remarkable performance. The simple fact that he
was standing there. The added fact that he was buoyant, confident. The
room was united in one thought. How does he do it?

"Now, if we balance the budget for next year, it is projected that we'll
then have a sizable surplus in the years that immediately follow. What
should we do with this projected surplus?

"I have a simple four-word answer: Save Social Security first. Tonight
I propose that we reserve 100 percent of the surplus—that's every penny of
any surplus—until we have taken all the necessary measures to strengthen
the Social Security system for the twenty-first century."

The Democrats leapt to their feet, cheering. Gingrich paused for a
discernible instant—then he, too, stood, applauding. The Republicans
looked at Gingrich and then at each other. Then they stood and applauded. In that instant, a trillion dollars silently shifted on the budget
ledger from the column marked "tax cut" to the column marked "Social
Security." The President had gained the upper hand in the fiscal debates
that would dominate the last years of his term. The presidential pulpit had
never been put to more effective use.

The rest of the speech offered an array of hefty proposals. A national
child-care program. A $5 billion spending plan to build new schools and
modernize old ones. A raise in the minimum wage. The Patients' Bill of
Rights to regulate HMOs. An aggressive scheme to regulate the tobacco industry, and a cigarette tax increase to pay for new programs.

It was a speech that would have been remembered as one of Clinton's
best under any circumstances. And under *these* circumstances, it was a display of remarkable grit. It was also piercingly sad. It was hard to escape
thoughts of what might have been.

The "post party" was now an elaborate affair. A long buffet was set out
in the State Dining Room. Jesse Jackson and other celebrities mingled with
dozens of administration officials. The President came in and clenched his
hands over his head like a fighter, as the hundreds around him cheered. He
was still standing.

NINETEEN

PARALLEL UNIVERSE

SNAPSHOT. It is sixth months later, July 28, 7:45 A.M.

The Roosevelt Room is filled for the morning meeting of the senior staff to the President. Erskine Bowles sits halfway down the long table, as he always does. Top assistants array themselves in more-or-less permanent spots. Usually, treasury secretary Rubin, the only cabinet member to attend, sits at the end closest to the Oval Office, before the fireplace, under the great portrait of Theodore Roosevelt on a rearing horse. Rubin reads through memos, marks up speeches, and keeps an ear cocked in case someone is proposing a tax cut or a steel import quota he doesn't know about. Gene Sperling and Janet Yellen, the head of the Council of Economic Advisers, flank him. Today, Rubin's not here, and Sperling is late. At the other end, closest to the door, sit the political and press operatives, slouching, the cool kids: Begala and McCurry. A few of us stand by the battle flags: those with the youngest children at home, who find it hardest to drag ourselves away to get there on time—me, Vice President Gore's chief of staff, Ron Klain, OMB director Jack Lew, Deputy Press Secretary Barry Toiv.

Stephanie Streett, the President's scheduler, reads out a list of events for the day, some public, most private. The President will be speaking at a memorial service for slain Capitol Hill police officers, then in the evening at a senior citizens dinner. General Donald Kerrick, a lean and impressive man who is the deputy national

security advisor, is next. King Hussein has come to the country for
cancer treatment. There is a meeting with the Japanese foreign
minister, and Sandy Berger is giving a speech. Larry Stein is the
legislative director—Clinton's fourth—and he talks about the
progress on Capitol Hill on the "Commerce, State, and Justice"
appropriations bill, which spends money for those departments.
"Riggs has an amendment on Title Two." On the Texas Low Level
Waste Compact, whatever that is, "We sent no SAP. We informally
support it." A SAP is a "Statement of Administration Position." In the
Senate, amendments to a banking bill have been "tabled."

Sperling's chief of staff, waiting for him to arrive, reports good
progress on the job training bill. Bruce Reed discusses an executive
memorandum expanding health care options for people with
disabilities. The anniversary of the signing of the Americans With
Disabilities Act is the next day. Judy Winston, executive director of the
race initiative, is sitting on a couch under a sweeping western
landscape. She reports on the initiative's activities that day: "The
Canadian secretary of state for multiculturalism and the role of
women will be here." Hillary's chief of staff reports, "She'll have a full
day of meetings, videos, photo opportunities, etcetera." The liaison
with cabinet offices reports that Secretary of Education Dick Riley will
give a speech on discounted Internet access for schools and libraries.

For me, for my colleagues, the rest of the day seems similarly
uneventful. There is great excitement about a bureaucratically
obtuse memo, sent out by the communications office, telling the
speechwriters: "The language of the Millennium, and the logo (until
we hear otherwise), is for millennium use only. Although we always
want to consider whether there is a millennium component in our
message opportunities, it is very important to the over-all strength
and infrastructure of the millennium project that it remain quite
distinct and separate from the WH and our day to day messages and
words that we use." It promptly leaked to the press. ("Does this mean
we can't say 'bridge to the twenty-first century' anymore?" one of the
writers asks. Speechwriter Jeff Shesol sends out an e-mail rallying
people to "Party like it's 1999," then panics that this, too, will leak.)
There is last-minute retyping of a eulogy for the two slain police
officers who stopped a gunman from terrorizing the Capitol, with a
beautiful concluding paragraph sent over by the President: "Our
words are such poor replacements for the joys of family and friends,
the turning of the seasons, the rhythms of normal life that should
rightfully have been theirs. But we offer them to you from a grateful
nation."

Another normal day at the most unusual of White Houses. For by any measure, this isn't a normal day. Monica Lewinsky is preparing to testify. Rumors of immunity are sweeping. By late afternoon, the word is on the news wires: she has made a deal with the prosecutors. And there is no discussion in this meeting (or any other meeting I attend that day).

IN THE MONTHS that followed the State of the Union, as the storm over Lewinsky raged, the White House was a house divided. A handful of people obsessed about the scandal, plotted legal and press strategy. But the vast majority of White House staff were deliberately kept walled off. It was vital that we keep working on policy, doing our jobs—in part so that the President would keep his job. It was an ironic but undeniable fact that the only place in America where you could have a two-hour conversation about Bill Clinton and the name Monica Lewinsky did not come up was in the White House itself.

We joked about living in a parallel universe. Clinton's determination to keep doing the public job of his presidency entailed, above all else, public appearances, a relentless reliance on the bully pulpit. One after another, the message of the day was hewed to religiously, sometimes two or even three a day. In one week in early March, the President spoke in public on disaster relief in California, on tax reform, on drunk driving, on food safety legislation, on Medicare reform, on the economy, and on health care, and announced the first woman commander of a space shuttle mission. One morning, he listened, red-faced, as a mother told how she saw her nine-year-old daughter struck by a drunk driver. That afternoon, he flew to New York to participate in the *Time* magazine anniversary celebration at Radio City Music Hall. As the scandal went on, the pace of appearances accelerated.

Reporters scorned Clinton, mocked his events—but they had no choice but to cover them. CNN would break into its programming and broadcast the day's speech on education standards in its entirety, as if the President were going to slip up mid-paragraph and start free-associating about the controversy. The evening news, with their high-calorie diet of stories about the scandal, felt compelled to include a few sentences from the President's policy statements, too. These daily sessions showed the world a confident, unshaken Clinton focusing on the work of the people. That was partly right. Clinton, to a remarkable degree, was able to focus on his work. And those around him focused obsessively on that, too.

Plainly, in private, the controversy was frequently on the President's mind. A briefing before a speech might begin with a withering comment

about Starr or the press, or a rueful aside about the mess he was in. Then Bruce Reed or Elena Kagan would begin with gun control or school safety. And Clinton—the cloud having passed—would bore in, asking questions, rewriting, sending aides to double-check facts.

The scandal did intrude in other ways. The empty chair at the morning staff meeting meant someone—you found out on the radio—was testifying before the grand jury. You did have the impression that somehow you had walked onto the set of a lurid soap opera.

At another level, though, the clamor that surrounded the White House was only the most intense, most absurd version of the din that had been growing louder for years. Coverage of presidents, indeed of all politicians, had been growing steadily more negative for decades.

At the outset of Clinton's term, a handful of television reporters would stand on the North Lawn of the White House to broadcast their reports. Now nearly two dozen cameras sprouted for regular "feeds." In the first days of the scandal, the reporters who stood on the lawn to cover the White House were drenched by rain. They trudged back indoors, literally caked in mud. The lawn was quickly covered with gravel.

THROUGHOUT THE SPRING, it seemed as if real progress might be made on two major issues highlighted in the State of the Union address.

Improbably, it appeared that there was a real chance for bipartisan action on Social Security after the election—as long as we could make sure there was no partisan action on the subject *before* the election.

As the President said at Georgetown University a few weeks after the State of the Union, Social Security was facing a "looming crisis." The baby boomers—that huge generation that had flooded the college campuses in the 1960s and the stock market in the 1990s—were slowly creeping toward retirement age. The number of senior citizens would roughly double over three decades. Clinton used a chart to point out the consequence. In 1960, there were 5.1 Americans working for every one person drawing Social Security. In 1997, 3.3 younger workers supported each Social Security recipient. At the current rates, in 2030, there will be two people working for every one person drawing Social Security.

Clinton had pledged to involve the Republican and Democratic members of Congress in a year-long effort to try to forge a consensus on Social Security. (Yes, a "national dialogue" on Social Security.) He scheduled a series of conferences around the country, taking Republican and Democratic lawmakers with him. They would begin probing the issue, testing the contours of a possible deal. These sessions were also supposed to postpone the debate until after the election. (Paul Begala explained what candidates

would likely say: "I am willing to do anything to save Social Security—anything except raise taxes or cut benefits. Anything.") Then, after the election, in December, there was to be a White House conference. Negotiations would begin in earnest in early 1999. In the meantime, as long as the Republicans did not spend the surplus on a tax cut, and banked it instead so that it could be used to save Social Security, we had achieved our goal.

At the same time, it appeared for a brief moment as if there would be a breakthrough in the struggle to restrict tobacco. Tobacco was the archetype issue for the post-modern presidency. In 1995, the Food and Drug Administration (FDA) had launched a drive to regulate tobacco, seeking to restrict advertising and marketing practices aimed at children. That executive action was now enmeshed in the courts. In the meantime, the state attorneys general had launched a high-profile series of lawsuits against the tobacco companies to recover $368 billion in health care costs from illnesses due to smoking. The attorneys general and the companies settled the case in 1997, with the firms agreeing to restrict their marketing and to accept FDA oversight of tobacco. The deal required sweeping legislation from Congress, including an increase in the tobacco tax. (Cigarettes were considered price-inelastic; higher prices would mean fewer young people would buy them.)

On April 1, the Senate Commerce Committee, chaired by Senator John McCain, passed a version of the bill, 19–0, that included a far steeper tax increase than the administration had sought. Tobacco companies pelted the legislation with ads. Soon it was withdrawn. One of the questions about 1998 was whether the legislative outcome would have been different had the scandal not intruded. I doubt that the tobacco bill would have passed in any case.

Meanwhile, our best chance at real campaign reform expired. The day after Clinton called for free TV time for candidates in the State of the Union, the chairman of the Federal Communications Commission, William Kennard, announced that the agency would move forward on the proposal. Members of Congress, prodded by the broadcasters, angrily threatened the FCC and virtually ordered it to back down. In the Senate, the leading tormentor was reform sponsor John McCain, who said he objected on the grounds of jurisdiction. The White House threatened to veto the lawmakers' efforts. But soon thereafter, wilting under industry pressure, the FCC retreated.

But the accumulation of presidential effort on tobacco, on Social Security, on education, and on health care served as constant reminders to the public of what they liked about Bill Clinton. His poll ratings kept climbing. Even though many people said they didn't believe him, his approval rating hovered above 60 percent.

ALL THROUGH THE SPRING, the independent counsel and the White House waged a fierce battle in the courts and in the press. Starr was seeking to compel Secret Service agents to testify about what they had seen while protecting the President; the struggle over that took weeks. Clinton's lawyers filed motions demanding investigations of leaks by Starr's office. Nothing new, really, was being revealed—as it turned out, the outlines of the case were clear in the first few days—but each twist and tumble of the investigation consumed days of coverage and speculation. We knew that the scandal was affecting what we said and when we said it. It wasn't always clear how or why. Someone would mutter, "We really need something for Friday," or "This just isn't strong enough," or "Don't worry. Nobody's going to hear this."

The President traveled to Africa, where he spoke before the South African parliament, expressed remorse over the U.S. response to genocide in Rwanda, and spoke at Gorée Island—a transshipment point for slaves headed to the New World. While he was there, Judge Susan Webber Wright dismissed the Paula Jones case before it went to trial. After that decision, the President planned a long-delayed press conference. The staff hesitated, waiting, worrying about announcing it. We were meeting in John Podesta's office. A few minutes after the announcement was made, the press reported that a judge had issued a ruling in the Lewinsky case. We continued a fitful discussion of Clinton's opening remarks.

Mike McCurry looked at me. "Look, Waldman. Don't take this the wrong way, but this is going to be the least consequential opening statement in history." It was. The press conference was consumed by questions about Lewinsky.

Then, improbably under the circumstances, Clinton had to perform his stand-up routine at the annual "humor dinners" for members of the press.

Mark Katz, the joke writer from New York, made his annual visit. He was anguished about the scandal, finding nothing funny in it. He expected us to be equally funereal. That spring it was a constant surprise meeting people from outside the government, outside the White House. They would ask, "How are you doing?" in a tone of solicitousness and concern. We knew we were spending our time on things other than Monica, but nobody seemed to believe it. The White House was still standing there every morning; the guards still saluted; the endless meetings droned on. It was unsettling to brush up against the way the rest of the country saw us, portrayed through the press.

The President's sense of humor was not naturally honed for the humor dinners. His strength was long shaggy-dog stories—whimsical tales

of colorful characters in Arkansas politics. This year Clinton had to project normalcy and a certain jaunty air in the midst of a hostile situation. "So," he began his remarks at the off-the-record Gridiron dinner. "How was *your* week?" Before the White House Correspondents Association, the unthinkable happened—something that had never occurred—the latest skirmish in the war with the press. A joke leaked. The joke—not a particularly funny one—had Clinton sending Congressman Dan Burton into space. The afternoon of the dinner, John King, the new White House correspondent on CNN, reported it. Most leaks were shrugged off. But leaking a joke—well, this had never happened. It demanded a witch hunt.

As we waited for the President to come down from the residence where he was changing into his tuxedo, angry staff members gathered in Ann Lewis' office. Several argued: Let's kill the joke. That'll punish the leaker—and take away King's scoop. But if our purpose now was to keep Clinton from going off-script, changing a joke now was the worst possible idea. We straggled over to the Map Room on the ground floor of the residence. The debate continued within a wider circle. I was frantic to resolve it before Clinton came in. A compromise was reached.

"There are barely forty days left in the 105th Congress as of tonight. This is a Congress with nothing to do and no time to do it in," Clinton said later that night to laughter. "But there will be one news item coming out of Capitol Hill next week. I met with Senator John Glenn recently to decide who should be the next distinguished member of Congress hurled into the far reaches of the universe. And we have our man. Godspeed, Dick Armey." Dan Burton remained safe on Earth.

THE BEST CHANCE for the President to give a "big" speech—one that might be covered by the press regardless of a breaking crisis, one that might even be excerpted in the newspaper—was during college commencements. The staff began planning possible topics months in advance, well before it was decided what schools Clinton would speak at. I organized a planning process that culled suggestions from different policy offices. Some topics— national service as a way to bring the races together, expanded voter registration, antitrust enforcement, the importance of American history and civics—were discarded. We sent a menu to the President, then discussed the options with him at strategy meetings. In the end, he chose to speak on immigration at Portland State and on the digital divide at MIT.

The administration was paying increasingly close attention to the Internet and its impact. In 1993, when Clinton assumed office, there were only fifty sites on the World Wide Web. By 1996, as he joked at a com-

mencement address that year, even his cat had a Web page. It was still seen, in many ways, as a novelty.

But as the decade accelerated, it became increasingly clear that America was being transformed. Clinton remarked in several speeches on how profoundly computers had remade the economy—"The high-tech industry employs more people today than the auto industry did at its height in the 1950s." At a speech before high-technology executives in San Francisco, he announced support of a moratorium on new taxation on the Web. Now he would address a growing problem. If opportunity would increasingly come from the ability to master computer technology, poor children would fall even further behind. We explored whether it made sense to call for universal computer literacy as a condition of high school graduation, but it seemed unwise to add yet another layer of requirements. (Also, with computers becoming ubiquitous and easier to use, the very concept of computer literacy was dated.)

A day before the speech, the schedulers let slip that the President had a few other things on his schedule that Friday. In addition to delivering the commencement address in Cambridge, the First Family would drive to Thoreau's Walden Pond to dedicate a nature center built by guitarist Don Henley of the Eagles.

Then there were the Kennedys. The weekend was the thirtieth anniversary of Robert Kennedy's death. The family was hoping that, since the President was in Boston, anyway . . . A visit to Congressman Joe Kennedy's house was arranged. Clinton would tape the radio address honoring RFK, to be broadcast the next morning. Then the press wanted a photograph of the President with Ethel Kennedy. That picture and the radio address text were released on Friday, along with the MIT speech and the Walden ceremony and a Walden conference call with youth. Plus, I was reminded, the new unemployment numbers would be coming out on Friday—and Clinton always took the opportunity to discuss economic strategy when the figures were released. So that was appended to the MIT speech.

Friday morning we were startled to open the news clips and discover that a major announcement was being made about the Internet—by the White House—endorsing a new system for giving out "domain names." Ira Magaziner had devoted the past several years to developing administration policy on the Net. He had promised John Podesta he wouldn't make any announcements that would conflict with the MIT speech, but the opportunity, apparently, was too juicy to pass up.

"Today," the President told the graduates, "affluent schools are almost three times as likely to have Internet access in the classroom; white students more than twice as likely as black students to have computers in their homes. We know from hard experience that unequal education hardens

into unequal prospects. We know the information age will accelerate this trend. The three fastest-growing careers in America are all in computer-related fields, offering far more than average pay. Happily, the digital divide has begun to narrow, but it will not disappear of its own accord."

ON THE EVENING OF JULY 7, consultant-pollster Doug Schoen stood at the projector and said, "Satisfaction in the direction of the country is up to 65 percent." Buddy barked. Clinton, sunburned in a black shirt and pants, waved at the dog. "He agrees. The real issue is what should the tone of July and August be, and what about the fall?"

Every year, the budget struggle between the Democratic President and the Republican Congress rolled toward a near-guaranteed showdown at the end of the fiscal year on October 1. By now the rhythms of the battle were familiar to Clinton. He looked forward to it with a confidence born of having bested the Republicans several years in a row. The Democrats were now in the enviable position of being the party most devoted to fiscal discipline, opposing tax cuts and other measures that might throw the budget out of balance—yet also supporting higher spending on domestic programs. Clinton's original economic synthesis of 1992, linking deficit reduction with increased investment, was finally coming to fruition, thanks to the balanced budget and the surging economy.

This year, the puzzle was whether the Republicans would want to make a deal, or resist until the end. We were operating under the assumption that the Republicans would resist. "But they could pull a '96, and give us our druthers," Clinton warned, recalling the sudden burst of compromise as the elections approached.

Gore—more combative by nature than Clinton—interjected. He urged a more direct attack on the recklessness of the Congress. "What they have done in the appropriations committees is as bad as what they did in '95." The difference? "They are a lot smarter now. They have built in fail-safe systems so that the government doesn't shut down, for example. They won't have nine of thirteen appropriations bills bundled into one continuing resolution this time. But they still have a lot of momentum driving them straight into a brick wall."

We ran through the issues that would be included in the spending bills. Clinton said the environment didn't really work as an issue unless people thought it was threatened—so congressional refusal to fund pollution controls adequately was not cutting as an issue. The environment never really hurt in 1992: "Bush, galumphing along, nobody thought he would really hurt the environment," he said.

The tobacco legislation looked doomed. The President was looking for

other ways to press the fight. Ever since the states had filed lawsuits against the tobacco companies to recover costs lost under state Medicaid programs, an obvious possibility was a federal lawsuit to recover costs to Medicare. But the possible suit raised legal and practical issues. It was not clear whether the government had the legal grounds on which to sue. It was quickly recognized that the topic should not be discussed in such a political setting. Gore strongly suggested that the decision had to be made strictly within the Department of Justice. "We have to be aware that they have a very different culture over there." (Left unstated was the fact that his brother-in-law, Frank Hunger, was the assistant attorney general for the civil division—and was one of the Department of Justice officials most cautious about a suit.)

"I haven't studied this in a while, but the states are able to bring lawsuits under their very broad parens patriae power," Clinton said offhandedly, showing off his law professor pedigree. The federal government might have a harder time.

Looking toward the election, Clinton felt he had found an effective way to frame both the Democrats and the Republicans—"partisanship versus progress." "People think that partisanship is the root of all evil. Partisanship is endangering the economy, partisanship is blocking the health care bill of rights." (Hell, the worst thing you could say about Stalin was that he was excessively partisan, Clinton joked.) This would inspire congressional Democrats to pass legislation and not just obstruct the Republicans. From now on, Clinton instructed us, all issues should be framed in this way. "This is the best slogan we've ever had."

THE "PHONY WAR" came to an end on July 28 with the news that Monica Lewinsky would be testifying before a grand jury. Within a few days, the President's lawyers had arranged for him to testify later in August.

Lewinsky testified. On August 6 there were press reports that she had signed a statement that she had had an affair with the President. That night, we had a scheduled political strategy meeting. Minyon Moore, the political director, quoted a folk saying as we walked to the residence. "Find the good and praise it," she said. "Find the good and praise it." "That's the problem," I replied, "finding the good." When we arrived, the room was empty. A few minutes later, Podesta and Bowles rushed back in from Clinton's study. "Not yet!" We scurried downstairs, awaiting a summons.

The Friday before his testimony, the White House's façade of normalcy was stretched thin. That morning, speechwriter Jeff Shesol and Ann Lewis gave Clinton a lyrical radio address honoring the victims of terrorism in Kenya. He recorded it, and then told them he wanted a new speech with hard news. "This just won't break through. It just doesn't do what I need

right now," he told them. Kris Engskov, his personal assistant, was trying to shoo people along and speed the President's schedule so that he could meet with his lawyers. "I know he has to be President," Kris snapped, "but he can't do that if he isn't President anymore."

Clinton was due to speak to labor leaders at a Democratic National Committee lunch at the Hay Adams Hotel across Lafayette Square. In the Oval Office before the speech, he called for his health policy advisor—and a set of charts he had used to explain the difference between the Democratic and Republican versions of the Patients' Bill of Rights legislation. The week before, he had instructed how to list the items in the legislation in speeches. "Follow Ronald Reagan's rule of lists. Reagan said: Start with your strongest item, go through the rest, and finish with a bang!" Today, his blue eyes burned in a worry-lined face. He wanted to stress that there were real differences between the two parties' bills—not simply, as the Republicans claimed, that the Democrats wanted to let patients sue their HMO. "Did you see the way the charts worked in Kentucky on Monday?" he asked. "I think it really made a difference."

At lunch it was a red-meat crowd, literally: a hearty steak lunch was served. The scandal was not mentioned, but it hung over the room. Halfway through, I dashed out, fearing suddenly that the wrong radio address might have been released to the public. (It hadn't.) Clinton was low-key but firm. We have the right issues, he told the labor leaders. We are united. Our agenda is right for the country. They applauded vigorously, seeming to hope to buoy him.

AS THE TESTIMONY APPROACHED, a weird solitude came over Clinton. I felt I couldn't help him: I had not been in the snows of New Hampshire, hadn't been called to defend him on TV, hadn't been one of those who were clearly tortured by the whole matter. On this matter the speechwriting staff was *not* needed.

I walked around the West Wing on August 17. It was ghostly. Most offices were quiet, doors closed. I stood at the open door of the empty Oval Office, cordoned off with a velvet rope. Outside, it was unnaturally dark, with rain pelting the windows. It looked as if a rather uncreative B-movie director had scripted the weather. I thought about the first time I had seen the office, bathed in light, six years before.

That night, Clinton addressed the country. An apologetic draft, apparently penned by Shrum, was not used. (It promptly leaked to the press, and appeared in full within days.) Instead, Clinton confessed his affair, insisted that his testimony had been "legally accurate," and lashed out at Starr, demanding privacy for himself and his family.

TWENTY

CONTAGION

EVERY FEW DAYS, in the morning staff meetings, Gene Sperling would issue a cryptic report on the fluctuations of a currency. "The Thai baht took a big hit today," he would announce. Or "Bad news from Brazil, the real is way down." (The staff would nod gravely, as if we knew whether there was, in fact, a Thai baht.) There were smudge marks of fatigue under Gene's eyes, and worry lines creased Rubin's forehead. Throughout 1998, as Washington was transfixed by the saga of the President and the intern—and as the White House struggled to keep to its recommended daily dose of message events—the world economy was spinning off its axis. The high-tech, global marketplace Clinton had worked to encourage into being was facing its first truly worldwide financial crisis.

Once upon a time, Richard Nixon could be heard snarling on his White House tapes, "I don't give a (expletive deleted) about the lira." Now, after the end of the Cold War, a president was expected to have mastered the intricacies of the global economy, so central to foreign and domestic policy. And that was especially true in September 1998—when both Clinton's presidency and the world economy were in crisis. He was scheduled to deliver a major speech before the Council on Foreign Relations.

FOR YEARS, the economies of developing nations—especially in Asia, but also in Latin America and the formerly communist countries of Eastern Europe—had surged forward. Foreign investment had flowed in. But for all the real growth, the newly booming economies were riddled with cronyism, corruption, and lax banking standards. At the same time, more than

$1 trillion in foreign currency transactions now took place each day, vast oceans of funds sluicing around the world in search of higher returns.

In the summer of 1997, the Thai currency collapsed, and foreign investors began pulling their money out. In the months that followed, economic crisis spread like a virulent disease from country to country. Economists called it a "contagion." In December 1997, just before the State of the Union address, Korea—then the world's eleventh largest economy—had threatened to default on its debt. An emergency loan from the International Monetary Fund, in exchange for drastic austerity measures by the government, had kept the economy from collapsing altogether. Rubin persuaded American banks not to call in their loans. But a full-scale panic was on. Not just for a bank, or a class of financial institutions, or even a country, the panic was now worldwide and affecting almost all the developing economies. At the slightest hint of trouble, money that had indiscriminately flooded in was now rushing out again. The loss of confidence in one country could be felt in the markets of another country half a world away.

Clinton, Rubin, deputy treasury secretary Larry Summers, Sperling, and the others had been working on the crisis for months. It was in the 1998 State of the Union that the President had warned that "far-off clouds" would soon affect the U.S. economy. Throughout the year, a quarter of the world had sunk into recession. To the surprise of the economists, the drop-off in exports to the Asian markets had not yet had a severe impact on the American economy. But delicacy was required: U.S. experts believed that in many instances sclerotic political systems, shady practices, and risky lending had brought the countries' crises on themselves. Structural reforms were needed. When the countries came calling to the International Monetary Fund, many administration officials were skeptical about throwing good money after bad. They worried about the "moral hazard" that arose if lenders believed that they would automatically be rescued. But concerns about global economic and political stability necessarily prevailed. So when the IMF devised a plan that would offer countries a way out in return for sometimes harsh austerity measures, the United States agreed.

In Indonesia, the austerity measures demanded by the International Monetary Fund helped lead to the fall of the corrupt government. Speculators threatened the economies of South America. In August 1998, the Russian economy flattened like a burst balloon. The U.S. stock market plummeted at fears of a worldwide recession. Each morning brought news of overnight drops on Asian markets followed by similar drops in the U.S. stock exchanges. Panic followed the sun in the twenty-four-hour global market. Liquidity—the ability to get loans and capital—began to dry up

around the world, as lenders feared the consequences of a collapse. It seemed possible that the situation could become a deflationary spiral, with stock values, prices, and wages plunging together. That was what had caused the Great Depression.

Until now, there was no benefit in having the President make a public show of his involvement in the issue. That would have signaled the markets that things were *really* serious. Instead, Rubin and his colleagues had handled it. Now, it was clear that the President needed to make a strong statement, conveying confidence and showing action. While the President was on a trip to Russia in late August, he decided to give an address in New York when he returned.

A SPEECH LIKE THIS is not written on the fly, or in a speechwriter's aerie. Each word matters. Sperling convened a rolling meeting in his office, bringing together Treasury and State Department officials, White House economists, and me to discuss nuances. Some of them were at ease in the thin atmosphere of the White House; Stuart Eizenstat, the under secretary of state, had been President Carter's top domestic aide. Others sat quietly, looking somewhat startled when their arcane expertise was suddenly called for. The door was always closed tight.

Treasury officials, who had been working for months on the financial crisis, were skeptical of bold moves announced for the sake of announcing bold moves. It was important that we not seem to discard all the previous steps taken. Anything less would signal panic, a lack of mastery, that itself would cause problems. A speechwriter who worked for Summers had drafted a detailed outline, vetted and approved by Rubin and his team, which spelled out the permissible line of argument.

The President, in turn, had a bias toward action, which was conveyed through Sperling. If he acted too alarmed, he might spook the markets and worsen the panic he was trying to forestall. But if he acted blasé, he risked being seen as a Herbert Hoover of globalization. "You don't understand. We need more. The President needs more," Sperling would insist to the Treasury officials—more new things to say, more announcements to make.

I wanted to ring the alarm bells—to state that this was the most severe financial crisis since World War II. Treasury aides pursed their lips. We can't say that, they explained. I had just proposed shouting "fire" in a crowded theater (or "sell!" in a trading pit). I crossed it out.

The speech had to inject a jolt of confidence into the world financial system. Just as during the bank panics of the 1930s, psychology was working against us. The other purpose was to persuade central banks simultaneously to lower interest rates around the world. The Treasury Department

was consulting closely with the U.S. Federal Reserve, which was independent but wanted to know what Clinton was going to say. In turn, the Fed and the Treasury Department were meeting with their counterparts in the G-8 group of industrial nations. If any one country slashed rates on its own, then funds would simply slosh from the dollar into a currency that paid higher rates. It was vital that the bankers all jump at once. Clinton's words would send the signal that coordinated lowering of interest rates around the world should begin.

The way that both these objectives would be accomplished was with a key phrase that had to be precisely composed. According to the Treasury officials, the desirability of an interest rate cut would be signaled by saying that inflation was no longer the greatest threat. The speech should say, "The balance of risks has shifted"—without saying from what to what. "That's nonsensical," I suggested. After much negotiation, we agreed that the President could say, "Low and stable inflation is critical to our economic health. But the balance of risks has now shifted. We must also guard against the danger of global deflation—the spiral downward of prices and economies that wipes out wealth and eats away hope within nations, and sows seeds of conflict among them."

Beyond that, something more fundamental and more interesting was going on in Clinton's mind. Once again—perhaps too late—he had begun to create a new approach to globalization. After the failure of fast track legislation in 1997, he had begun to press for a new direction in trade and global economics. In Geneva, in May 1998, at a meeting of the World Trade Organization, he urged that it open its operations to public scrutiny. I had flown to England to write the address. It incorporated many of the arguments, and even some of the proposals, we had fought for when I ran Ralph Nader's lobbying office. Clinton quoted Supreme Court Justice Louis Brandeis: "Sunlight is the best of disinfectants." At the suggestion of Larry Summers, he said, "We must do more to ensure that spirited economic competition among nations never becomes a race to the bottom—in environmental protections, consumer protections, or labor standards. We should be leveling up, not leveling down." Privately, he was even more emphatic. We did not create the WTO, he said, "so that it could impose the economic theories of Milton Friedman on the rest of the world."

Since the global economy was exhibiting the same boom and bust qualities that the national economy had suffered before strong national regulation was created to stabilize markets, Clinton wanted to make a broader case. The world economy needed the kind of order and structure that had protected the domestic economies of the United States and other countries.

As the raw force of the market had ripped through the world, a variety

of proposals had gained currency. Some, including the financier George Soros, wanted a global central bank to regulate the swings of expansion and contraction. Soros had sent Clinton the galley proofs of his book on globalization. Clinton had underlined it heavily and commanded Sperling to read it.

Others wanted forms of capital controls, to stanch the flow of funds in and out of countries. The approach proposed by the United States had been different. Rather than trying to dam up the flow of capital, the U.S. goal was to regulate it by requiring openness, strict banking safeguards, accurate accounting techniques, and an end to systematic corruption and bribery. This approach looked like the safeguards introduced in the securities markets in the 1930s, on a global scale. But it fell short of having a global enforcement office, or a worldwide central bank. It wouldn't be enough, ultimately. But in the effort to tame the wild forces of global markets, it was a start.

On Friday, September 11, I sat at my computer, trying to work on the speech. But it was hard to concentrate.

That morning, the President had addressed a somber gathering of religious leaders in the East Room. He had stayed up until 4 A.M., writing out remarks about the Lewinsky matter in longhand, and he had read them in a husky voice. His first speech about it had not been contrite, he acknowledged. He had not said he was sorry. He had struggled with his anger for weeks. He apologized to his family and, for the first time, to Lewinsky. He had, he said, "what my Bible calls a 'broken spirit'—an understanding that I must have God's help to be the person that I want to be."

A few hours later, the Starr Report was released and posted on the Internet. The independent counsel had sent the Congress a report, and without reading it, lawmakers had voted to release it to the public. It was a lurid narrative, far more graphic than necessary to prove a legal or constitutional case. It was clear that the prosecutor was trying to sandblast Clinton from office. The reaction over the next few days would be telling.

That weekend, we were worried about Brazil. Working from home, I joined in a series of nonstop conference calls to plan for the speech, to report on the negotiations with the central bankers, and to monitor the increasingly dire South American situation. I was warned not to draft language that seemed to promise international support for Brazil's currency. We could not be sure that nation would hold.

Sunday morning, Sperling called me with extensive comments. Late that afternoon, I went to the White House and worked on a secretary's computer in the paper-strewn outer office in the economic advisor's suite. At 9 P.M. the President called Sperling over to the residence to tell him he had cut and rewritten the speech. I stayed behind, working on the draft. Gene

returned. Clinton wanted more discussion of the human toll of the financial crisis. He wanted me to look at a *Washington Post* series reporting how the entire middle class of many Asian nations had suddenly been plunged into poverty over the previous year. There were empty office buildings in once thriving cities.

A few hours later, the President called again. Now he would be coming over to the Oval Office. Sperling and I brought a new copy of the speech down, through darkened halls, past locked offices. A Secret Service agent stood at the door and let us in. "Please close the door behind you," he said. Gene and I stood in the bright office, alone. That weekend, people across the country were reading about that office.

Clinton came in from the patio, dressed in sneakers, gray shorts, and a Martha's Vineyard T-shirt. An unlit, frayed cigar was in his mouth. He talked about the speech, the problems faced by Asian governments, the unnerving impact of stock market gyrations on middle-class people who now had their wealth tied up in the market. I suggested that about six months ago, a lot of people had looked at their portfolios and suddenly realized they were now wealthy. Now they would feel a great loss if the market plunged. At one point, he alluded to his personal "mistakes" and gratefully recounted the support he had gotten from friends.

The audience tomorrow would be testing him. Much as the Congress had looked into his eyes earlier in the year, these captains of finance and the media would be measuring Clinton. "When you talk about the global capital markets—that's the second and third row" of the audience, I joked. "The media types are people like Tom Brokaw and Diane Sawyer." He nodded and chewed on his cigar.

We moved out into Betty Currie's darkened outer office. It would be a big day tomorrow.

"I think the markets will react favorably tomorrow," Sperling told him. "Why?" "This speech, somewhat. And also the diminished sense that you will leave office." Clinton listened intently as Sperling explained: "The market went up on Friday because there were no surprises in the Starr Report."

I told him that the financiers had a much more acute sense of alarm about the contagion than did the general public. I reported on a conversation I had with a leader of the Council on Foreign Relations. "The crowd there is very nervous about the financial situation."

"Me too!" Clinton replied quickly. Though frankly, at that moment he didn't seem scared at all—happy to have something other than the scandal to talk about. After a detailed grilling on Japan, its markets, and its banking reform policies, he left. Silently, through darkened halls, we walked back upstairs.

The flight to New York is a short one, about an hour. Time on Air Force One seems to move more slowly than on other airplanes. Although passengers are urged to sit in their armchair-style seats for takeoff and landing, there are no seatbelt lights, and people wander through the plane at will. This morning, Clinton continued to edit the speech at his desk. Hillary sat on the couch, watching him.

The operators who fly on board the plane patched through a call from the Treasury Department. (Despite the high-tech accouterments, the phones were less sophisticated than the ones on the back of a seat on the Washington–to–New York shuttle — you have to hold down a "talk" button to be heard.) Mid-level Treasury officials pulled a classic bureaucratic move: suddenly, strenuously objecting to their own language. We can't say "deflation" at all. Too scary.

Sperling and I went to the President's cabin to tell him. He chafed at the timidity, then he shrugged and suggested, "with a quarter of the world's economy in recession." I went to the office in the back of the plane and typed out the phrase. In the motorcade on the East River Drive, Sperling shouted into a cellphone with a Treasury official in London to find out whether the G-8 finance ministers had reached an agreement on a statement. He was still trying to find the answer when we pulled up to the council. We were ushered into a tiny office, where the President sat at a table as Rubin and I hovered over him. Gene held a cellphone up to one ear and covered the other with his hand, trying to hear London. The joint statement by finance ministers wasn't quite ready.

Worse, now we couldn't say the balance had shifted to risk of "recession." Clinton finally struggled out with "Clearly the balance of risks has now shifted, with a full quarter of the world's population living in countries with declining economic growth or negative economic growth."

If you had been kidnapped, blindfolded, and deposited in the library of the Council on Foreign Relations and asked to guess where you were, you might arrive at the right answer pretty quickly. The paneling was dark, the curtains thick. I sat on the side, with my head resting against the frame of a portrait of some august mandarin. The room was crammed with luminaries, about a hundred strong. Ted Sorensen, George Soros, Richard Holbrooke . . . the owner of U.S. News, the editors of Time and Newsweek. Tom Donahue, the former head of the AFL-CIO, turned around and pumped my hand.

The audience was polite as the President entered the library. Pete Peterson, an investment banker and former Republican commerce secretary, began by telling the President: "From Main Street to Wall Street, people sleep better because Bob Rubin is the secretary of the treasury." The applause was so vigorous that Clinton stifled a laugh.

"This is the worst financial crisis in fifty years," Peterson declared. Clinton got up, thanked him, and continued: "I agree with what Pete Peterson said—this is the biggest financial challenge facing the world in a half century." "Ha!" I quietly elbowed the person next to me. Treasury had made me take it out, but Pete Peterson, for God's sake, had put it back in. The world economy might collapse, but for that moment, it seemed as important that I was proven right.*

Clinton read the speech in a strong voice, dutifully at first, then picking up speed and emotion as he reached the list of policy items. Steps to spur growth, a doubling of World Bank support for the social safety net in depressed Asian countries, and pledges to use IMF emergency funds to help keep the contagion from spreading to South America.

He was not interrupted once for applause. But the audience seemed impressed, if grudgingly, and even more, relieved that someone was taking charge. After he finished, hands reached out, quiet murmurs of thanks were offered. Then, from the back of the room, came a booming voice. David Bloom of NBC called out, "Mr. President. Will you accept a censure by the Congress?" Usually, when reporters shout out rude questions over the heads of an audience—say, teachers in the Rose Garden—they will hiss, or murmur, or shake their fingers. Here, the crowd literally, audibly went, "Harrumph," as if someone had belched in the House of Lords. The audience members slowly turned around. The reporters in the back of the room looked back at their bosses. No more questions.

Clinton and Rubin were pleased with the speech and its reception. There was one more bit of business to conclude: what Clinton should say about the death of George Wallace, which had been reported earlier in the day.

Wallace personified the Old South, the South that Clinton had broken with. On the day he announced his candidacy for president, Clinton spoke about how his native region had been kept down, held back, by racism and the clever ruse of pitting white working-class people against blacks. Now one of the speechwriters had drafted a brief eulogy and faxed it to me, but it was off, too laudatory of Wallace. I intercepted the President as he was heading back into his holding room. "You should think about what you are going to say," I warned him. "I would think you would want to say that he had a long journey, but ultimately brought people together." Clinton recounted a time when he and Wallace briefly overlapped as governors. "It was at the National Governors Association meeting, during the

---

* Two years later, it appears that the crisis might not, in fact, have been the worst in a half century (unless you had the misfortune of living in an Asian country). That honor still went to the oil shocks of the 1970s, or the Latin American debt crisis of the 1980s.

1980s. The Republicans were saying 'let the states do it.' They sent two assistant secretaries up to this meeting. And I had this resolution—it was on unemployment disability insurance. There was this truck driver with a sixth-grade education who was disabled, and they said that he could get a job as a computer programmer! Anyway, I had a resolution, and we needed the sixty-seventh vote. So I called Wallace. And he got up two hours early, because it was so hard for him to get ready in the morning and get dressed. He got up two hours early to cast that vote. So I'll always remember that."

Clinton looked intently at me. "And he did wrong—and he asked for forgiveness."

I flinched and looked away. I tried to recover quickly. "Well, he started at the bottom and was moving in the right direction."

Clinton leaned in. "No, no, he started here"—he pointed at the wall with his finger—"and went like this"—he traced down, then back up. "No, no, believe me. I know the history of that region." Wallace had begun as an economic populist, then turned to racism mid-career. In his later years, after being shot, he returned somewhat to his more progressive roots and sought the support of Alabama's black community. I wondered what he would have made of having a tutorial on redneck history taught in the hallway of the Council on Foreign Relations on the East Side of Manhattan.

The economic crisis was not over. But in this instance, dispatching fleets of words, not warships, an American president was able to help turn the tide. It was a new world, a world in which global markets mattered more than traditional statecraft. And I remember thinking that if the President, at that moment, had not understood it, we would have been in big trouble.

I WAS STRUCK, one Saturday two weeks later, watching Clinton, Rubin, and their deputies arrayed around the big table in the Cabinet Room. I had seen so many pictures of Kennedy and McNamara hunched over this very table, plotting a response to Khrushchev and Castro. I felt as if I were watching an economic Cuban Missile Crisis. One false move and the whole economy could vaporize.

The President was due to address the IMF and World Bank annual meeting in Washington. The Council on Foreign Relations speech—with the accompanying rate cuts—was beginning to have the desired result. But the world economy was still rattled. More action, visible to all, was needed. I was writing a speech that would spell out the next steps. But more than anything, it would be a pep talk to the shaken finance ministers who were gathered.

"I am very concerned about a credit crunch—a loss of confidence,"

Clinton began the meeting. In New Hampshire in 1992, during the presidential primaries, a "credit crunch" had helped crush that state's economy—and Clinton formed strong views during that time. His orientation, philosophically and temperamentally, might be to ease up a bit on standards to make sure banks kept lending. Rubin pointed out that the banks had earlier been risky in their lending. Larry Summers explained, "The answer is not to raise capital regulations" to clean up the banks' books. "The short-term solution is *more* capital."

Summers tried to explain the ultimate issue. "Brazil is $80 billion in debt and deficit. They need to pay $40 billion. What is there to do? Normally, you roll over the debt—borrow more to pay off the existing debt. After all, Brazil's government debt takes a smaller share of its economy than does ours. But the key is confidence. It's like an LBO [leveraged buyout] gone bad. When that happens to Macy's, someone works it out. But when every institution in the country is in trouble, that's not so easy." Rubin explained that what was needed was a kind of international Chapter 11, referring to the provision of the bankruptcy code that lets companies put off paying some debts while staying in business. Clinton understood. "If you don't have that you will have much more contraction than you would otherwise have. There will be a rejection of markets, and that will spiral."

When confronted with a complex issue—the subtle hydraulics of international finance—I never saw Clinton betray bafflement or a lack of understanding. What he did do was to translate the subject into some metaphor or example that he could use to explain it. He recalled a plan that he had formed while governor during a farm crisis. Arkansas had taken equity positions in troubled farms for three years, providing capital so that the farmers could pay off their debts. Summers, the former Harvard professor, nodded. "That's the right idea, to talk about swapping debt and equity. Though in Arkansas, not *all* the banks were in the hole."

Looming over all these discussions was the continuing sclerosis of Japan's economy. If Japan had not allowed itself to drag through nearly a full decade of economic recession, the Asian economies would be selling their products to their biggest regional economy. But a series of failed governments had proven unable to challenge the big economic interests—from the rice farmers to the government bureaucrats to, above all, the badly overextended banks. There was a constant, continuous-loop debate over how hard to push Japan. The foreign policy types saw that nation as our most important regional ally. The economic types—many of whom, including Rubin, had done business there and thought that hard bargaining was respected—wanted to press them to fix their economy.

That Saturday morning, Gore rustled his papers. "Let me know when it's time for me to explode," he said. Clinton laughed. "Any time. We've

switched roles." Usually Clinton vented his temper, and Gore punctured it with humor. Not today. Gore demanded that a strong message be sent to the Japanese that they needed to get moving. And he pointed out that in the coming months, as inexpensive Asian imports would continue to flood into the United States, "We face enormous pressure regarding steel." The steel companies, steelworker union, and politicians from states like Pennsylvania were already demanding that measures be taken to block the surge of inexpensive steel. The pressure would grow only worse. We had to act now or we would be in a terrible position later. (It was unstated but obvious that "later" was when Gore would be running on his own.)

Finally, the talk focused in on the speech itself. Clinton recalled conversations with other leaders who wanted a meeting of heads of state; Rubin pointed out that none of them knew what they would do if a meeting actually occurred. It was a fascinating dance. Neither wanted to confront the other, especially in front of so many subordinates. Clinton and Rubin had a relationship of deep respect. Rubin thought that Clinton, whatever fretting he might do about the political consequences, invariably did the right thing on the economy, even if it was unpopular. Clinton respected not only Rubin's track record, but also his sense of calm, his personal rootedness. (That summer, the *New York Times Magazine* had published a glowing profile of Rubin, focusing on what he called "probabilistic" decision making: since you'll never be right all the time, you must recognize that fact and weigh your actions accordingly. Clinton mock-groused to his Treasury chief, "When Rubin does that, they say he's prudent. When I do it, they say I'm indecisive!") Gently, they pushed back and forth. Eventually, no leaders' meeting was held.

I knew that Clinton saw the challenge to the world economy as a fundamental one. I knew that he thought the mission was as significant as the one that had confronted the nations after World War II. The speech to the IMF was even more explicit: we needed nothing less than a global New Deal.

He began with a penned-in interposition: "We must put a human face on the global economy." It was a deft line, and seemed to be borrowed from his student days, backpacking through Eastern Europe, when Czechoslovakia struggled to create "socialism with a human face" (before the experiment was crushed under the treads of Russian tanks). He continued, "An international market that fails to work for ordinary citizens will neither earn nor deserve their confidence and support. . . . Just as free nations found a way after the Great Depression to tame the cycles of boom and bust in domestic economies, we must now find ways to tame the cycles of boom and bust that today shake the world economy." He cited the strong Federal Reserve, the Securities and Exchange Commission, and strong bank regula-

tions as brakes on marketplace irrationality that have worked in the United States. "Now, though we understand that the realities and the possibilities in the international marketplace are different, some of the same functions clearly need to be performed. We must address not only a run on a bank or a firm, but also a run on nations."

It was a farsighted speech, one that—if it were implemented—could change the nature of the world economy. Its vision would not take hold during Clinton's term. As the sense of crisis abated, the reform spirit faded among world powers. In any case, the speech didn't get much attention. That same day, the House Judiciary Committee voted to move forward with impeachment proceedings.

"WE NEED A GARDEN HOSE." In yet another strategy session in the residence, Clinton leaned forward with his elbows on his knees and repeated a refrain I had heard from him many times. Gore agreed. "We really have to work at this. We need a garden hose."

The Rose Garden didn't need watering. Instead, we were searching for ways to explain a difficult, internationalist policy to a balky public. And the "garden hose" had taken on the status of a political legend. In 1940, Franklin Roosevelt faced an agonizing political choice: how to help England stand against Hitler in the face of an oppositionist Congress and isolationist country. Polls then were primitive, but FDR devoured them, and they showed how far ahead of popular opinion he was. He devised lend-lease—the idea of providing destroyers to Britain. "Suppose my neighbor's home catches on fire, and I have a length of garden hose four or five hundred feet away," FDR had said at an Oval Office press conference. "If he can take my garden hose and connect it up with his hydrant, I may help to put out his fire. Now what do I do? I don't say to him before that operation, 'Neighbor, my garden hose cost me $15; you have to pay me $15 for it.' What is the transaction that goes on? I don't want $15—I want my garden hose back after the fire is over."

Now, with the election approaching, the congressional session drawing to a close, and the world economy continuing to sputter, the Congress was refusing to appropriate the funds to meet the U.S. obligation to the International Monetary Fund. Republican lawmakers were critical of the IMF on an array of shifting grounds, charging that it had made matters worse in the developing countries by insisting on austerity, that it needed internal reforms, even that it had raised taxes in foreign nations.

At the beginning of the year, public support for IMF funding was weak. Penn's polls had found it the least popular part of the State of the Union. For years, working people had been told that their jobs were being

gobbled by Asia's "tigers." Now the Asian economies were anemic, and we were asking those working people to bail them out, lest their economies drag down the world. It was not, to say the least, an intuitively obvious point.

So Clinton was looking for homespun arguments. Earlier in the year, Gore had tried. At a strategy session for the State of the Union, he offered, "If you've got a business community in a small town, and one store catches fire, you put the fire out before it spreads." Even though the other businesses are your competitors, if you don't stop the fire, it can consume you as well.

Now, Clinton stepped up his campaigning for IMF funding. We offered the metaphor of the fire department, another nod to FDR. "We can have an honest debate about the best ways to put out the economic fires abroad, but there should be no doubt about whether we give the fire department the resources to do the job," he said in the Rose Garden. That night he spoke at a fundraiser in Philadelphia. "I never thought I'd come to Philadelphia, or go anyplace in America in a political election and say, 'The big issue is: are we going to fund the IMF?' Most Americans don't know what the IMF is. Sounds like those people that make bowling equipment," he joked. "I say to you, if you want to keep the American economic recovery going, if you like the way it's gone the last six years and you'd like to have a few more years of it, then America has to lead the world away from the brink of the worst financial crisis in decades. And that means we have to pay our fair share to the fund that will do it." When he repeated the "fire department" analogy in the speech before the IMF itself, it made the evening news.

To our amazement, support for IMF funding had become an applause line in the President's stump speeches. The public's awareness of the global economy and its impact was deepening. Penn's polls showed that it was now a popular proposal—in part as a surrogate for general nervousness over the direction of the economy.

Two days after the speech to the IMF, the political and policy advisors met for our weekly strategy session. The election was a month away. The press, which had spent September demanding Clinton's resignation, predicted electoral doom for the Democrats. On average, a president's party loses twenty-seven House seats in a midterm election, more if the election takes place in a second term. Robert Novak, the political columnist, had warned, "Dreams of recapturing control of the House have been replaced by nightmares of a 20-seat Republican gain or worse. The election of an unprecedented 60 Republican senators, able to break filibusters, is possible."

That day, the full House of Representatives voted to proceed with an impeachment inquiry against the President for the Lewinsky affair. The debate was harsh and the vote was along party lines.

The Republicans had stumbled badly on the budget. The new fiscal year had already begun, yet they had not managed to pass most of their spending bills. Clinton—having triumphed repeatedly in the government shutdown of 1995 and since—had the upper hand in negotiations. The challenge to set aside the surplus had worked: the budget included no major tax cut. The Republicans were acceding to Democratic demands on issue after issue. "They're basically bringing money to us in a wheelbarrow," he joked. The President had always argued to other Democrats that they should try to pass their agenda, rather than letting it fail for political reasons, since there would always be something to fight about later. "Here is what I want to say," Clinton said, looking especially to me. " 'What is this election about? IMF funding. Social Security. The environment. And the teachers.' " He dictated passages on different issues to use in his speeches. On education: "If we're gonna have smaller classes, we need somewhere for them to teach."

A week later, the Republicans relented and agreed to the full $18 billion for the IMF that the administration had requested. It was part of a budget deal that was concluded on the Democrats' terms—substantively, and even more so, politically. In the State of the Union in January, Clinton had proposed hiring 100,000 new elementary school teachers so as to reduce class size. There were studies—though not, surprisingly, overwhelming in number—showing that smaller classes make a difference in the early years. (It is plain to any parent who has ever worried about his child's public school, however. In fact, Republican governor Pete Wilson of California had first made it a major issue.) The Republicans waited until it was the last major proposal outstanding, then resisted it. For four days, Clinton and the Democrats pounded, and then, predictably, the GOP caved. For the very first time in his presidency, Clinton had gained political traction on education.

On election day, the Democrats scored a victory that was in its way as decisive and unprecedented as the defeat they had suffered in 1994. Newt Gingrich had predicted the GOP would gain thirty seats. (If they had, we would have argued that was the historical norm.) But the Democrats gained five seats, putting us within eleven seats of a majority. This was the first time that an incumbent president's party had gained seats in the midterm election of a second term since 1822. (Indeed, it was only the second time in the twentieth century that an incumbent president's party had gained seats at all in a midterm election.) A few days after the election, Gingrich announced he would be leaving Congress.

The financial crisis had begun to abate. Korea and Thailand, countries with thriving democratic governments, were beginning to recover the most quickly. The waters lapped at Brazil's walls, but then receded. The

IMF's new "facility," which would make funds available early in a crisis, helped calm the markets. Investor confidence began to return. The forceful exertion of leadership—through actions, and words—had worked.

A FEW WEEKS LATER, I sat with the President and a few others in the Oval Office. It was the first planning session for the 1999 State of the Union. (I now had a new deputy chief of staff to work with: Maria Echaveste, a talented lawyer who was the former head of the Office of Public Liaison. I felt a bit like a jaded British civil servant. *Do you know how many deputy chiefs of staff have told me to get the speech in on time?*) John Podesta was now chief of staff. Rahm was gone. Paul Begala would be leaving soon.

And I was optimistic. Foolishly so. Assuming that the impeachment was resolved, Clinton was in a commanding position, more so than any other president in his seventh year, dominating the agenda, gaining seats in a midterm election, with his popularity high and the country strong. The President winced a bit when I said that to him.

"Apart from the investigations," I added.

TWENTY-ONE

IMPEACHMENT

DECEMBER 16, 1998, was one of the most bizarre days in my time in the White House—a day of universes, not parallel, but colliding.

The impeachment vote by the House of Representatives was scheduled for the next day. On Capitol Hill, and in the Counsel's Office and Legislative Affairs Office on the second floor of the West Wing, a dozen lawyers and lobbyists sweated over phones and vote counts, watching the margin of victory slip away. Meanwhile, on the ubiquitous televisions that droned throughout the West Wing, CNN was reporting that Saddam Hussein was preventing the UN weapons inspectors from doing their job in Iraq. As reports swirled of a looming missile attack from the United States and Britain, Trent Lott, the Senate Republican leader, went on TV to denounce the move as a diversion from impeachment.

Our universe was floating in an office down the hall. At 4 o'clock, in the domestic policy advisor's suite, the wonks were crammed around a table, spilling onto chairs and perched on the edge of Bruce Reed's desk. We were gathered for a meeting to lay out possible "free ideas" for the 1999 State of the Union, which was to be delivered in little over a month. "Free" ideas were those that didn't have significant budget impact. Vice President Gore's domestic advisor, David Beier, rattled off a list of technology proposals. "An international Y2K Corps." Improved crime forecasting and crime fighting, using computers, in the crime bill. Jose Cerda, an aide to Reed who worked on crime policy, discussed proposals to put laptop computers in police cars. What about farm policy, repairing the agricultural safety net? Sally Katzen of the National Economic Council had been negotiating with Congress. We couldn't propose a bill, she explained. "All we

can say is, 'Work with me to figure out how to do it.' " Dr. Neal Lane, a physicist who served as the science advisor, discussed ethics rules covering cloning and the use of animal genes in humans. "Cow people?" "Yes," he said wryly, "cow people."

I wrote down the issues and grilled the policy experts as they presented, but I was distracted. Four or five times, I got up to call my office. The speechwriters had been asked, belatedly, to help draft arguments against impeachment for lawmakers to deliver on the floor of Congress. They were eager to do it, wide-eyed at the chance to help. I finished phoning in my edits and sat down.

Reed was explaining a proposal to challenge states to keep more teenagers in school by raising the compulsory school age, when heads began turning. A few people were pointing at the TV set, which was on, silently, behind me. There was the President, speaking from his desk, directly below us in the Oval Office. Someone turned up the sound.

"Good evening. Earlier today, I ordered America's Armed Forces to strike military and security targets in Iraq. They are joined by British forces. Their mission is to attack Iraq's nuclear, chemical, and biological programs, and its military capacity to threaten its neighbors. Their purpose is to protect the national interest of the United States and, indeed, the interest of people throughout the Middle East and around the world."

We watched silently. When the President was finished, and the commentators began feverishly analyzing the air strike and its impact on impeachment, the "mute" button was pushed again. We were mute, as well. After a few seconds, we began discussing education policy again, agriculture policy, electricity deregulation. Gene Sperling leaned over to write on my notepad, "Just when you think things are as weird as possible, it gets weirder."

WHEN WE HAD BEGUN WORKING on the speech a few weeks earlier, it had seemed an oddly calm, almost uneventful time. With this, my fourth State of the Union as chief speechwriter, it was now a smooth ride along well-worn tracks.

On December 3, 1998, President Clinton flew to Rhode Island. On a windy point in Narragansett Bay, surrounded by Democratic politicians, he would announce new water-quality grants. I was along for the ride not because any last-minute tweaks were needed on a perfunctory speech, but to serve as a visual Post-it note. Every time Clinton saw me, it was supposed to remind him to work on the State of the Union.

The policy councils had sent him a compendium of memos with dozens of policy proposals for the State of the Union — far too many for any-

one to absorb, even someone as avid as Clinton. Consulting with Reed and Sperling, I had condensed the dozens of pages into a three-page summary of what seemed to be the most promising items. But even then, Nancy Hernreich and Doug Sosnik, the president's counselor, thought he wouldn't likely look at it. I sat in the staff cabin, looking plaintive as the President strolled up and down the aisle. Sosnik brought the memo to him in the front cabin. "What did he say?" "He said, 'I haven't had time to read it. How can I comment on it if I haven't had time to read it?' " Apparently, my presence had its desired effect. A few minutes later, Clinton's personal aide waved at me and pointed to the front cabin.

The President was sitting behind his horseshoe-shaped desk. A CD boom box, flanked by jewel boxes containing jazz, country, and rock CDs, played softly. The memo was spread out before him. "This is very good," he said. His instructions were simple. For the themes of the speech, look at the transcript of the remarks he had made a few nights before to the Democratic Leadership Council. In it, he had proclaimed that the "Third Way" was now the successful governing strategy not just for the Democrats, but also for the British Labour Party and other progressive parties in Europe. Then he wrote out an outline of the State of the Union, neatly numbered, with issues under each category. He handed it over. I thought about years before—in 1993, in 1995, when he thrashed about. At that moment, 12,000 feet aloft, he seemed to know exactly what he wanted to say.

But back in Washington, the impeachment was grinding on. It was hard to believe, but the Republicans in the House were determined to impeach Clinton. Speaker Gingrich's sudden abdication meant that nobody was in charge—nobody to negotiate or wave a yellow flag of caution. Robert Livingston, a dyspeptic congressman from Louisiana, was now the presumptive Speaker—but with the Republican grip on the majority so slim, he could lose the post if he lacked only a few votes. Tom DeLay, formally number three in the Republican hierarchy as party whip, was actually in charge. He was a partisan. He hated Clinton. And he was determined to see him impeached.

As the impeachment gathered momentum, our parallel universes became ever more distinct—and the intersection among them became ever more surreal. After one session with the President, Reed, Sperling, Kagan, and I went upstairs to Bruce's office. We wondered at the reputed battles among the lawyers over who would get to talk at the impeachment hearings. "You would think it would be a matter of who draws the short straw," Reed laughed.

The whole staff was watching Clinton to see how he was reacting; his emotional swings would be magnified by our own. The evening that the lawyers argued for and against his impeachment before the Judiciary Com-

mittee, Clinton convened another strategy session in the residence. These meetings studiously avoided discussions of impeachment or foreign policy. In jeans and a sweater, Clinton was working hard to be cheery. "Wasn't that a great day? We had an event over at the USDA to unveil [former agriculture secretary Mike] Espy's portrait. And we had a great budget meeting. While the world has been consumed with other stuff, I have been having a great time!"

In the Roosevelt Room on the day the impeachment debate began on the House floor, Podesta convened the senior staff meeting. "This is going to be a hard week," he warned, adding, "We've had harder." Charles Ruff, the President's counsel, spoke from his wheelchair in the corner. "Let a few of us slug it out, and the rest of you do what you do for the country. The most helpful thing is for us to be able to say to a member of Congress, 'Look at what the country is doing, look at what the President is doing.' " The routine relay of reports from different offices continued. Podesta looked at Sperling. "Gene, how's our 'bipartisan Social Security process'?" The room erupted with laughter. Sperling joined in mirthlessly.

"Hey," shouted Greg Craig, one of the impeachment lawyers, "can you just give us ten votes?" In fact, the bitter impeachment struggle was on the verge of destroying the chance for progress on entitlement reform. Just a few days before, at the White House conference on Social Security, Republican lawmakers had buttered up the President, telling him that only he could lead a national effort for reform. Now they were voting en masse to impeach him.

The next day—the day he was originally scheduled to be impeached, before the Iraq air strike put off the vote—Clinton met with the budget team in the Cabinet Room. He looked as gray as his suit. Presidents famously age with the cares of office. It was not that he had previously been immune to that trend; rather, that he looked too young at first, and then through the years of his term, he matured into the slightly craggy look we expect in a chief executive. Now, he just looked old.

Congressional jihad or not, the calendar dictated that Clinton would have to begin making the final choices among new programs to include in his annual submission to Congress—the new programs that would make up the State of the Union. Jack Lew, the new budget director, read off a list of dozens of items for the budget or the speech, and the President gamely struggled to pay close attention. Lew explained his negotiations with different agencies. "We have settled with DOD [Department of Defense]," he explained, as if discussing a labor negotiation with a particularly prickly union.

"Is this real money?" Clinton asked.

Gore, sitting next to him, gave impassioned mini-speeches about his

priorities. "Overall, the science and technology budget is gonna cause a real plop," he explained earnestly.

Staff members tried different gambits to catch the President's ear. One was to joke about gaming the process. "We wanted to leave you something to give the agencies when you meet with them," Lew explained. As the meeting droned on, Doug Sosnik put his head on the table. Clinton himself appeared to nod off.

Saturday, December 19, 1998, I knew, would be a date that would live in history, or infamy, or both. The day of the impeachment vote. Though it was a weekend, I put on a sober pinstripe suit and headed to the office. Two blocks from home, I switched on the car radio. Robert Livingston, the presumptive Speaker, was on the House floor. Evidently, a pornography magazine was planning to report on *his* extramarital activities. Now he was resigning, as Democrats shouted "no!" and Republicans sat in stunned silence. I jammed on the brakes and ran to a pay phone to call my wife. The capital seemed consumed by madness.

The day, incongruously, was crammed with meetings. We were going to show that we were keeping to our normal routine, even if that meant treating a Saturday as if it were a Tuesday.

I went to Room 180 in the Old Executive Office Building. Once it had been Nixon's hideaway office, home to some of the most lurid cover-up conversations. Now it was a tidy, high-ceilinged conference room. This first meeting of the day was with the "outreach" offices—the aides whose job was to communicate, handhold, and prod the constituencies important to the White House: labor, women, minorities, business lobbyists, Democratic officials. I made a presentation on the themes and some of the substance of the State of the Union. The meeting was desultory and depressed. We were holding it to say we were holding it as much as anything else.

Paul Begala was in his small office in the basement of the West Wing, decorated with a stuffed deer head and photos of civil rights heroes John Lewis and Barbara Jordan. Begala had written a speech for Clinton to give if he was impeached. The President had torn it up, and asked him to come over to the residence with a tape recorder so that he could dictate a new speech.

Upstairs, the Roosevelt Room was filling. Instead of waiting for all the new policies to be announced in the State of the Union, once again we would peel them off, announcing them one by one throughout January to fill the news vacuum that was supposed to exist. (This year, that vacuum would be rather crowded.) It was hard to concentrate. After a few minutes, I quietly returned to Begala's office. Mark Penn was sitting on the couch, reading a draft of Clinton's statement. We suggested a few changes, and

then the three of us watched the impeachment vote on Begala's television screen. I paced around Paul's office — which took about two seconds — and dropped wearily onto the couch next to Penn, sitting square on a plastic tray containing the pollster's half-eaten, ketchup-smeared lunch. The Vice President's photographer peeked in to take pictures. By a vote of 228–206, the President was impeached.

It seemed dreamlike — and it was. It simply did not feel like a real impeachment. A real impeachment was not on a party line vote, by a lame duck Congress. A real impeachment was not about lying about sex. It seemed to me to be an act of constitutional vandalism. At the same time, it was deeply dismaying.

The unreality deepened as the day went on. A few hours later, busloads of Democratic members of the House of Representatives pulled up at the White House. The visit had a primal political purpose. The Republicans, recognizing they were unlikely to convict Clinton in the Senate, wanted to stampede him into quitting. A poll published in the *Washington Post* earlier in the week showed that while the public opposed impeachment, it might support a presidential resignation to spare the nation a trial. Clinton and the Democrats wanted to end that speculation. First they met in the East Room; then they trooped out to the South Lawn for a pep rally. The President walked with his head bowed.

Gephardt and Podesta spoke. The Vice President called Clinton "one of our greatest presidents." Clinton said he was committed to bringing the nation together. "It's what I've tried to do for six years; it's what I intend to do for two more, until the last hour of the last day of my term." Standing to the side, realizing that the press would watch White House staff for any reaction, we clapped enthusiastically.

And then, of course, no impeachment day would be complete without a gala black-tie holiday party on the South Lawn. By a cruel quirk of scheduling, the Clintons' big fete for senior officials and top financial supporters was scheduled for that night. It was held in a heated tent on the South Lawn. John Podesta deflected condolences. "He'll be the first president in a century to be acquitted," he said through gritted teeth. There was a long line for a photo with the President and First Lady, who sat and smiled through hundreds of photos.

Then, improbably, almost absurdly, it was back to work on the State of the Union. The President would have to give a speech to the House that had just impeached him, and to the Senate that was putting him on trial.

One morning, I was sitting at my computer. Not typing, but staring. Writers refer to the "terror of the blank page" — the gnawing fear that comes from trying to start a story or a book, and not knowing where to begin. I was facing the terror of the blank screen. I had typed the heading:

PRESIDENT WILLIAM J. CLINTON
STATE OF THE UNION ADDRESS
UNITED STATES CAPITOL
WASHINGTON, D.C.
JANUARY 19, 1999

And in the upper-left-hand corner, I had typed "Draft 1." And then I stared.

At that moment, a reporter came on the all-news channel on the TV that was murmuring in the corner. I turned up the sound. "They are hard at work on the State of the Union," he reported breathlessly. "They are already passing back and forth a third draft. The big issue is whether to say anything about impeachment." I nearly had whiplash. Was there another draft? I picked up the phone and quickly dialed around the building. There wasn't another draft, was there? Apparently not.

It was a stark reminder—if any were needed—that this State of the Union was anything but ordinary. It was a bit of a surprise that the Congress invited him. From our perspective, there was never any real question as to whether Clinton would speak: Of course he would. It was the best chance he had to remind the public of the part of his presidency that they not only liked, but strongly supported. Unless the Democrats whispered to us that they wanted us to pull back, we wouldn't miss it for the world. At no point in the entire month did the writers operate under any assumption other than that Clinton would speak.

Nor was there any question either over whether Clinton would address the Lewinsky issue. He wouldn't. He didn't want to, and it would have made little political sense. Also, it would have been improper, given the trial.

Clinton had no intention of giving a meek, apologetic speech. He would present an aggressive policy agenda. Most dauntless of all, we were working in secret—as we had done the year before—to spring a surprise on entitlements. For a year, Clinton had sought to fuzz the sharp political lines on Social Security, putting off the real engagement until after the congressional election. By now, bipartisan negotiations were supposed to be well under way. Only the President could get the debate moving again. And with the budget surplus growing at a breathless pace, Clinton needed to frame the debate once again or lose the momentum to a Republican tax cut, which had already been introduced. The centerpiece of the speech would be a proposal for how to divvy up the surplus.

On December 22, the Tuesday after Clinton was impeached, he met with us in the Cabinet Room. Days before, as the undecided votes had broken against him in the House, Clinton had looked haggard. Today, he had pulled himself together again, focusing on the work at hand.

Sperling began. This was, he said, above all, a timing problem. The proposal would have to be defensible on its own terms, but recognizably an opening bid in a long negotiation. We had to hold the Democrats together, but leave enough room for a final compromise with the Republicans. "This is one of the most difficult strategic decisions we've faced."

We were finally grappling with the nettlesome question of how to repair Social Security. The Republicans had made clear they wanted to chip away at the program, or eliminate it, in favor of individual investment accounts. These private accounts, they argued, would offer a higher return than Social Security did. Any final deal would likely have to meet their need to show some private investment. But progressives feared that the true purpose of such individual accounts was to undermine support for the universal, guaranteed Social Security benefit.

Some liberals, in turn, also wanted those higher returns but wanted the Social Security trust fund itself to invest in private stocks and bonds, just the way a state pension fund would. This would raise the specter of substantial government investment in the stock market. Private investment, however designed, looked like a sure bet in 1999, with the helium-powered rise in the stock market. And it is true that, over thirty years, stocks are a good investment. But what would happen if the market dropped over a long period of time? What if a worker had the bad luck to retire during a bear market?

Gore was emphatic. "Our mission must be to defeat individual accounts," he said heatedly. They would undermine Social Security. He doubted there was a way to make such a scheme work. "It's like the 'progressive' sales tax. It won't be progressive by the time they finish with it." Gore parodied the supposed drawbacks of the current, supposedly low-return Social Security system. "No, it's much better for your great-grandchildren to have to go on the Internet and compare price earnings ratios!"

For days, "special issues" meetings were held in Sperling's office. Rubin, Summers, and other top economic officials trooped in and out. Two thorny issues consumed the discussion. One was the proposal—which we expected the Republicans to make if we didn't—to wall off the "Social Security surpluses." When measuring deficits or surpluses, for years the government had counted both funds raised from the payroll tax and all other funds. Social Security administrator Ken Apfel and some economists wanted that money segregated, out of the budget, so that it could never be used to fund the rest of the government (as had been the case since the early 1980s). I was deeply alarmed by this. A year before, Clinton had stood before the country and Congress and proclaimed—using the customary measurement of the budget—that the budget was balanced. We couldn't

seem to back off from that claim. I wrote out in block letters, quoting the previous year's speech, and held it up: "1998: THE DEFICIT, WHICH WAS ONCE ELEVEN ZEROES, IS NOW ZERO. 1999: THE DEFICIT, WHICH WAS ZERO, IS NOW ELEVEN ZEROES."

"He can't go before the country and say, 'Oh, my biggest accomplishment? Never mind.'"

The other struggle was over how large an investment the Social Security trust fund could make in private stocks and bonds. One option was impossibly large: devoting half the trust fund to private investment. Others were smaller. Each change in one part of the proposal scrambled the numbers in another. Vexing issues proliferated. If the government controlled large blocks of stock, would Congress try to force companies to stop selling cigarettes? Or stop paying for abortions through their health plan? Wouldn't this look like socialism? Mark Penn (who was not present for these meetings) had polled voters to see how much private investment was too much. We could safely propose some, but proposing too much would sink the plan.

At the last planning session in Sperling's office, the pieces finally came together. When Social Security was created in the 1930s, the New Dealers argued that it would be supplemented by individual savings, and also by pensions. The Treasury Department had been working on an individual investment scheme that was separate from Social Security—what John Podesta dubbed a universal pension. (That was supposed to make it more acceptable for Democrats, who knew that unionized workers have both Social Security and a private pension.) Now the Treasury Department presented its plan for the pensions, in the form of savings accounts subsidized by tax credits—and to the surprise of everyone in the room, they were able to draw up a plan that was highly progressive, benefiting the poor the most. Sperling's process had stumbled onto a way to subsidize savings by working-class families. Bruce Reed, who had girded to argue for some form of individual investment, looked at the proposal and said, "Wow." The liberals, who had been prepared to blast it, nodded in agreement. Sperling also reported that Gephardt liked it, as long as the individual pensions were clearly not part of Social Security.

On January 6, the day before the impeachment trial was to begin, Clinton met with the economic team. Sperling, with Summers at ease in his seat next to him, laid out the options for Clinton, rehearsing the subjects that had consumed hours of debate. Should Social Security be put off budget? "Oh, we're not going to do that," Clinton said quickly. Sperling then laid out a plan for significant investment of the trust fund in the stock market. "Oh," Clinton said offhandedly, "that's too much." At the height of impeachment, in a minute's time, he had quickly disposed of the political

and policy headaches that it had taken his advisors weeks to thrash out. "Let me just say that, conceptually, in principle, I like this," Clinton continued. "I have three concerns." He then proceeded deftly to identify three flaws in the plan. "This will only keep Social Security solvent for fifty years. Is that going to be seen as serious? From the point of view of serious Democrats — not 'individual account Democrats,' but people who care about Social Security." Clinton briskly rattled through the checklist, outlining other issues, some of them technical, that needed to be addressed.

Podesta pointed out that the surplus was growing so large, it could extend the life of Social Security and Medicare by ten years each "without doing anything else." "This is the easiest meeting we ever had," Clinton retorted. He was rolling now, entertaining his troops. "Money cures a lot of problems. This is an illustration of one of Clinton's Laws of Politics: When someone tells you 'it's not a money problem,' it's someone else's money."

Working off the outline that the President had prepared on that flight in December, I finished a first draft a week before the speech. The policy agenda was the most far-reaching since his first years in office. Education spending would be recast so that federal funds would go only to those communities that had stopped promoting children from grade to grade if they had not mastered their material. Senior citizens, faced with skyrocketing prescription drug costs, would receive a new drug benefit in Medicare. It set out a vision of an active government that nonetheless lived within its means, focused on education, modernizing entitlements. It was also striking, as several newspapers were to point out, how similar the priorities, as measured by the budget, were to the initial goals set out in 1992. Over two terms, Clinton was finding that he could accomplish more through incremental steps than by charging up the hill.

The draft was very long. In the morning, Clinton called for the speech, so that he could have two hours to read it before the discussion with a larger group. Reed, Echaveste, and I brought in a copy, still warm from the photocopier. "How long is this—two hours? It can be the first filibuster State of the Union. Maybe it will come out of our twenty-four hours." The White House had been allotted twenty-four hours for a defense in the impeachment trial.

Later in the day, the writers, policy advisors, and others crowded into the Oval Office. The opening, as drafted, was not very good. These first few pages were always of great interest to Clinton—they were where he spelled out his philosophy, proclaimed the direction of the country. Each year, he labored over them endlessly. That morning I had written a new version and brought it to the session. Before Clinton had time to criticize the draft, I began the meeting by telling him, "Here is a new beginning. The version you have is inadequate." Clinton took the new draft, looked at it, scanned

the old one. "Oh. Yes. This is much better. Much better." We worked off that one. As we left the meeting, Paul Begala whispered to me admiringly, "Wow. You did that to yourself. Impressive."

The next day, January 13, was the eve of the opening argument by the House managers who were prosecuting Clinton on the Senate floor.

We had our most extensive prep session with the President yet. For the first time, the full plan for the surplus was fleshed out. Six out of ten surplus dollars would be used for Social Security. Part of that money would be invested in the stock market. The plan would also devote 15 percent of the surplus for Medicare. Since the Republicans had already agreed, in effect, to save the surplus for Social Security, this raised the bar—posing their tax cut not only against Social Security but also against Medicare. Both Social Security and Medicare would need fundamental structural reforms. But these investments should make that easier, not harder.

The most complex proposal was the universal pension—the Democratic help-the-little-guy version of individual accounts.

Clinton wondered about the order of the policies in the speech: jumping from Social Security, back to Medicare, back to retirement savings. "It's weird," Clinton said. "If you think about it rationally, we're going flip-flop-flip." Podesta reminded him that the Democrats would support the pensions only if they were separate from Social Security. "You can't underestimate how sensitive our friends are." Clinton assented.

Bob Shrum had now joined the discussions. James Carville and he, along with Clinton's original pollster, Stanley Greenberg, were spending their days in Israel, advising the Labor Party candidate for prime minister, General Ehud Barak. Shrum was learning the details for the first time. "You know," he said, "if you call it a universal savings account, the acronym would be USA. It would light up in people's consciousness."

There was a brief silence as everyone in the room thought, *Why didn't I think of that! Or I was just going to say that!*

"You're a great American!" Clinton said. "USA. 'It's your USA account.' You can see people talking ten or twenty years from now, saying, 'How much money do you have in your USA account?' " I lightly suggested an alternative. "Universal Social Security Reform accounts. USSR." Clinton started singing the Beatles song "Back in the USSR." That night, in my office, bearing our instructions from the President, we had one long rewrite session, with Shrum, Penn, and the others.

The next day, the trial began. Clinton worked doggedly on the draft. Instead of long gab sessions, we traded versions back and forth. "We cut at least three thousand words out of the last draft," I wrote him. "It is still too long (if delivered, it would be about fifteen to twenty minutes over). But we are definitely getting there."

The next day Clinton sent the speech back, with a yellow Post-it note: ASAP.

> I cut another 515 words. 43 more if you take ones at the begin-
> ning and end in parentheses. BC
> → Pls make Δs and get me another copy by 2—we can do more
> in prep.

At the bottom of each of the seventy-five large-type pages was a tidy row of numbers: the running total of words cut.

There were some outstanding questions. Chief among them was, who would sit next to Hillary in the First Lady's box? Clinton's State of the Unions had evolved into increasingly elaborate spectacles. Like a Busby Berkeley musical, each new version had to surpass the last one. Maria Echaveste, the deputy chief of staff, had organized a painstaking process. Representatives from every office in the White House came and presented long lists of possible people. For years, Clinton's White House simultaneously telecast its broad message to the suburban middle while keeping party constituency groups as happy as possible through assiduous cultivation. A presidential visit, tickets to the Kennedy Center, an autopenned greeting for an annual meeting. Or a seat in the First Lady's box.

Reagan's "heroes" displayed plucky individualism, grit, personal heroism. Clinton's tended to highlight a more communitarian set of values: people who worked in their communities, public employees. In 1993, Alan Greenspan had sat next to Hillary as the President unveiled the economic plan. In 1996, in the wake of the government shutdown, the federal worker who was shut out of his office in Oklahoma City was highlighted, and in 1997 and 1998, teachers and students involved in education reform. This year, the key issue was the aging of America—the key policy areas Social Security and Medicare. But how do you put a human face on that? The Social Security administrator? Some really old people? We wondered whether any of the original recipients of Social Security or Medicare were still alive. (They weren't.) One office proposed a hundred-year-old woman who was still practicing medicine. "That's admirable," I said, trying to keep a straight face. "It really is. But don't you think people will start thinking right away, 'How's her malpractice insurance?' "

What about a military officer who flew missions over Iraq? Absolutely, the National Security Council representative said. Moreover, we would highlight one of the women combat pilots. "There are women pilots?" several people asked in surprise. Apparently, it was not well known, but the ban on combat did not extend to women pilots. (Hearing this, John Podesta

was alarmed. Did the Pentagon really want to draw attention to this? The NSC was instructed to check into it.)

We searched for a fresh way to dramatize Clinton's call for racial unity, which would be a major part of the speech. Names were tossed out. Apparently, there was a lobbying campaign urging the White House to invite Rosa Parks, the former seamstress whose refusal to give up her seat had sparked the Montgomery bus boycott forty-five years earlier. I suggested Mark McGwire and Sammy Sosa, the two baseball sluggers who had each chased Roger Maris' record of sixty-one home runs in a season — and egged each other on to top it. Throughout the ugly year of 1998, they had shown sportsmanship and grace. After each meeting, we had a lengthening list, but no sure winners.

Through that weekend, the President rehearsed in the family theater. He would begin each session by announcing how many words he had cut. (Then, reading through, he would invariably add many more back in.) He was rewriting paragraphs as he went along. But the speech was now, in essence, done. In contrast to the almost unbearable tension of the year before, this year, at least, he knew days in advance that the speech would probably go well. I sat confidently at the computer in the family theater, whispering assignments to individual speechwriters, calling them down to sit next to me when sections they had worked on were being discussed.

As the President rehearsed and rewrote, he sharpened two key elements of the argument.

We noticed a half-submerged feature: The way the plan worked was to pay down the publicly held debt of the federal government, and then dedicate the interest savings to Social Security and the other priorities. In so doing, over time, the plan would pay off the debt, a revolution in fiscal policy. Whenever the government runs a deficit, it has to borrow by selling bonds to the public. The United States has been in debt since 1835. In the twelve years after Reagan's tax cuts, the accumulated national debt quadrupled. As a share of the economy, publicly held debt had doubled from 1981 to 1993. Interest payments were the third-biggest single government expenditure. By retiring the debt, hundreds of billions of dollars a year spent on interest payments could now go to Social Security and Medicare. It married severe fiscal discipline with the progressive goal of strengthening entitlement programs without radical cuts. Most ingenious, paying off the debt was what would happen if Congress did nothing—no reform, no tax cut. Liberal critics would warn that an obsession with paying off the debt resembled Calvin Coolidge–style Republican orthodoxy. But the economic and political allure was simply too great.

Clinton also seized on an argument that effectively blunted the still-

loud calls for a tax cut. Not that all tax cuts are bad; in fact, we support some. But we should deal with the tough issues of Social Security and Medicare before turning to a tax cut—"first things first." William Safire wrote that the phrase, repeated in the speech, "gripped the nation and is doing its job of persuasion."

The guest list for the First Lady's gallery was finally taking shape, too. The idea of a female pilot was scotched; it would look like a jarring attempt at social engineering rather than a simple salute to the military. We finally decided to call McGwire and Sosa. McGwire said no. But Sosa—who had traveled with Hillary to his home country of the Dominican Republic to bring flood relief the previous year—would attend. We hoped—and expected—that Sosa would blow a kiss to Clinton, just as he had to his mother after every home run.

Yet the absurdity of the situation kept intruding. On Sunday morning, the political talk shows were full of demands that Clinton cancel the speech. That evening, I was summoned to Betty Currie's office to go over some edits with the President. We stood in front of her desk, and he leaned in on me to show me his changes. Gradually, I became aware of a growing noise. Soon, it was so loud, I couldn't hear the President. Finally, I turned. All around us were a contingent of the President's lawyers, laughing, bantering, and preparing for their next day's cameos on the Senate floor. I could see that the President—for all his surface calm—was under increasing pressure. As a year before, I was amazed at how he could keep going.

January 19. Game day. The morning was silent and tense.

Paul Begala had been busy with impeachment and had not played his customary role in preparing the address. The morning of the speech, I dropped by his office. "I am very worried that it's too long," he said somberly. "Well, the only way to deal with that now is to cut policies, not words," I agreed. We went up to the chief of staff's office.

With Podesta, we drew up a list of topics to strike out altogether: computers in the classroom, a paragraph on the wonders of science and funding for scientific labs; the paragraph discussing the coming NATO summit in Washington; some of the education proposals. I wrote a memo to Clinton proposing that these cuts be made. When I returned to my office, Tommy Caplan wandered by, genial. He had been staying with the First Family for a few days. He agreed to take the memo up to the President directly.

Clinton wanted to talk to Michael Sheehan alone, in the Oval Office. But the press office needed a photo of Clinton at work, and it wouldn't do to have a consultant in the picture. So Maria Echaveste and I rushed over to the Oval Office. We were ushered in, and stood by the desk, waiting for the President. When he came in, he looked trim, dignified, and confi-

dent. But as I watched him hold the speech, I could see how tired he was. We discussed cuts that could be made. He was loath to strike policies altogether. For all his worries about length, he knew the political calculus that had gone into each paragraph—and could argue endlessly about the vital policy importance of . . . well, of just about anything. He scratched out lines and found ways to cut hundreds of words while saving the policies.

Suddenly, there was a loud clattering and scraping. A dozen photographers and television cameramen were pressed up against the French doors to the Oval Office, herded by a nervous-looking press office assistant. I straightened up and moved closer to Clinton for the shot. It was hard to keep from laughing.

From there, we went to the family theater for the final rehearsals. The theater was filled—speechwriters, policy aides, the staff members from Arkansas who had been with him the longest. Erskine Bowles, Rahm Emanuel, and Don Baer were there. It was like the final episode in a sitcom where all the stars who left the show come back.

For days, our mission had been to keep the process orderly, precise, and calming to Clinton. He needed to feel that the speech was in good shape—that in an almost impossibly difficult situation, the speech would carry him, and he wouldn't have to carry the speech. Then, the afternoon of the speech, the traditional chaos suddenly erupted.

For days, the President had noticed each time a budget figure changed. Education spending had been described as $20 billion, now it was $16 billion. Why? (It depended on which programs were counted.) The description of Africa trade policy kept sliding from the section on trade to the section on foreign policy—with different political consequences for trade legislation depending on how it was framed. The amount of the projected surplus kept changing. And today, the amount of the surplus that would be devoted to Social Security was recalculated downward by several percentage points.

Some of the changes were welcome. For weeks, Reed had been working with the Justice Department, trying to get them to agree on language announcing a lawsuit against the tobacco companies. The department was still insisting on a period of study. It would not allow the President to announce a suit—merely to report that they were considering how to do a suit. Reed kept pressing. Finally, the day of the speech, the language was ready. We had omitted any mention of the tobacco suit from the circulated drafts. Even the inner circle did not get this language. When he got to that part of the speech, in the family theater, Clinton coughed and skipped to the next page. "What happened? He missed a page," people grumbled behind us. The secret was holding.

Late in the afternoon, word came from the First Lady's office. Rosa

Parks was now in the box! (Apparently, if we hadn't invited her, she would have been sitting with Speaker Dennis Hastert's wife.) "June! Get on that computer and write a tribute to Rosa Parks!" Shrum sat with a pen, writing, while June Shih worked on a keyboard. They compared notes and gave me a draft, which I trimmed and typed in. There was last-minute lobbying on family planning language. Clinton had wanted the language changed or removed, but was told that outside groups had already been notified.

The sudden lobbying, the shifting numbers, the last-minute changes left Clinton rattled. He went up to the residence to change his clothes and shower—and he was not in the right frame of mind.

That morning, Charles Ruff, the President's counsel, had begun the President's defense. In the afternoon, the Senate adjourned the trial so that the senators could prepare to walk across the Capitol to the House Chamber for the speech.

At eight-thirty, Paul Begala and I waited in the Map Room on the ground floor of the residence for the President. Before an antique mirror at the north end of the room, we bent over a table, comparing the copy that had been entered into the teleprompter with the bond paper reading copy that sat in a blue felt-covered box. Aware of every second, we wrote each change into the President's copy by hand.

Clinton and Hillary arrived and saw us. The President—in a blinding white shirt and telegenic blue tie, his hair sprayed into place—was edgy. "What did you do? Are the changes entered?"

"We put Rosa Parks in, but only one sentence," I explained, trying to sound confident. "We switched back to the way you wanted in the other paragraphs." Clinton looked unimpressed. Paul Begala tried again. "Sir, Rosa Parks is in, family planning is the way you wanted it. Africa trade is in the Africa section. Sir, we've given you your speech back." Clinton exhaled and relaxed. "Yeah, this is a pretty good speech, isn't it?" It was a complete change in mood. Hillary stood behind him, smiling and pleased.

The motorcade pulled up to the Capitol, and the President's party swept into the imposing marble pile. After standing around for a few minutes in the lobby, we began to move, the presidential entourage sweeping in Clinton's wake. As we walked along the echoing corridors, Jeff Forbes of the scheduling office sidled up next to me. "Jeff, we need to check one thing. Are the widows of the Capitol Police officers in the box with Mrs. Hastert?" The officers who had been killed in July were to be honored.

"Yes." I was relieved. One more item checked off. "But the names in the speech are wrong," he said.

I nearly landed flat on my face. "*What?!* Can we find out the right names?" Forbes, an experienced political organizer, smiled beatifically. "I'm having that done right now." Clinton went into the Speaker's office to

greet the leaders of the House and Senate. I paced up and down in the hall, chilled and sweating. A man I had never seen before ran up the marble stairs from the basement and handed me a note with the right name for the widows. "Wen Ling Chestnut," not "Wei Ling Chesnut" as the speech draft had it. I slipped into the Speaker's office as unobtrusively as I could, following Clinton's photographer. The President was in a garrulous group, laughing and talking with Trent Lott, Don Nickles, and Strom Thurmond. I found Kris Engskov and had him neatly change the spelling on the text. Clinton never knew. A minute later, Trent Lott looked up at the clock. "Oh, it's nine o'clock," he said chirpily. "I guess it's time to go."

The House chamber was tense—and less crowded than usual. Empty seats were visible among the Republicans. They could barely bring themselves to clap as the President walked in.

Clinton began with a salute to the widows of the slain police officers. And then he paid tribute to the new Speaker. "Mr. Speaker, at your swearing-in, you asked us all to work together in a spirit of civility and bipartisanship. Mr. Speaker, let's do exactly that." He turned around to Hastert and stuck out his hand. The Illinois congressman, caught unawares, rose and shook it with a goofy grin. The entire Congress applauded.

Instead of a lofty, theoretical opening, Clinton began again with an itemization of the country's remarkable good health. "For the first time in three decades, the budget is balanced. (Applause.) From a deficit of $290 billion in 1992, we had a surplus of $70 billion last year. And now we are on course for budget surpluses for the next twenty-five years. (Applause.) Thanks to the pioneering leadership of all of you, we have the lowest violent crime rate in a quarter century and the cleanest environment in a quarter century. America is a strong force for peace from Northern Ireland to Bosnia to the Middle East.

"Thanks to the leadership of Vice President Gore, we have a government for the information age. Once again, a government that is a progressive instrument of the common good, rooted in our oldest values of opportunity, responsibility, and community; devoted to fiscal responsibility; determined to give our people the tools they need to make the most of their own lives in the twenty-first century—a twenty-first-century government for twenty-first-century America.

"My fellow Americans, I stand before you tonight to report that the state of our Union—is *strong*."

I turned to Mark Penn, standing with me at the back row of the chamber. "All across America, people are watching their TV sets," Penn said, "and saying, 'They want to impeach him? Are they crazy?' "

Clinton set out his plan for the budget surplus, reading quickly at first but then loosening up as he grew more confident. For the Republicans, this

was root canal. In previous years, when Clinton would issue a challenge, the Republicans would look to Speaker Gingrich for a cue. If he rose, they rose; if he sat silently, so did they. Gingrich knew the issues as well as Clinton did. Now, they looked at the Speaker's chair and saw ... Dennis Hastert? When Clinton made a proposal, the Democrats would leap to their feet. Republicans would peer at Hastert. He, in turn, would squint into the audience, looking for Tom DeLay, the majority whip, who was really calling the shots. DeLay would applaud. A second or two later, Hastert would stand, applauding. A second or two after that, the Republicans would stand—by which time the Democrats were already sitting down. It was the DeLay delay.

With each proposal, the Republicans grew more sullen. When Clinton proposed ending the rule that limited earnings for Social Security recipients—a measure long backed by the GOP—I heard one congressman sitting near me blurt out, "That's incredible," his fists balled in fury.

About halfway through the speech, the President turned to tobacco. The lawmakers read the prepared speech, unobtrusively spread on their laps as he called on Congress to pass the anti-smoking legislation. Then he continued, "Smoking has cost taxpayers hundreds of billions of dollars under Medicare and other programs," beginning the section that was not in the printed text. Heads snapped up. "You know, the states have been right about this—taxpayers shouldn't pay for the cost of lung cancer, emphysema, and other smoking-related illnesses—the tobacco companies should." The Democrats edged forward. "So tonight I announce that the Justice Department is preparing a litigation plan to take the tobacco companies to court—and with the funds we recover, to strengthen Medicare." The chamber exploded. Democrats began jumping up and down, cheering, as if they were at a basketball game. The Republicans were flattened back in their seats, as if by G force. It was a powerful moment—a reminder, in terms as stark as the Constitution allowed, that *he* was still President, that *he* didn't need Congress for everything, that he wasn't pulling back from anything. It was a signpost of how the domestic presidency had evolved in Clinton's terms.

For all the rancor of the preceding weeks, as the speech went on there was an increasing sense of genuine comity. Clinton's sunny disposition was defusing the tension in the room. When he introduced Rosa Parks, and the small woman, with her white hair tied in a bun, rose, lawmakers from both parties cheered and cheered.

Clinton concluded:

Perhaps, in the daily press of events, in the clash of controversy, we don't see our own time for what it truly is—a new dawn for America.

A hundred years from tonight, another American president will stand in this place and report on the state of the Union. He — or she — (applause) he or she will look back on a twenty-first century shaped in so many ways by the decisions we make here and now. So let it be said of us then that we were thinking not only of our time, but of their time; that we reached as high as our ideals; that we put aside our divisions and found a new hour of healing and hopefulness; that we joined together to serve and strengthen the land we love.

The processional back to the White House was triumphant. Sammy Sosa graciously enthused, "That was the sixty-seventh home run!" (Though it did occur that he probably says that at least four times a day. "This award from the Cook County Chamber of Commerce . . . is the sixty-seventh home run.")

My wife and I sat next to Rosa Parks to have our pictures taken. When I saw Clinton, I told him how much it meant to our six-year-old — who had learned the story of the bus boycott in school — that Rosa Parks was still alive. "It's interesting," he said, still pumped with adrenaline. "It's an easier story for kids to understand than Martin Luther King. They can all understand having to sit in the back of the bus."

On February 12, 1999, the Senate voted to acquit the President. Neither of the charges received even a majority of votes. A move for a congressional censure petered out. The President dictated a statement over a speakerphone to a group of us in John Podesta's office, then tweaked it standing at his desk in the Oval Office. He spoke in the Rose Garden. "Now I ask all Americans — and I hope all Americans — here in Washington, and throughout our land, will rededicate ourselves to the work of serving our nation and building our future together."

Tested by his own conduct and the bitter efforts of his opponents, Clinton's new approach to the presidency, his new brand of government activism, had proven itself remarkably durable. It was a new alloy that revealed its tensile strength only under the pressure of the past year — pressure that could have broken this presidency and the man who held it.

TWENTY-TWO

FAREWELL PARTY

Six months later, I told the President I was leaving the White House.*

In 1999, there had been a return to normal: a return to the by-now solid ground of Clinton's public presidency. At first, the calm was strained, as though dinner party guests were trying to act as if nothing was wrong after a huge, door-slamming row. There were the continuing public rituals. A month after his acquittal, at the Gridiron dinner, the President announced that he was releasing his memoirs now, instead of waiting until he left office. He held up mock book covers: *I'm OK, You're OK, They're Out to Get Me. Bill Clinton, in My Own Words—As Told to a Team of Ghostwriters. Beyond Hope.* And the one "chosen" for his memoirs: *My Story—And I'm Sticking to It.*

Two unfolding tragedies seemed to fire Clinton with new purpose.

After years in which Serbia's Slobodan Milosevic had terrorized his neighbors and the other ethnic groups within his country, he was beginning a slow-motion massacre in Kosovo. NATO, led by the United States and Britain, launched a fierce bombing campaign in an attempt to stop it. For weeks, the high-tech weapons of the Western alliance pummeled Belgrade and Serb troops, seemingly to no avail. Hundreds of thousands of refugees poured into neighboring countries. The President repeatedly reminded us how Jimmy Carter had himself become a hostage to the Iran cri-

---

* There are protocols for such things. I didn't actually tell the President; I told John Podesta, the chief of staff. We agreed to keep the news secret for a while. Eventually, he told the President, to whom I sent a letter, just in case. Only then would the news be released in the way that mattered, by giving it to Al Kamen, a *Washington Post* columnist whose "In the Loop" was a de facto job board.

sis, and pressed to keep up his domestic schedule of events and meetings. But it was apparent that he, too, was increasingly drawn in. I got the sense that, for all the anguish over the refugees and the second-guessing over how negotiations had broken down, he was relieved to feel morally sure. "What's the point of having all this popularity if we don't use it for something like this?" he asked at one point. In his speeches, he drew the parallels between the ethnic hatreds in the Balkans and the history of racism in the United States. It was a high-stakes campaign, the first military engagement NATO had ever waged. It was roundly denounced as a failure. (The House voted to end the bombing, and to double funds for it, on the same day.) But the sorties and missile attacks were more effective than we realized—or perhaps the Serbs were reacting to the planning that had begun for a ground invasion. On June 9 the Serbs agreed to withdraw from Kosovo. It was the first successful intervention to forestall ethnic mass slaughter in Europe in a century.

In the middle of the Kosovo campaign came Littleton, Colorado. For years, even as overall crime dropped, a series of horrific school shootings had erupted with seasonal regularity. Drugs and gangs terrorize children in cities every day, with little outcry. But these murders, in Paducah, Kentucky, Jonesboro, Arkansas, and Springfield, Oregon—placid communities in the heartland, finally shook the public. On April 20, we were meeting with the President in the Oval Office on the international economy. He was puzzling over some particularly dense language, complaining, "I understand this stuff, and even I don't understand it." Just before, we had learned about a massacre unfolding at a large suburban high school outside Denver, which we had seen on cable news. All told, twelve students and a teacher, and the two student gunmen, were dead. In the Oval Office, the President spoke on the phone to the governor of Colorado and to a local official at the scene. "This is President Clinton," he said, raising his voice so she could hear him on her cellphone. "I just wanted you to know that the whole country is praying for you and watching you." He urged her to reach out to grief counselors. "You know, you'll have kids who heard [the gunmen] say something and then didn't do anything, and they'll be consumed with guilt. You know, unfortunately we have really had a lot of experience with this." After it was clear the children were out of the school, he spoke to the nation in the Rose Garden. "Saint Paul reminds us that we all see things in this life through a glass darkly, that we only partly understand what is happening. We do know that we must do more to reach out to our children and teach them to express their anger and to resolve their conflicts with words, not weapons." The struggle for gun control measures—continuing the battle with the NRA that helped cost the Democrats their majority in 1994—consumed much of the remaining time of his term. He pressed,

first, for mandatory trigger locks to keep children from being able to use guns, a law to require that all sales at gun shows be subject to the Brady law's five-day waiting period and background check, and other steps. (In his 2000 State of the Union, he would call for the licensing of all handgun owners.)

THAT SUMMER, the tensions of seven years dissolved as I prepared to leave. There was a birthday cake on Air Force One, a last ride on the President's helicopter, a farewell to the White House operators who had placed thousands of calls.

A few days before I left, my colleagues gave me a going-away party in the State Dining Room. Under the crystal chandeliers and the portrait of Lincoln, with waiters circulating among friends and colleagues and family, it was sentimental and humbling.

(Life in Washington: A few days later, the *Washington Post* actually ran a story about the party on the front page, explaining that at White House farewells, the importance of the departee could be gauged by whether revelers were served . . . shrimp. A color picture of a shrimp accompanied the story. For the record: You pay for your own going-away party. I didn't want to fork over the money for shrimp. I had pastries, and they were very nice. *I could have had shrimp.*)

As at any office going-away party, there were gag gifts and roasts. On behalf of my colleagues, the six speechwriters, Jordan Tamagni gave me a gift mocking our propensity to use the same material, over and over. It was a T-shirt emblazoned with the "emblem of the speechwriting department," the recycling symbol. Bruce Reed and Gene Sperling staged a mock *Jeopardy* game. They were my friends, the two policy aides who had traveled with Clinton in 1992, who now, in their early forties, in many ways held dominant positions in government.

The President spoke. After warm words, he presented a framed page from an actual speech retrieved from the National Archives. Before delivering it, he had crossed out every line in thick black pen. Now, across the top, he had written, "Mike—One of your better efforts." The audience roared. For all the glory of writing for Bill Clinton, everybody knew that he gave his own speeches—rewriting, improvising, making them his own.

When it was my turn, I thought back over the seven years. I teased Reed and Sperling, "Two of the finest public servants it has been my privilege to know," as Nixon said of H. R. Haldeman and John Ehrlichman. I told my friends that I wanted to write and think about what I had seen. I concluded, "Bill Clinton has not only been a good president, but he will be seen as being a very important president."

The next day, I saw him off one last time. He was flying to Arkansas and then St. Louis for yet another series of speeches. First he read a statement on the budget and answered reporters' questions. I stood beneath the awning, half in shadow, my usual place to watch. Clinton was, if anything, more spirited than usual, his voice booming through loudspeakers, Marine One sitting in bright sunshine. After shaking hands with some spectators, he loped toward the helicopter, arms swinging, saluted smartly, and ducked in. His retinue climbed in as the doors pulled shut. I could see his profile through the window, animated, chopping the air for emphasis, trying to persuade.

AFTERWORD

I OFTEN THINK ABOUT BILL CLINTON, sitting at his desk in the Oval Office, surrounded by two busts of FDR, two more of Lincoln, a bust of Kennedy, of Truman, and of Yitzhak Rabin. Presidents stare at history, and it stares back at them. With his term drawing to a close, and the election of his successor at hand, the debate over Clinton's legacy is already well under way. When I say I think he will be seen as an important president, not just a successful one, what do I mean?

There are the obvious reasons, good and bad. The stunning economic expansion, the longest in history. The fact that he was reelected—itself a rarity for a Democrat. Real, measurable social progress, with crime plummeting, the welfare rolls cut in half. The bad as well. The failure to pass health care reform. The loss of the Congress. And he was only the second president to be impeached.

All these things matter. But I think history will focus on four other things.

First, Clinton changed the office, transforming the way a president uses the bully pulpit to lead.

We're still accustomed to thinking of presidents the way political scientist Richard Neustadt describes them in *Presidential Power and the Modern Presidents*, as towering figures using their power to rally support—and, together with the voters, persuade Congress to enact their dreams. Above the stairwell in the White House pressroom hangs a case holding dozens of pens used by Lyndon Johnson to sign the Great Society into law. The display seems to insist: *this is what a President is supposed to do.*

But as we have seen, it's hard to be a modern president in post-modern times.

With the Cold War over, the chief executive has lost the aura that came from knowing the fate of the earth hinged in the Oval Office. Clinton faced an emboldened, oppositionist Congress for three quarters of his two terms. In fact, voters have chosen divided government for twenty-six of the past thirty years. Even when it wants to cooperate, Congress, consumed by partisanship and with power dispersed among dozens of key lawmakers, is more fractious than ever. Then there were the investigations, by six special prosecutors and myriad congressional committees, tangling the White House in a profusion of subpoenas, controversies, and mini-crises.

Above all, Clinton had to contend with a hypercompetitive, hyperactive, scandal-obsessed media. One academic study showed that news reports on presidential candidates grew twice as negative, all in the decade *before* Clinton ran. Time itself seems to have sped up. When German U-boats sank our merchant ships, Woodrow Wilson had weeks to decide how to respond before plunging us into World War I. As late as 1992, the Clinton campaign War Room was considered so sharp, so quick, because we responded to charges within the same "news cycle"—within a day after they were made. Now the news cycle has shrunk to minutes.

Amid this din, Clinton had to try to govern. Presidents have to work harder to be heard at all. They can no longer order up an Oval Office address without wrangling with the television networks for time.* At the same time, presidents and their words are more exposed than ever.

One day, we invited Ted Sorensen, JFK's brilliant counsel, to meet with the speechwriters. We asked him for his advice. "Well, I would eliminate the department of speechwriting," he said; a separate office crammed with writers was wrong. Speeches on farm policy would best be written by the agriculture secretary, and so on. We were baffled. How many speeches would they produce for President Kennedy? "One or two a week," Sorensen answered. We wrote one or two a day.

"But didn't he go out into the Rose Garden? Didn't he speak there?" We all had seen the picture of him shaking young Bill Clinton's hand.

"Oh, sure," Sorensen replied. "But we wouldn't give him something [prepared] for that."

Now, when a president walks into the Rose Garden, his words are beamed around the world live by CNN, MSNBC, Fox, CNBC, C-SPAN, and a dozen Internet sites. And while in 1962, reporters might have been

---

* A recent example: the President's request to deliver an Oval Office address on U.S.-China relations in May 2000 was rebuffed by two of the three networks. *Are you crazy? It's sweeps month!* Eventually, he canceled the speech.

standing at the back of the gathering, they would never have dreamed of shouting over the heads of the Girl Scouts or Boys Nation delegates, "President Kennedy, what about Marilyn Monroe?"

In the teeth of these challenges, Clinton transformed the way a president speaks to the country. He has to speak more often, and always to make news, no matter how small. Speeches are no longer thunderbolts hurled from Olympus. Instead, they are a steady purr, one or two or even three a day. The White House is not just the object of coverage by news networks—in effect, it has itself become a twenty-four-hour cable news channel. It is expected to generate programming.

Partly to fill the need for "message," partly because Congress was so resistant, Clinton pressed the boundaries of the executive presidency as well. Welfare reform was already largely in place through waivers granted to the states by the time it was enacted by Congress. The drive for national education standards injected the presidency into a previously local issue. Increasingly, we turned to regulation, as in the struggle against the tobacco industry—which began with an unprecedented move by the Food and Drug Administration to regulate tobacco, and concluded with a lawsuit against the tobacco companies, with a slew of presidential speeches and events in between.

There is one major exception to all this: Clinton elevated the State of the Union address into the template for a year's worth of initiatives. This speech was now the only time a president knew he could speak directly to the public. As the daily speeches shrank in stature, the annual address to Congress grew in heft as well as in length.

Clinton does not leave a long trail of chiseled phrases. Heroic words come from dramatic times. Frequently his speeches read like what they are: transcripts of a highly persuasive man trying to win a listener's agreement. The prose of policy, not the poetry of rhetoric, was what mattered. Speechwriting and policymaking were fused together again to a degree not seen in years. In all this, as journalist Jacob Weisberg has perceptively argued, Clinton readjusted the presidency, "making adjustments demanded by the historical moment." The bully pulpit is still a president's most powerful tool, but after Clinton, it will be used differently—and that is one change that likely will long outlast his administration.

Second, Clinton changed the Democratic Party. The Democrats in 2000 are a different party than they were in 1990. That transformation was not easy. Unlike Tony Blair, who was able to remake the British Labour Party by dramatically striking socialist dogma from its constitution, Clinton had to try to lead in the vague and informal American system. It was fascinating to watch up close as he tugged at his balky party, sometimes letting the rope go slack, other times being pulled by it himself. He kept

modernizers and Old Democrats together. He was a one-man coalition. Still, eight years after he decried the "brain-dead policies of both parties," and after constant collisions with the congressional remnants, he has worked a transformation of the Democratic Party that seems irrevocable. My own journey from Naderite to New Democrat seems somewhat emblematic; for most Democrats, except on trade, the Third Way has become the only way.

It is now second nature for liberals to talk about responsibility as well as opportunity. Few politicians would blithely propose bushels of new programs in a way that was second nature, say, to Hubert Humphrey. Clinton methodically addressed the issues that had bedeviled Democrats for decades. The party is no longer identified with out-of-control government, welfare, crime, or stagflation. Republicans had used these images and issues to pit white and black working-class voters against one another for years. The divisions that had defined American politics for a generation have been supplanted. The wedge has lost its edge.

Clinton wanted a realignment, but he never even achieved a majority of the popular vote—he is the only president ever elected twice without one. Repeatedly, he would mull electoral coalitions. "I love issues where independents side with Democrats," he would say. Like other minority presidents, he has been what political scientist Stephen Skowronek called "preemptive," seizing issues, ideas, and language from the other party. (That also unhinges the other party.)

Some condemn Clinton for shedding the party's core commitments. If unreformed welfare defined the Democrats, then that was a problem, not an answer. A stronger argument against Clinton's party leadership is empirical. Since 1992, the Democrats have been losing elections. It's too much to say that he destroyed the party in order to save it. More precisely, given the conservative electorate, the Democrats lost their congressional majority far later than might have been expected. The rebuilt, repositioned Democratic Party is far stronger than it would have been had it continued to trudge along the old path. By the 1998 elections, an ideologically united party had regained much of its lost electoral ground.

It is certainly conceivable that this change in the Democrats is not permanent. If the party loses the White House, it would be easy to imagine a return to fundamentalism among the congressional remnant. Or the party's submerged ideological fissures could emerge again. Still, there is just as good a chance that a fundamental modernization of the party's message and program has occurred.

Historians will note a third change: Clinton pointed the United States firmly—and irrevocably—toward the global economy. Paradoxically, by recognizing that markets are more powerful than presidents, he gained new

power over the economy. His legacy is not so much the duration of the prosperity as the new policy approach that helped create it.

The prosperity of the 1990s was more than just an uptick in the business cycle, more than just a Nasdaq bubble. Beneath the froth was the hard reality of economic transformation. There was no World Wide Web to speak of on the day Clinton took office. While a century ago, most people worked on farms—and a half century ago, nearly four out of ten often worked in factories—now most people are what Peter Drucker has called "knowledge workers," working in some way with computer technology. The biotech revolution is next, with the mapping of the human genome and the stunning prospects for health that it portends. As Clinton said repeatedly, this all portends social change on a scale matching the industrial revolution a century ago.

No president can claim full credit for an economy. In much of the twentieth century, presidents could tell themselves they had the ability to spur growth or step on the brakes, but by the 1990s, faceless markets could upend seemingly settled arrangements. Still, Clinton forced through two changes, from his first weeks in office, locking in a policy that *did* help unleash the boom.

Clinton was an accidental fiscal disciplinarian. By balancing the budget, he learned that in a world of dynamic capital markets, fiscal discipline is now a powerful stimulus. He did it in a way that took genuine political courage, and that produced an immediate benefit in the lives of ordinary citizens. Lower interest rates were followed by a spike in business investment, which ballooned as a share of the economy. That we are now debating whether and how to pay off the national debt suggests the lasting impact of this step.

And by insisting on open trade, he kept the United States facing outward—blocking the retreat from engagement that is always an appealing option after a long, albeit mostly bloodless, war. The U.S. economy is vastly more linked to the global marketplace than it was two decades ago—more exports, more imports, greater dominance by our culture and commerce. That was far from obvious in 1992. It would not have happened if a Republican president had been in office, since the Democrats likely would have united in opposition to trade. Nor would it have happened if this Democrat had followed the congressional party's fundamentalism. Only a New Democrat like Clinton could have passed NAFTA and GATT, for better or worse.

It is clear that issues of globalization and technological change will mark the politics of the next generation. The issue will not be whether to globalize but how. Clinton consistently articulated one view—open trade, yes, but also action to improve education, labor standards, and the environment. There was some action to match these words. But if we are truly

going to expose people to the "gales of creative destruction" of economic change, in years to come we will have to be far more serious about giving them the skills they will need to thrive. We will need to find a way to bring order and law to the global economy.

Through all this, perhaps most fundamentally, Clinton framed a new vision for what government should do, and persuaded people to agree. The era of opposition to big government is over.

For the first time in decades, there is now a rough consensus — government should be smaller, should follow fiscal discipline, but should actively try to solve problems. The anti-government, anti-tax movement that drove the Republican Party was the most potent political force of the past quarter century. After first misjudging its continuing fierceness, Clinton tamed it. By balancing the budget and reforming welfare, Clinton drained off the most toxic anti-government sentiment. By seizing the spotlight after the Oklahoma City bombing, and standing against the Republicans during the government shutdown, he staged a morality play reminding middle-class voters what they gained from government. The drip-drip of Rose Garden events, announcing incremental steps on issues such as child care, crime, health care, and consumer protection, all sought to restore confidence that government could do something. Clinton never sought or won any sweeping reorganization of government. The shifts have been subtler, but real. At the same time the budget was balanced, spending on education and training doubled. While the welfare rolls were cut in half, the Earned Income Tax Credit that helps the working poor doubled.

As important as the change in government is the change in the public's reaction to it.

The best clue was the electorate that didn't bark. When the President vetoed a $792 billion tax cut in the fall of 1999, voters yawned. Indeed, some criticized him for *following* public opinion by nixing a tax cut. Trust in government as measured in polls has slowly crept up. Most tellingly, none of the major candidates who sought the presidency in 2000 (Gore, Bush, McCain, Bradley) ran as a Reaganite foe of "big guvmint." Of all the things he said, I think most of what Clinton said one night in the residence, writing the State of the Union in 1998: "FDR saved capitalism from itself. Our mission has been to save government from its own excesses. So that it can again be a progressive force."

AFTER EIGHT YEARS, OF COURSE, there is unfinished business.

For me, the greatest personal and professional disappointment comes in the area of campaign finance. In the upcoming election, a torrent of corporate money will wash away whatever remains of the election laws. It is per-

haps the only social problem that has gotten markedly worse over the last eight years. I still believe this trend threatens the vitality of our democracy. For all the fulmination about Clinton's fundraising, he wasn't worse than the other politicians of his day. But he himself set the expectation that he would be better. He did want reform, especially when he thought he could achieve it, but it did not fire his moral passion — the kind of energy needed to break through entrenched resistance. We missed our moment in those first months of the first term. Yet, had we pressed forward with a public financing plan while simultaneously seeking a tax increase for deficit reduction, we would have courted a firestorm. Looking back, the very fact that I was tapped to run the effort was probably a bad sign. (Now that I am forty, giving a thirty-two-year-old that much responsibility seems foolhardy.)

The failure to enact reform will have political consequences as well. Throughout American history, energy has come from third parties. The cycle repeats: An existing majority party doesn't meet a perceived need. A disgruntled chunk of that coalition breaks off. Whichever major party can corral that breakaway faction and absorb its energy can become a new majority. The 1920s Progressives became the 1930s New Dealers. The George Wallace breakaway led to Nixon and Reagan. The Perot breakaway from the Republican Party, thus far, has not yet been resolved. Oddly, neither party really absorbed his reform agenda. John McCain did so briefly within the Republican Party, but flared out. The outcome of the 2000 race — and the races that come after — may depend on whom these reform-minded voters choose.

In other areas of social policy, where there has been more progress, it may well be that we too readily blurred the line between purposeful incrementalism and timidity. Widening inequality is the ugly hallmark of the new economy, though the gap has finally stabilized and even begun to narrow a bit in recent years. More people lack health insurance today than in 1993. To a greater or lesser degree, the administration tried to address these issues, but with only partial success. After two decades in which median income dropped, working families finally saw their incomes begin to rise in the mid- to late 1990s. We face the risk that, when the economic boom comes to an end, as it will, we will look back and ask, is that all that could have been accomplished? The true test may come not in this presidency but in the next one. Only a decade from now will we know whether Clinton's time clearing the underbrush opened the way for a wave of progressive activism or was wasted energy.

CLINTON CHANGED THE PRESIDENCY. Did the presidency change him? Here, I return to my own perspective. It differs from many who have

known him and written about him. I didn't fall in love at first, only to feel betrayed and disillusioned later. Instead, exposed to him over many years, I grew steadily more impressed.

Clinton has powerful personal strengths: his intellect, his love of history, his understanding of policy. Beyond its value as political theater, he does, in fact, feel people's pain. His personal flaws, obviously, are also very real. I suspect that the only difference between his and those of other presidents is that we know his now, rather than having to wait twenty or thirty years to find out.

Journalists and novelists have speculated whether these strengths and weaknesses flow from the same well of personal history. Perhaps, but that wasn't my experience. The chaos and overreaching of the first months in office were typical of new presidents, if an extreme case, a function of institutional and party pressures. Over time, Clinton learned the job. And as president, he was cautious, sober, and reasonably well organized. His temper was overrated. When his personal life crashed so noisily into the parlor of that well-ordered presidency, it was, in part, so startling to many of us around him because it was so unexpected.

There is much simplistic talk about character. Clinton has asked to be judged on his public work, on whether he has fought for the interests of the country as president. Time and again he pressed through policies that he thought were needed despite public opposition—from the tax increase in the 1993 budget, to NAFTA, to military engagement in Haiti, Bosnia, and Kosovo.

But character has another facet. He kept his head during a harrowing economic crisis. He never gave up, and he instilled that determination in those of us around him. That grit is a form of character, too—the highest kind.

During impeachment, there was a widely circulated joke. If Clinton were the *Titanic*, the iceberg would sink. His opponents still fume about the Clinton luck. Clinton liked to cite the words of an athlete: "The more I practice," he would say, "the luckier I get."

In the end, I come back to his enormous persuasive power, the effervescent force of his words. At his best, Bill Clinton was able to make a listener feel that the turbulent currents of change could carry us forward. The hopes he set on that first election night in Little Rock were high, too high. He did not meet them all. But I am convinced history will show he met more of them than we realize today.

ACKNOWLEDGMENTS

IN A SPEECH, the acknowledgments come at the beginning. In a book, they usually come at the end. I have no long list of county commissioners and party dignitaries to thank. Instead, I have a community of colleagues and friends. Without them, I could not have joined in the exciting work of speechwriting for a president—and without their help and support, this book would never have happened.

I want to begin by thanking President Clinton for giving me an unparalleled opportunity to serve. As this book makes clear, I believe his substantive achievements are undervalued—and from watching him, I learned a great deal about grace under pressure. Vice President Gore and Hillary Clinton were supportive throughout.

I was also lucky to have true friends with whom I shared the most exhilarating years I expect to have. Bruce Reed and Gene Sperling are dedicated public servants and generous friends. Don Baer tapped me to be chief speechwriter, and was my partner, mentor, and confidant. George Stephanopoulos hired me, inspired me, and taught me a great deal. Mark Penn tutored me about the fascinating American mind. Jordan Tamagni was a gifted writer and a trusted friend. I am grateful for their many hours of shared effort, which entirely shaped this account.

The presidential speechwriters with whom I worked were brilliant, funny, and dedicated—working under more pressure with less ego than one might imagine: Terry Edmonds, Jordan Tamagni, Josh Gottheimer, Jeff Shesol, June Shih, Lowell Weiss, Paul Glastris, Jonathan Prince, Carolyn Curiel, David Shipley, Laura Capps, Gabrielle Bushman, and Paul Tuchman, as well as David Kusnet, Alan Stone, and Carter Wilkie.

Friends and colleagues read all or parts of the manuscript: Cliff Sloan, Jon Cuneo, Mara Liasson, Elena Kagan, Roland Lewis, Eric Alterman, David Dreyer, Jordan Tamagni, Bob Boorstin, Matt Cooper, and David Frankel. Many participants in these events helped me sharpen my memories and perspectives, including Don Baer, Lael Brainard, Taylor Branch, Chris Dorval, Rahm Emanuel, Jeffrey Frankel, Tom Freedman, Al From, Pamela Gilbert, Gary Ginsberg, Nancy Jacobson, Mark Katz, Ron Klain, David Kusnet, Jon Orszag, Mark Penn, Jonathan Prince, Bruce Reed, Robert Reich, Ricki Seidman, Jeff Shesol, June Shih, Gene Sperling, George Stephanopoulos, and Fred Wertheimer.

As I gaze at my bookshelf at the great works of contemporary history, thirsting for inspiration, I come to realize that they have one thing in common: Alice Mayhew as editor. She is justly a legend. Her attention to detail, gift for felicitous compression, and rich historical knowledge helped me enormously. I want to also thank her colleagues at Simon & Schuster, especially Roger Labrie, K. C. Trommer, Brenda Copeland, Steve Messina, and Charlotte Gross. Thanks also to David Rosenthal, the publisher of Simon & Schuster's hardcover trade division, who was my editor on a previous book. My agent, Rafe Sagalyn, was unflagging, honest, and enthusiastic.

This book is the product of my memories, the President's speeches, and notes from my time in the White House. It also draws on the work of several perceptive journalists who helped shape how we in the Clinton administration saw ourselves. Jacob Weisberg's *New York Times Magazine* article on the Clinton presidency "The Governor-President," deeply influenced me (in and out of government), as did the work of Ron Brownstein, E. J. Dionne, and Jonathan Alter. Carol Gelderman's *All the President's Words* is an excellent history of presidential speechwriting. William Safire, the dean of ex-speechwriters, encouraged me to write this book. I was inspired by his book, and those of other predecessors, including Dick Goodwin, Ray Price, Samuel Rosenman, Robert Sherwood, Ted Sorensen, Peggy Noonan, and Harry McPherson.

I wrote this book while teaching at Harvard University. At the Institute of Politics, I benefited from the support of Alan Simpson, Jennifer Phillips, Kathy McLaughlin, Tim Wilkerson, and Ronda Jackson, and from the insights of my fellow fellows: Jim Edgar, Ray Strother, Dan Lungren, Claudia Winkler, and Katie Whelan. At the John F. Kennedy School of Government, I would like to thank Professor Thomas Patterson for inviting me back to teach; Professors Roger Porter, David Gergen, and Jeffrey Frankel for their insights into the presidency; my faculty assistant, Alison Kommer; and the students in my class on speechwriting.

I never worked directly for Robert Rubin at the White House, but

since leaving government, I have had the privilege of working for him on a part-time basis. He has not read this work and bears no responsibility for the views I express here. I would also like to thank his assistant, Joann McGrath, for her help.

Mark Green, New York's public advocate, was especially generous with his support and encouragement. Thanks also to Carla Cohen and the staff of the Politics and Prose bookstore, for letting me camp out in their coffee shop.

My deepest thanks go to my family. My parents, Martin and Sandra Waldman, were avid and careful editors. They leavened their unconditional love with savvy advice. My brother, Steve, found the time to help shape, read, and edit this manuscript while moving to New York and starting beliefnet.com, and his wife, Amy, also provided perceptive comments.

My wife, Liz Fine, was my partner and colleague in all the work I describe in this book. She is my best friend and my best editor. Liz passed up many opportunities for herself during these years because of our family. After I left the White House she had every reason to expect a break, only to find that I was working harder than ever. She is remarkably kind and generous. I could have done none of this (the job, the book, life) without her, nor would I want to.

Our three children, Benjamin, Susannah, and Joshua, were born during the Clinton administration—proof that we had at least three nights off. I wrote this book, in part, so that they would someday understand what I was doing all those years.

INDEX

ABOUT THE AUTHOR

MICHAEL WALDMAN was President Clinton's Director of Speechwriting from 1995 to 1999 and served as Special Assistant to the President for Policy Coordination from 1993 to 1995. Previously a public-interest lawyer and writer, Waldman is the author of *Who Robbed America? A Citizen's Guide to the S&L Scandal*. Since leaving the White House, he has taught at the John F. Kennedy School of Government at Harvard University. He lives in Washington, D.C., with his wife and three children.